Jill L. McNish, PhD

Transforming Shame
A Pastoral Response

Pre-publication
REVIEWS,
COMMENTARIES,
EVALUATIONS . . .

"**A**n essential book for pastors and counselors or anyone who has felt the pain of feeling inadequate. Rooted in her experience as a priest, pastor, chaplain, and preacher, Jill McNish argues compellingly that the core ministry of the church does not involve sin and guilt, but the creative transformation of shame, exemplified in Jesus' crucifixion. In a clear and engaging style, McNish integrates theological, psychological, and biblical perspectives with personal reflection, case histories, and a profound perceptiveness and pastoral sensitivity. She argues that contemporary ministry in general must be informed by insights from depth psychology, especially in dealing with shame. Readers unfamiliar with depth psychology will find this book a clear and accessible introduc-tion; more experienced readers will discover a freshness of insight and presentation that makes familiar concepts new. McNish examines the nature, origins, and universal human experience of shame toward an understanding of the potential of shame to be a marker on the path of transformation. This book challenges pastors and other religious leaders to understand not only the shame of others, but their own shame, and to learn how to hold on in the 'Godless vortex,' and to discover the grace of God that can transform it."

Rev. D. Andrew Kille, PhD
Co-chair, Psychology
and Biblical Studies Section,
Society of Biblical Literature;
Author, *Psychological*
Biblical Criticism

More pre-publication
REVIEWS, COMMENTARIES, EVALUATIONS . . .

"McNish develops a complex and original analysis of the transformative power of shame. She guides her readers through a series of psychological, spiritual, and theological reflections on the toxic mutations and healing potential of shame. She exposes it as a product of the tension psyche and spirit, functioning both to isolate us and to unite us in community. The gospel narratives provide a touchstone for her innovative analysis: she convincingly argues that the psychic power of shame is the key to understanding the Christ event. Drawing upon the wisdom of a diverse array of theorists—from pastoral counselors to philosophers and theologians to depth psychologists—McNish shows how shame can lead us to honor our humanity and connect us with divinity."

Diane Jonte-Pace, PhD
Professor of Religious Studies
and Associate Vice Provost,
Santa Clara University

"McNish's book offers a page-turning analysis of a ubiquitous, but repressed, aspect of human life—the experience of shame. McNish enlists depth psychological and theological insight to spell out the difference between toxic and, surprisingly, healthy shame. The book is a thesaurus of interdisciplinary research. It enlists the insights of depth psychologists from Freud to Jung to Erikson. It constructs a portrait of the shame of Jesus as a fatherless son in first century Palestine, employing the insights of social-scientific studies on honor and shame systems in first century Mediterranean culture. It fascinates us with familiar verbatims of counseling clients caught in the vise of shame and its concomitant spiral of suffering self-doubt. *Transforming Shame* concludes with a rich and comprehensive bibliography that can keep us reading for a 'shamefully' long time."

Wayne G. Rollins, PhD
Adjunct Professor of Scripture,
Hartford Seminary

"In *Transforming Shame*, McNish juxtaposes the ubiquity of the shame experience in human life and the Christ event, a paradigmatic model of the representation and transformation of shame toward renewal of life itself. Her comparison of Saul, who died of shame, and David, who survived his guilt, is a wonderful illustration of a problem that continues to this day, that our formal religious rites and practices provide resources for the guilty to confess their wrongs and experience forgiveness, but leave the shameful stranded, bereft of comfort, and lost in their own self-condemnation. For McNish, however, this need not be cause for despair. Instead, she testifies in this compelling book to the various ways that ministers may 'make space' through informal acts of attention and care for those whose shame has become an unbearable burden. McNish brings clarity and depth of understanding to a dimension of our human experience whose very ubiquity tends to impede such illumination and insight."

Donald Capps
William Harte Felmeth
Professor of Pastoral Psychology,
Princeton Theological Seminary

Transforming Shame
A Pastoral Response

Transforming Shame
A Pastoral Response

Jill L. McNish, PhD

The Haworth Pastoral Press®
An Imprint of The Haworth Press, Inc.
New York • London • Oxford

Published by

The Haworth Pastoral Press®, an imprint of The Haworth Press, Inc., 10 Alice Street, Binghamton, NY 13904-1580.

AUTHOR'S NOTE
While all of the pastoral examples described herein are in a very real sense "true," details have been greatly altered and composites have been created. Therefore, no true life individual example can be identified or inferred in this document.

Cover design by Brooke R. Stiles.

Library of Congress Cataloging-in-Publication Data

McNish, Jill L.
    Transforming shame : a pastoral response / Jill L. McNish.
        p. cm.
Includes bibliographical references and index.
    ISBN 0-7890-2152-8 (hard : alk. paper)—ISBN 0-7890-2153-6 (soft : alk. paper)
    1. Shame—Religious aspects—Christianity. 2. Patoral psychology. I. Title.
BT714.M36 2004
253.5'2—dc21
                                                                                2003005005

For my parents

ABOUT THE AUTHOR

Jill L. McNish, MDiv, PhD, is an Episcopal priest engaged in parish ministry, spiritual direction, and adjunct teaching. She is presently on the faculty of the Pastoral Studies Program of Blanton-Peale Institute in New York City.

CONTENTS

Acknowledgments

I tender deep and heartfelt thanks to my advisor, Professor Ann Belford Ulanov, for her help and patient guidance of me in this work, as well her support and the gift of her extraordinary example during all of my years at Union Theological Seminary, New York City. She is the most awesome teacher I have ever known. I also gratefully acknowledge the many hours spent and the invaluable input of the other members of my dissertation committee, Dr. Harry Fogarty, Dr. Robin Scroggs, and the Reverend Dr. Margaret Guenther. Many thanks also to Barbara Rasero for her patient reading and rereading of chapters, for sometimes understanding what I was trying to say before I knew how to say it, for consistently insightful comments and suggestions, and for all of her encouragement and positive "mirroring." Thanks to the Right Reverend John S. Spong, whose early and constant support of my academic work and my priestly ministry first made the impossible seem possible. Thanks to all of my parishioners, directees, patients, and students who have enriched my life, opened and fed my heart, my mind, and my soul. Thanks to my daughters Elena and Cristina for the many sacrifices they made as I pursued the dream of this project, for keeping me grounded in reality, and for preventing me from ever taking myself too seriously. Last but certainly not least, thanks to Patricia Nachtigal for a lifetime of love, patience, companionship, and support.

Chapter 1

Introduction

When someone asks me what I am working on and I say shame, it tends to stop the conversation. The response is typically a polite, "Oh, shame; that's nice." I find shame is not a topic that evokes most people's lively enthusiasm. Nobody wants to talk about it. There is a sense that even to talk about shame is shaming. I confess that I came to this topic reluctantly myself. It was as if *it* came to *me,* and I finally had to accept that this was the topic I needed to pursue.

My perspective is that of a pastor, priest, and teacher in the institutional Church and a spiritual director. I have taught students in college and seminary settings. I have worked as a chaplain in short-term psychiatric units. This issue of shame just kept hitting me between the eyes. It was not something I was looking for, but the fact is that virtually every depressed person I spoke with presented either directly or indirectly with issues that I came to identify as shame issues. When I started reading more about it, I saw it everywhere.

Around the same time that I was coming to this insight about the ubiquity of shame as an element of psychic suffering, I was preaching on a weekly basis in the churches I was serving. When you are the solo pastor in a small church, it means that you preach just about every Sunday. You slog your way through that lectionary week after week. As I worked through all those passages, I began to notice that not only were my parishioners, directees, students, patients, friends, and colleagues dealing with issues which could be seen directly or indirectly as shame issues but also that many of the events from the gospel which I was preaching about—i.e., events in the life, ministry, and death of Jesus of Nazareth—were most fundamentally about shame. When the lectionary passages did not directly suggest shameful circumstances for Jesus, they often implied something shameful in the lives and circumstances of people he was engaged with, ministering to, or speaking about in parables.

I have come to believe that understanding the psychic and spiritual phenomenon of shame and its centrality in human life is key to understanding the psychic power, meaning, and transformative potential of the Christ event. My general heuristic assumption—that is, the reason I study the interface of psychology and religion—is that I believe understanding the psychological underpinnings of the lived faith experience gives us courage. It gives us a place to stand in the midst of shame and other psychic suffering by providing us with insights about how God may be working in the human psyche and what God has done for us in the incarnation. Working at the intersection of theories of depth psychology and lived religious experience, I propose positive, life-giving potential for shame.

This book draws upon scriptural descriptions of the life, words, trial, and passion of Jesus to demonstrate that he—or at least the figure that the gospelers describe—experienced the sting of shame at many points in his life and death. It discusses theological understandings of the human shame experience, and it attempts to relate these understandings and lived spiritual experiences to the psychological underpinnings of shame in human life, as proposed in the theories of depth psychologists.

I believe that shame is an integral and inevitable part of the human condition and indeed is at the core of most profound religious conversion experience. In that sense, shame can draw us to God. Depth psychologists, theologians, and mystics have independently discovered that when shame experience is honestly confronted instead of bypassed and defended against, it is transformative and revelatory of identity because it is the affect closest to the experienced self. As one follows and connects the insights of depth psychologists, theologians, and mystics, one sees that shame arises most fundamentally from the tension between the understanding of the human finite, creaturely nature, and the consciousness that comes from being created in God's image. On another and parallel level, there is a fundamental tension in human life between the competing desires for separation and union, between wanting to pull apart and longing to draw close, between wanting to be part of the collective and wanting to be one's own most authentic and creative individual person. This tension, which ultimately may play out in the experience of oceanic unity with the Absolute, as well as through truly creative and abundant life, is central in religious experience and, I believe, central to the meaning and paradoxes of shame. It is in our confrontation and negotiation of shame that this tension is resolved. This is so because the affect of shame has the paradoxical property of being both a uniting and dividing force. Shame is a uniting force because it moves us to try to fit in and conform to societal conventions and standards. It is a dividing and isolating force because it moves us to seek privacy in our physical lives and creative impulses. In its more pathological forms, the processes of shame may separate and isolate the individual altogether. Thus, shame pulls us into society even as it separates us from society. One aspect of shame serves social adaptation and ensures membership in human society through conformity; the other seemingly opposed attribute of shame ensures that the collective does not violate the individual's boundaries of personal integrity and is responsible for the maintenance of privacy in our thoughts and ideas.

This book also looks briefly at the tendency of the institutional Church to unhealthily exploit, even if unwittingly, the shame affect in human experience. I propose some ways for the Church and its ordained representatives to begin to use shame more constructively to facilitate its transformative potential in individuals and to build up the Body of Christ. It is recognized, however, that this work only begins to scratch the surface in raising issues and proposing strategies for the consideration of the Church on the subject of how it might more effectively facilitate the resurrection and transformation of the shame affect. It is my hope that future work will go farther in proposing liturgical reform and methodology for pastoral caregivers in helping people to confront and transform shame, thereby growing in relationship with themselves, with one another, and with God.

The great Rollo May once said that an important part of healing is "utilization of suffering." This is an invaluable insight for pastors, especially when we feel tempted to cop out by taking the "There-there-things-are-not-so-bad-Jesus-loves-you" approach. May also noted that, "a human being will not change his or her personality patterns, when all is said and done, until forced to do so by suffering. . . . Suffering is one of the most potentially creative forces in nature."[1] Shame is a cause of great suffering in human life. The idea that suffering has creative potential is hopeful and optimistic. It is therapeutic for pastoral caregivers to set this reality before those to whom they minister—especially in a society in which many assume that happiness is the ultimate (and most realistic) human value, and that it is somehow neurotic not to be feeling happy most of the time. As John Hick once noted, "The capacity to find God in suffering and defeat as well as in triumph and joy is . . . the special genius of Christianity."[2] This is most particularly and obviously true with the shame experience. The central figure of the Christian faith suffered the worst imaginable shame—the public exposure and shame of the cross—and was transformed (i.e., resurrected) in and through that experience. We too can be transformed—spiritually and psychologically—if we face shame honestly.

Chapter 2

Shame in the Gospel Accounts of the Life, Ministry, and Death of Jesus

O sacred head, now wounded,
With grief and shame bowed down;
Now scornfully surrounded
With thorns, thy only crown.

> Paul Gebhardt, *Passion Chorale* (1656),
> based on twelfth-century Latin hymn, st. 1.

We read Thee best in him who came
to bear for us the cross of shame;
sent by the Father from on high,
our life to live, our death to die.

> From Hymn 455, *Episcopal Hymnal* (1982)

Some modern scholars, including Andries Van Aarde and Donald Capps, have convincingly asserted that, by reason of the unusual and unorthodox circumstances of his conception, the historical Jesus was not a completely accepted member of the house of Israel. Van Aarde understands there to have been seven categories of Israelite men based upon their parentage and the circumstances of their birth. Priests, Levites, and full-blooded Israelites made up three of these categories.[1] "Illegal" children of priests—i.e., children of priests who had married prohibited women—and proselytes made up the fourth category. The fifth group was "made up of bastards, the fatherless, foundlings and those made eunuchs by human agency."[2] The sixth group included those who for physical reasons could not have sexual intercourse, such as born eunuchs, men with deformed genitals, and hermaphrodites. The last group consisted of non-Israelites who by definition were "impure and outside the covenant and thus excluded from any kind of social relationships" with Israelites.[3]

Van Aarde believes that Jesus belongs in the fifth category. He writes that "the historical claim may therefore be made that in terms of the criteria of the period of the Second Temple, Jesus was regarded as being of illegitimate descent."[4]

> The image of Jesus as the fatherless carpenter, the unmarried son of Mary, who lived in a strained relationship with his village kin of Nazareth, probably because of the stigma of being father-less and, therefore, a sinner, fits the ideal type of the fifth category.[5]

If this is true, Jesus would have been without "proper covenant membership" in the house of Israel. People in this fifth category were those "of doubtful parentage, perhaps even of disreputable descent. Thus, their membership in the true Israel was . . . suspect"—and they were therefore "not allowed to enter the congregation of the Lord in terms of the ideology of the temple. . . ."[6] This view accords with that of other contemporary scholars, including the significant work of Jane Schaberg in her book, *The Illegitimacy of Jesus: A Feminist Theological Interpretation of the Infancy Narratives.*[7]

It is not my intent to enter into the thicket of the doctrine of the virgin birth of Christian faith or the direct fatherhood by God of Jesus by the instrumentality of the Holy Spirit. This is of not the concern of the present work. Here I am concerned with how the circumstances of Jesus' birth would have been construed by his own historical community and by the gospelers. Joseph is not a factor in what are believed to be the earliest sources (Thomas, Q, Paul, and Mark).[8] The later gospels of Matthew and Luke go to great pains to attribute divine and virginal conception of Jesus. Thus, it may well be that central to the historical Jesus' identity in first-century Palestine was an illegitimate and fatherless status.[9] Mark—the earliest gospel—refers to Jesus as "son of Mary" (Mark 6:3) and does not mention Joseph at all. Matthew and Luke refer to Jesus parenthetically as Joseph's son, and "[s]ince later traditions are intent to show Jesus' divine origins (John 1:1-18; Hebrews 1-2), the general New Testament tendency is to obscure the factual origins of Jesus while 'theologizing' them."[10]

Honor and shame were (and still are) pivotal values of the Mediterranean world of which Jesus of Nazareth was a part. Bruce Malina and Jerome Neyrey have elucidated the centrality of the honor/shame dynamic in their article "Honor and Shame in Luke-Acts: Pivotal Values in the Mediterranean World."[11] "Honor," they write, "is the positive value of a person in the eyes of his or her social group."[12] *Ascribed honor* (as distinguished from *acquired honor*) is honor that a person has because of his or her kinship, not because of any effort or achievement of his or her own. To "be shamed" was to be publicly stripped or denied honor. However, to "have shame" was positive, especially for women. It is a good thing to care about one's honor. Most human beings think it desirable to "have" shame; however, we do not want to "be" shamed.[13]

The first-century male ideal, the honorable man, was

> one who knows how to live up to his inherited obligations. He neither encroaches upon others nor allows himself to be exploited or challenged by others. He works to feed and clothe his family. He fulfills his community and ceremonial obligations. He minds his own business in such a way as to be sure no one else infringes upon him, while looking for possible advantages for himself.[14]

The quantity of honor available in the first-century Middle Eastern community was perceived as fixed and finite. Thus males were continually jousting to maintain, and if possible increase, the honor that they had. Acquiring honor typically meant taking it from someone else. There was frequent challenge and response, "a sort of constant social tug of war, a game of social push and shove" to protect honor and test the possibility of acquiring more of it at someone else's expense.[15] We see this jousting in some of Jesus' conversations with Pharisees and Sadducees. For example, in Matthew 22:24-34, the Sadducees attempt to trick him by asking him whose wife a woman will be in the resurrection after she had married seven brothers. Jesus effectively silenced them with his response. It is only by fully understanding the centrality of the honor/shame dynamic in first-century Palestine that we can begin to appreciate the radical, countercultural nature of Christ's life and work, and the agony and isolation that his convictions, his teachings, and his choices must have caused him.

There is a cultural difference between the concepts of honor and shame for men and women in Mediterranean culture. A male's honor is at stake in the sexual purity of his mother, wife, daughters, and sisters. *"The sexual purity or exclusiveness of the female is embedded within the honor of some male."*[16] Thus, regardless of whether we believe that Jesus' conception came about to a virgin through the instrumentality of the Holy Spirit and without any involvement of a male human being, if Jesus' conception and birth were viewed by his community as unorthodox, it surely would have affected his worldview, as well as the way he would have been viewed in the world into which he was born. Capps puts it this way:

> If Jesus was viewed as illegitimate by villagers, and was therefore the victim of considerable social ostracism, this would have affected his marriageability, his occupational prospects, his chances of an education, and, of course, for participating in the religious life of the community. In that case, we would not be surprised if what most scholars believe happened did in fact happen, that is, he left Nazareth to make his "home" in Capernaum; that he probably did not marry and father children of his own.[17]

What does it mean if the most important person in Western history, the one that Christendom proclaims as part of the Godhead itself, was born with the shame and stigma of illegitimacy, in the context of an honor/shame Mediterranean culture for which the virginal purity of a woman bore "almost mythical importance"?[18]

It is also informative to take a brief look at Jesus' genealogy as set forth in the first chapter of Matthew. It is, of course, acknowledged that this genealogy is not historically "factual." Nor can we even say with certainty that the individuals whose names appear in the genealogy were actual historical figures. However, as will be developed later, their stories as recorded in the Hebrew scriptures are true in the mythic sense; they rose up from the collective and were preserved in oral and written tradition for hundreds of years. The characters are bearers of archetypal truths, if not historical truths. In religious life—life in the spirit—symbol and mythic truth are the most important truths.

We can look at the gospel accounts of the birth, life, ministry, and death of Jesus of Nazareth on least four levels of "reality." First is the level of factual historicity. Most of the historical Jesus has been permanently lost to us, although historians and archaeologists can with some credulity uncover realities of the cultural and material world in which he lived. The second level of reality is the experience of Jesus by people who knew him or had contact with him in his own time. The third level of reality is seen in the reformulation and reworking of the story of Jesus of Nazareth by those who wrote about him decades after his life. The fourth level of reality is the psychological, archetypal meaning with which scripture is experienced by us today. This experience can be enhanced by understanding something of the social and material world in which Jesus lived.

I contend that on whatever level of reality one views and experiences the Christ event, one is inevitably confronted with the centrality of the shame dynamic, and that this fact must be seen as significant to understanding the enduring power of Christianity.

In an honor/shame culture in which a man's honor was dependent upon the perceived sexual purity of his mother (and other women in his family), what does it mean if Jesus was not only the illegitimately conceived offspring of Mary but, according to explicit (although largely ignored) biblical witness, also descended from a long line of women who had conceived some his ancestors by extremely unorthodox—shameful—sexual means?[19]

Tamar, the foreign wife of Judah's elder sons Er and Onan, was widowed by both brothers before she had children. When her father-in-law Judah refused to give her his third son in marriage, Tamar tricked her father-in-law into sleeping with her by disguising herself as a prostitute. By this route she conceived and bore him twin sons, Perez and Zerah (Gen. 38:6, 11, 13-30). Perez is a direct ancestor of David and Jesus (Ruth 4:12; Matthew 1:3).

The prostitute Rahab, also a foreigner and a traitor to her own people—in fact an inhabitant of Jericho, which was conquered by Joshua with her assistance—married Salmon (Joshua 2:1-21; 6:25), also a direct descendent of David and Jesus (Matthew 1:5).

Ruth, the Moabite (another non-Israelite) who in desperate need to provide for herself and her beloved mother-in-law Naomi and to continue her deceased husband's (and Naomi's) line, presented herself and her body to Boaz (son of Rahab and Salmon). She ultimately became the mother of Obed (Ruth 4:15). He, in a direct line, fathered Jesse, who fathered David—the ancestor of Jesus of Nazareth (Matthew 1:5).

Then there was Bathsheba, whose relationship with David was shameful for the Davidic line because she was taken by David through a sequence of adultery, conspiracy, and murder (2 Samuel 11:1-12:25). According to scripture, this union was displeasing to God (2 Samuel 11:27). David's taking of Bathsheba resulted in the illness and death of the first child she bore for him. It was the cause of David's fall, his repentance, and his redemption. King Solomon, the son of David and Bathsheba, was another ancestor of Jesus (Matthew 1:6).[20]

It has been noted that although Rahab, Tamar, Ruth, and Bathsheba were all deficient in "the most important honorable quality for females, that is sexual exclusivity," nevertheless, "midrashic and postbiblical traditions present them in a more positive light."[21] Their dramatic presence may be indicative of a central theme of this book—shame transformed by grace: "God intervened, not only in their relationships with men in their lives, but also to transform their lives from those of questionable, if not sinful, natures, to states of innocence and virtue."[22]

Our Christian legend tells us that Jesus himself was born among animals, in the muck of a manger, filled as such places inevitably are with animal smells and animal excrement. Perhaps first-century peasants would have experienced all of this as quite ordinary, but the undeniable fact remains that Jesus was not born to parents of high estate. Author and theologian Jack Miles once went so far as to write in a *New York Times Magazine* article that "for most of the hundreds of millions who . . . will hear the story again on Christmas Eve, what counts in it is neither theological nor historical, but psychological."[23]

Jesus of Nazareth's shame did not end with the humble—even unorthodox—circumstances of his conception and birth. When stripped of the romantic Sunday school gloss that 2,000 years has affixed to it, his earthly life, by the standards of his day, was a shameful failure. He lived in a Jewish enclave in Palestine:

> Honor and shame are the constant preoccupation of individuals in small-exclusive societies where face to face personal, as opposed to anonymous, relations are of paramount importance and where the social personality of the actor is as significant as his office.[24]

What does this mean in the Mediterranean context in which the historical Jesus was born, lived, and died?

> The point of honor is the basis of the moral code of an individual who sees himself always through the eyes of others, who has need of others for his existence, because the image he has of himself is indistinguishable from that presented to him by other people. . . . Respectability, the reverse of shame, is the characteristic of a person who needs other people in order to grasp his own identity and whose conscience is a kind of interiorization of others, since these fulfill for him the role of witness and judge. . . . He who has lost his honor no longer exists. He ceases to exist for people, and at the same time he ceases to exist for himself.[25]

In a culture in which one's identity and honor were circumscribed by the honor of one's family and the performance of one's designated role as son, husband, brother, or father, Jesus' life and earthly ministry were so unorthodox that, according to Mark, the earliest and perhaps most historical gospel, his relatives came to collect him, "for people were saying, 'He has gone out of his mind'" (Mark 3:21). When Jesus heard that his mother and his brothers had come for him he rejected their claims on him, saying, "'Who are my mother and my brothers?' And looking at those who sat around him, he said, 'Here are my mother and my brothers! Whoever does the will of God is my brother and sister and mother'" (Mark 3:33-35). This "public exposure of strained family relationships challenges Jesus' honorable standing since all sons should honor their father and mother."[26]

Jesus' earthly ministry was so marginal that he literally had "no where to lay his head" (Matthew 8:20). His ministry was liberally punctuated by episodes of abandonment and rejection, which, as will be discussed, are sine qua nons of shame. The very prologue to John tells us that "He came to what was his own, and his own people did not accept him" (John 1:11). Luke is even more explicit, saying that the people in his hometown tried to throw him off a cliff when he came to teach them (Luke 4:29-30).

Assuming that he was unmarried in his thirties when he is believed to have begun his earthly ministry, his private life too would have been most unusual and problematic. Jews did not (and for that matter do not to this day) exalt a single, celibate life as holy.[27] There is no place for "holy virgins" in Judaism. The people of Israel are expected to marry and produce offspring for the community. However, Van Aarde contends that a man who had been conceived outside of marriage could marry others like himself but would have been "disqualified from marrying into the 'true Israel'—those associated with temple worship."[28]

Jesus ate and otherwise associated with impure and defiled people: prostitutes, tax collectors, lepers, persons inhabited by demons, Samaritans, and Gentiles. He conversed openly with women—Mary and Martha, the Syrophoenician woman, the woman at the well. He allowed "impure" women to touch him—the woman with the hemorrhage, the prostitute who anointed his feet with her tears and with costly perfume.[29]

The life's ministry of the one whom Christians have for 2,000 years identified as part of the Godhead was, by its own terms, a dismal failure. "He was despised and rejected by others; a man of sorrows and acquainted with infirmity" (Isaiah 53:3). By the account of the gospels, he endured an agony of doubt and anguish in the Garden of Gethsemane, and he endured it completely alone: his friends and followers dissociated from the hour of his emotional torment by falling asleep (Matthew 26:36-46; Mark 14:32-41; Luke 22:39-46).

The shame of Jesus appears in its most horrifying and explicit form in the gospel Passion accounts.[30] He was taken captive by Roman soldiers and interrogated, whipped, spat upon, mocked, and crowned with thorns by their authorities, who all the while were being goaded on by religious authorities of his own sacred temple and by a mob of his own people, who in the last analysis did not spring to his defense but instead shouted, "Crucify him!"

In his hour of excruciating need, his closest friends and followers betrayed and/or deserted him, abandoning him to public execution by an occupying authority with the help, complicity, and active participation of his own people. Death by crucifixion was unspeakably, archetypally shameful:

> The chief reason for its use was its alleged supreme efficacy as a deterrent; it was, of course, carried out publicly. . . . It was usually associated with other forms of torture, including at least flogging. . . . By the public display of a naked victim at a prominent place . . . *crucifixion also represented utmost humiliation, which had a numinous dimension to it.* With Deuteronomy

21:23 in the background [31] the Jew in particular was very aware of this. . . . Crucifixion was aggravated further by the fact that quite often its victims were not buried. It was a stereotyped picture that the crucified victim served as food for wild beasts and birds of prey. In this way his humiliation was made complete. What it meant for a man in antiquity to be refused burial, and the dishonour which went with it, can hardly be appreciated by modern man. (emphasis added)[32]

John Dominic Crossan has likewise conjectured that one of the reasons for the shameful horror connected with crucifixion in the ancient world was that the victim would not be properly buried. Instead, typically, the flesh would rot and/or be buried in a shallow grave, often becoming food for wild dogs and other beasts that waited at the foot of the cross.[33]

Shame is about belonging and fitting in. It is about exposure and vulnerability. As James and Evelyn Whitehead have noted, "At the beginning of Christianity looms the shameful public execution of a naked Jesus. This startling memory must indicate a special contribution of Christianity for the healing of social shame."[34]

What was Jesus thinking as he hung naked from the tree of shame, in agony, publicly exposed, and unspeakably humiliated? Of course we will never know; the gospel narratives display little or no interest in his psychological life, and thus his actual, historical personality "must remain an unfathomable enigma."[35] But the testimony of two of the gospel narratives put these words in his mouth: "My God, my God, why have you forsaken me?" (Matthew 27:46; Mark 15:34).

What had Jesus expected to accomplish with his life's ministry? Much has been written in conjecture about this, but perhaps nothing more eloquent or with a greater internal sense of truth than this, from Albert Schweitzer's *Quest of the Historical Jesus:*

There is silence all around. The Baptist appears, and cries, "Repent, for the Kingdom of Heaven is at hand." Soon after that comes Jesus, and in the knowledge that he is the coming Son of Man lays hold of the wheel of the world to set it moving on that last revolution which is to bring all ordinary history to a close. It refuses to turn, and He throws Himself upon it. Then it does turn; and crushes him. Instead of bringing in the escatological conditions, He has destroyed them. The wheel rolls onward, and the mangled body of the one immeasurably great Man, who was strong enough to think of himself as the spiritual ruler of mankind and to bend history to His purpose, is hanging upon it still. That is His victory and His reign.[36]

It would not be an overstatement to say that Christianity literally had its birth on the altar of shame. Some might protest that Jesus—the second person of the Trinitarian Godhead—did not experience shame, and that this was his glory. I do not see any support for this contention, at least in the synoptic gospels. In any event, to contend that he did not experience this fundamental part of the human experience would seem to me to deprive the incarnation of its power and meaning. The issue for me is not whether he experienced shame because, as will be discussed, shame is an ontological part of being human— and Jesus' life certainly contained more than its share of shaming circumstances—but rather how he dealt with the experience of shame.

It has been noted by biblical historical critics that the Bible was not written from a psychological perspective, i.e., it is virtually devoid of the kind of explicit psychological character development and observations that modern people would expect to find in contemporary storytelling. Bruce Malina observes that "people described in the New Testament, as well as those who described them, were not interested in or concerned about psychological or personality information."[37] However, the fact that ancient people might not have had much if any interest or understanding of themselves as psychological beings does not mean that they were *not* psychological beings, or that our current-day attempt to understand the psychic meaning of the religion which is our inheritance from them is invalid. Ancient people did not understand much about the workings of the human nervous system, but that does not mean they did not have nervous systems. Experts tell us that a culture existed in first-century Palestine in which the honor/shame dynamic was central. The question is this: What is its origin in the human psyche? My answer would be that the honor/shame dynamic, and all of the elaborate rules and mechanisms that supported it in that time and place, arose from the shame affect that is an ontological part of being human. In other cultures, the shame affect manifests itself in different ways. For example, in our own culture we see it manifested in the pursuit of material wealth or in efforts we make to be viewed as successful in our work or in the elaborate attempts some of us make to maintain physical attractiveness and a youthful appearance.

The transformation and redemption of shame was and remains central to the power of the Christian faith tradition. In Jungian terms, one might say that a shame archetype was constellated around Jesus of Nazareth in first-century Palestine, and the power of that archetype has remained undiminished for some 2,000 years. It is within this basic Christian context and framework—that is, never losing sight of the shame inherent in the life, ministry, and death of the One whom we now worship as part of the Godhead—that I hope to explore the spiritual, theological, and psychological implications, ramifications, and consequences of the affect of shame. If I am correct that much of Jesus' life, ministry, and death as transmitted to us in scripture was "shameful" according to the mores of his historical time and place, this becomes very important to understanding the psychic meaning of Christianity. Carl Jung aptly articulates it this way:

> Christ would never have made the impression he did on his followers if he had not expressed something that was alive and at work in their unconscious. Christianity would never have spread through the pagan world with such astonishing rapidity had its ideas not found an analogous psychic readiness to receive them.[38]

This is not to say that one needs to believe in the historicity of the gospel accounts of the life, ministry, death, and resurrection of Jesus of Nazareth, and the many references herein to events set forth in the gospel accounts certainly need not be taken as belief in their literal occurrence. I do not doubt the historical reality of Jesus of Nazareth, but neither is it necessary to accept whole cloth the historicity of the gospel narratives. The figure of Jesus and of Christ the Redeemer has vast archetypal meaning. It is the archetypal meaning of his life, ministry, death, and resurrection which has spoken most powerfully and deeply to Christians that have lived in the twenty-one centuries since the historical person of Jesus walked on this planet.

The persons who wrote the gospel accounts of the life, ministry, and death of Jesus were not so concerned with the historical person of Jesus of Nazareth as with finding ways to present their experiences of him and/or of the risen Christ.

At a very early stage, . . . the real Christ vanished behind the emotions and projections that swarmed about him from far and near; immediately and almost without trace he was absorbed into the surrounding religious systems and moulded into their archetypal exponent. He became the collective figure whom the unconscious of his contemporaries expected to appear, and for this reason it is pointless to ask who he "really" was.[39]

I want to avoid seeming to suggest that Jesus was "nothing but a myth"—i.e., a fiction. I do not hold myself out as a biblical scholar, and I leave it to others more qualified than myself to determine what events in Jesus' life as recorded in scripture, if any, were historical facts that could have been televised by CNN, had CNN existed at the time. However, myth is not "fiction"; in fact, myth and symbol are what express the deepest, most profound, and ineffable truths. Following Carl Jung, I would "go so far as to say that the mythical character of a life is just what expresses its universal human validity."[40] What I contend here is that the events of Jesus' life, ministry, death, and resurrection as recorded in the gospel accounts reflect the gospelers' experience of him and of the risen Christ as archetypal events.

Had there not been an affinity—a magnet!—between the figure of the Redeemer and certain contents of the unconscious, the human mind would never have been able to perceive the light shining in Christ and seize upon it so passionately.[41]

As the foregoing brief summary shows, the gospel narratives are shot through with the shame dynamic and how Jesus dealt with this dynamic. The life of Jesus of Nazareth "became a sacred symbol because it is the psychological prototype of the only meaningful life, that is, of a life that strives for the individual realization—absolute and unconditional—of its own law."[42] In part, as will be seen, this must surely mean a life in which shame experience is honestly confronted, without resort to shame defenses, and transformed.

An emerging sense of the centrality of the shame dynamic in human life—and why the Christ event as told in the gospel narratives continues to be experienced so powerfully after twenty-one centuries—came to me in the course of my work as a priest and particularly in my pastoral work with persons hospitalized in short-term psychiatric units for depression. I began to notice that virtually every individual with whom I spoke in my capacity as chaplain and pastor seemed to be filled with a sense of what I identified as shame. Here are just a few examples:

A nineteen-year-old African-American woman from the inner city said that she was "evil"; there was a "demon" inside her. She had never done well in school, could not get or keep a job. She said that as a schoolchild she had been mocked and humiliated. She had been, she said, "fat, ugly, and stupid." Boys had taken advantage of her sexually even as they mocked her, and her parents had once called upon the services of an exorcist to cast out the demon in her.

A middle-aged man suffered from a depression so severe and intransigent that even electroshock treatments or pharmacology could not touch it. He felt deep shame that he was often unable to go to work, that his illness had made him unable to support his family, that the family home was in foreclosure, and still there were many days when he could do no more than stay in bed and pull the covers over his head. "You have no idea," he told me, "the courage it takes every day for me to refrain from killing myself."

An eighty-six-year-old Roman Catholic widow of Polish descent, a mother, a grandmother, and a great-grandmother, reticently told me her depression came from the realization that she was an evil and sinful woman. Why? Because she often fantasized about the nubile bodies of young women.

A young woman was deeply depressed out of a sense of profound shame for which she could find no redemption. She said that when she was an adolescent, she had engaged in sexual activity with a female cousin two years older. In her judgment of herself, this was depraved and disgusting beyond expression. Nothing could remove the stain of that memory.

A vigorous and well-read ninety-three-year-old Jewish woman had worked all of her life as a teacher. She was beloved by nieces, nephews, and many friends. She had put her head in an oven and tried to kill herself because she "could not do anything anymore and was good for nothing."

Another elderly woman, deeply depressed, sat in her room all day alternately railing against the hospital and its staff and stating that she was a terrible person, had never been any good, was evil to the core, and just wanted to die.

An elderly man suffered deep shame because he was retired and was no longer supporting his family with a paycheck. He felt that he had not given his children enough financial help with their educations and would not be leaving them a big enough estate. He also felt profound guilt toward his wife because they could not go out to dinner or do much traveling as other retired couples do. The sense of shame toward his wife was severely compounded by the fact that his depression made him "no fun" for his wife to live with in their old age.

A middle-aged suburban woman, a social worker, who was married and the mother of six, was hospitalized for depression so severe that for many days after her admission she did not talk at all, lying silently on her bed. This was her first real bout with mental illness. Finally, she told me that she could not cope with shame that she felt because her eighteen-year-old daughter had "run off" with a married man. She was convinced that her entire community was gossiping about it. She obsessed about how this relationship could have been going on without her knowing about it and how she could have raised a daughter who would do such a thing.

A young Hispanic woman professed hatred of her parents, then confessed unbearable feelings of shame associated with promiscuous sexual activity and an abortion she had had as a teenager.

An elderly man—a devoted husband, father, and grandfather, a faithful churchgoer and a retired fireman—was admitted for deep depression soon after an anniversary of the Allied invasion of Normandy. He told me that he could not live any longer with the shame and horror he felt about acts he committed as a teen-aged infantryman during World War II, more than fifty years prior, and with the shame of the long life he had lived while so many of his pals had died in their youth.

A Roman Catholic woman gifted with great intelligence and a number of academic degrees wanted to commit suicide because, she insisted, she was "no damned good and never has been any good." Until five years before, she had suffered from a serious drinking problem, which she had conquered. She could neither take pride in this accomplishment nor derive any sense of self-worth from it. She was, she said, "selfish, unloved, and unlovable." She said that she had "never given a damn about anyone else, and nobody ever gave a damn about me." She could not believe in the obvious caring of a friend who visited her daily or of her brother who was also trying to help her.

A woman of great religious devotion was repeatedly hospitalized for depression. She expressed deep shame stemming from having been molested as an adolescent by her stepfather.

A fifty-year-old man who had recently lost his job due to corporate downsizing was hospitalized for back pain which was so severe that he could not get out of bed, but for which doctors could not find a cause. He talked incessantly about his failure as his family's breadwinner and his inability to make love to his wife.

A highly educated and accomplished sixty-year-old African-American woman, a devout Baptist, had never been able to enter into meaningful or mature intimate relationships. Her parents had beaten her and emotionally abused her throughout her childhood, while demanding perfection from her in every undertaking. This history, together with societal racism, combined to make her feel shamed, worthless, and dirty. In her job, she dominated and controlled every meeting, alternating between aggressive rage and self-deprecating withdrawal. The men she permitted herself to be involved with tended to be weak, immature, ineffectual, and dependent.

Encountering these individuals in the cauldrons of their most severe emotional crises awakened me to the centrality of the shame dynamic in my pastoral work in parishes and in providing spiritual direction. I came to believe that the "pathological" obsessions of persons hospitalized for depression were really not that different from the fears and concerns of many of my parishioners, particularly those who suffered any degree of depression. The difference was much more one of degree than of kind. Furthermore, because the individuals in the short-term psychiatric unit were by definition in the midst of severe crisis, they were more open about what they were thinking and feeling than was the average parishioner presenting himself or herself in a pastoral care situation. Their issues and pathologies were better crystalized than were those typically present with so-called normal people. Carl Jung once noted that "in mental cases we can observe all the phenomena that are present fleetingly in normal people in a cruder and more enlarged form." Then, in a footnote following this observation, Jung added:

> When I was still a doctor at the psychiatric clinic in Zurich, I once took an intelligent layman through the sick wards. He had never seen a lunatic asylum from the inside before. When he had finished one round, he exclaimed, "I tell you, it's just like Zurich in miniature! A quintessence of the population. It is as though all the types one meets every day on the streets had been assembled in their classical purity."[43]

And so I began to look more closely at the pastoral encounters I was having in parish ministry, and I concluded that there too the shame dynamic was writ large on many of them—perhaps most of them. The present work attempts to put this dynamic in psychological, theological, and spiritual perspective, to relate this ubiquitous shame dynamic to the scandalously shameful life of Jesus, and to articulate possible ways for ordained ministers and, more generally, the institutional Church, to respond to the endemic shame dynamic—as pastors, priests, teachers, and fellow human beings.

This book develops the thesis that shame is a necessary and ontological part of the human condition: it arises at its most fundamental level out of the conflict between human consciousness and spirit and the fact that human beings are, at the same time, out of nature and are thus finite and subject to the needs, longings, desires, joys, and agonies of the flesh. Most fundamentally, awareness of one's own mortality and powerlessness to avert it means that the body is the primary focus of archaic shame; it is "the seat of our inability to master the world."[44] It will be developed that shame is a boundary phenomenon, and as such it helps us differentiate ourselves from nature and from one another, at the same time guarding our privacy and our intellectual and emotional integrity. Shame can become pathological, undergirding and dominating the entire personality, making it impossible to feel either part of the collective or an individual in one's own right, and whether this happens depends upon the vicissitudes of one's personal history, perhaps combined with certain aspects of inborn temperament.

The experience of shame can be salvific, redemptive, and transformative. The place of shame is the vortex of feelings between isolation and desire for unity and longing to express one's creativity and individuality. Concomitantly, it is the place of tension between the body and its needs, desires, finite nature, and consciousness. The shame vortex is experienced as the *godless* place because it is a place of suffering. Yet if it can be tolerated and negotiated honestly, without ferocious deployment of shame defenses (see Chapter 5), it is at the core of transformation and much authentic religious experience. At the very center of the Christ event is the experience of shame and the transformation of shame. Much of the life, passion, and death of Christ as it is handed down to us in the gospels takes place in the shame vortex. Transformation of shame is a large part of the psychic meaning of the Christ event, what Christianity is about. Transformation of shame is the experience of grace. Thus, transformative Christianity is really not about sin and guilt; it is about transformation of shame experience. The great saints and icons of Christianity have used the Christ event to transform shame and experience grace. The more completely they have done this, the deeper their experience of grace and unity with God.

In order to understand the experience of shame and the religious and spiritual implications of it, this book explores the psychological meaning, implications, and etiology of shame. This will be undertaken in Chapters 3, 4, 5, and 7. Understanding the ubiquity and psychological meaning of shame can help us to create religious meaning. Psychological theories can verify our experience by giving us a footing, a place to stand, while we look for where, how, and why God may be present and working in our lives. The methodology that will be used for contextualizing theories of depth psychology in theology and religious experience will be discussed in Chapter 6. Finally, I attempt to set the experience of shame in the context of scripture and Christian theology in Chapter 8, and then in Chapter 9 reflect upon the role of the institutional Church in helping its people to make meaning of shame and experience grace from shame's transformation.

Chapter 3

What Is Shame? Toward a Working Phenomenological Understanding

Shame need not crouch
In such an Earth as Ours;
Shame—stand erect—
The Universe is yours!

Emily Dickinson, #1304, c. 1874

In a case that came before the United States Supreme Court in 1964, the Court was called upon to define obscenity in order to consider what speech was protected by the First Amendment. Justice Stewart said, "I shall not today attempt to define the kinds of material I understand to be embraced within that short-hand definition; and perhaps I could never succeed in intelligibly doing so. But I know it when I see it."[1]

One can plow through the voluminous literature pertaining to shame and read a bewildering array of definitions of it. Like obscenity, it may be that we well "never succeed in intelligibly" pinning it down but, also like obscenity, we will "know it when we see it."

At the most basic level, shame is "connected to the very fact of one's humanness."[2] I believe that most fundamentally shame always arises directly out of indirectly, out of life in the body. When we trace any instance of shame through, we find that it invariably has reference to the needs, desires, situation, or condition of the body. It arises out of the uniquely human experience of being a creature, yet feeling somehow that one is spirit and of God as well. It most likely begins with an infant's dawning realization of its helplessness and dependency, coupled with its desire for omnipotence. "For shame involves the realization that one is weak and needy in some way in which one expects oneself to be adequate."[3]

One task that needs to be undertaken early on in this discussion is that of making whatever distinctions need to be made between guilt and shame. A commonly articulated distinction, and the one that I accept, is that guilt has reference to an action perceived as wrong, whereas shame has reference to the self ("self-consciousness"). When a person feels guilt, he or she has a sense of having made a mistake; of doing something that culture or his or her own superego says is wrong, or he or she has failed to do something dictated by culture or superego. In religious terms, one might think of the words of the general confession in the Episcopal *Book of Common Prayer,* in which one confesses guilt for "what we have done, and for what we have left undone."[4]

Shame, on the other hand, is *self-referential.* Regardless of what a person has "done" or "left undone," to a greater or lesser extent he or she experiences himself or herself as inherently, ontologically flawed in the core of his or her being. Again, the *Book of Common Prayer* is helpful in illustrating this. In the ancient locution commonly known as "The Prayer of Humble Access" which occurs at the conclusion of the eucharistic prayer, the assembled congregation says,

> We do not presume to come to this thy Table, O merciful Lord, trusting in our own righteousness, but in thy manifold and great mercies. We are not worthy so much as to gather up the crumbs under thy table.[5]

The earlier (1928) version of the *Book of Common Prayer* currently in use in the Episcopal Church in the United States was even more explicit in referring to an ontological sense of shame in its worshipers. After confession of wrongful acts and omissions committed, which might justifiably create a sense of guilt, the general confession in that prayer book contained the declaration that "there is no health in us."[6]

Simply put, one feels guilt for *making* a mistake. Shame is a felt sense of *being* a mistake. "Guilt allows for retribution and atonement, shame does not."[7] In Helen Lynd's early and monumental contribution to the shame literature, she notes:

> Guilt is centrally a transgression, a crime, the violation of a specific taboo, boundary, or legal code by a definite voluntary act. Through the various shadings of meaning there is the sense of

the committing of a specific offense, the state of being justifiably liable to penalty. In the usual definitions there is no self-reference as there is in shame. [8]

Merle Fossum and Marilyn Mason state the difference similarly:

While guilt is a painful feeling of regret and responsibility for one's actions, shame is a painful feeling about oneself as a person. The possibility for repair seems foreclosed to the shameful person because shame is a matter of identity, not a behavioral infraction. . . . For many people shame exists passively without a name. [9]

Biblical examples that come to mind which illustrate the distinction between shame and guilt experiences are Kings Saul and David. Saul's downfall might be seen as the consequence of his exaggerated and unremitting sense of shame. Saul failed to obey God's supposed command in matters that would strike most of us as trivial, if not downright understandable. He failed to kill all of the enemy's sheep and cattle, saying that he had intended the animals as a sacrifice to God (1 Samuel 15). When this infraction was pointed out to him by the prophet Samuel, Saul experienced a withdrawal of God's love from him, the withdrawal of his sense of being chosen as God's anointed King of Israel. He was filled with envy for young David, who had felled Goliath. He was driven mad by "an evil spirit from the Lord" which "tormented him" (1 Samuel 16:14). Ultimately, his own sense of insecurity, exposure, flawedness, and unworthiness resulted in the loss of his kingdom to David. Clearly, the shame dynamic was operating in Saul in pathological proportions. Yes, there was guilt, too, for disobeying God's commands, but that guilt was fused with shame—and ultimately it was shame that brought Saul down.

An example of guilt would be King David's reaction to being shown by the prophet Nathan that his adulterous taking of Bathsheba and engineering the death of her husband in battle was grievously wrong and a violation of God's law. When David's sins were illuminated for him, he said, "I have sinned against the Lord." Nathan replied, "Now the Lord has put away your sin; you shall not die." When the first child of the union with Bathsheba became ill, "David fasted, and went in and lay all night on the ground." He remained fasting and in isolation for seven days; his servants were afraid that he would kill himself. But after he learned that the child had died, he "rose from the ground, washed, anointed himself and changed his clothes. He went into the house of the Lord and worshiped" (2 Samuel 12:16-20). Then David "consoled his wife Bathsheba, and went to her, and lay with her; and she bore a son, and he named him Solomon. The Lord loved him" (2 Samuel 12:24).

In David, we encounter a man who experienced and atoned for a grievous wrong he had committed—indeed by most standards a much more grievous wrong than the one Saul had committed. Having repented, however, David continued to feel God's love; he still experienced himself as a valued person before God. He resumed his life, even to the extent of returning to the bed of Bathsheba and fathering with her a second son who inherited his kingdom and became an ancestor in the direct line of Jesus of Nazareth (Matthew 1:6-7).

There was, of course, a terrible price paid for David's sin. The first child died. David's innocence was over. The Davidic dynasty and the Kingdom of Israel were tragically wounded (2 Samuel 12:11). Sin and human brokenness usually has this kind of systemic effect on communities for many generations. This, indeed, is the premise of family systems theory.[10] Nevertheless, unlike Saul, who was driven mad by shame, David was able to continue his life—chastened but with a sense of forgiveness, still a worthy and beloved person before God.

Sylvan Tompkins is often quoted for this powerful description of the affect of shame:

> [S]hame is the affect of indignity, of transgression and of alienation. Though terror speaks to life and death and distress and makes of the world a vale of tears, *yet shame strikes deepest into the heart of man. While terror and distress hurt, they are wounds inflicted from outside which penetrate the smooth surface of the ego; but shame is felt as an inner torment, a sickness of the soul.* It does not matter whether the humiliated one has been shamed by derisive laughter or whether he mocks himself. In either event he feels himself naked, defeated, alienated, lacking in dignity or worth. (emphasis added)[11]

"In general, then, guilt involves less experience of the self than shame. Shame is about the self; guilt involves activity of the self, with less perceptual feedback from the self's activity."[12]

Yet it would be clearly incorrect to separate shame and guilt from each other: they are often tangled up together and exist in a state of fusion. If a person has done something wrong, he or she can feel both guilty and ashamed of himself or herself at the same time. As Helen Block Lewis put it, the guilty self is saying,

> How could I have *done* that; what an injurious *thing* to have done; how I *hurt so and so;* what a moral lapse that *act* was; what will become of *that* or of *him* now that I have neglected to *do* it, or *injured him.* How should I be *punished* or *make amends?* Mea culpa![13]

The shamed self, on the other hand, would say: "How could *I* have done that; what an *idiot I am*—how humiliating; what a *fool,* what an *uncontrolled person*—how mortifying; how unlike so and so who does not do such things; how *awful and worthless I am*."[14] The phenomena of guilt and shame "enter into the attitudes of most people, and often into the same situation."[15] If one is a shame-bound person, even the smallest infraction will trigger a sense of unworthiness. Shame and guilt can easily by fused, and shame does often arise out of guilt.

In his 1963 book *Affect, Imagery and Consciousness, The Negative Affects* Sylvan Tompkins numbers "shame-humiliation" as one of six innate "negative affects." The six negative affects posited by Tompkins are: fear/terror; distress/anguish; anger/rage; dismell (the experience of revulsion triggered by smell); disgust; and shame/humiliation.[16]

By the word *affect* Tompkins means "a physiological mechanism, a firmware script" that is dependent on "chemical mediators that transmit messages, and on the organizing principle stored in the subcortical brain as the affect program." Thus, "no matter what shame or any other affect 'means' to us, it is essential for us to keep in mind that we are dealing first and foremost with a mechanism that is initially free of meaning."[17]

Affect theorists following the work of Sylvan Tomkins believe that shame is "the most recent affect to develop through the process of evolution, with the possible exception of tears leaked when we are 'overwhelmed by emotion.'"[18] If it is the case that only human beings feel shame, it seems plausible to suggest to those who believe in a God who is a force in human life that God has implanted shame in the human creature as a way of drawing us into relationship with God-self. In fact, in the Judeo-Christian tradition, shame emerges in the very first story of humankind's relationship with God. The story of Adam and Eve's expulsion from the Garden of Eden is the story of their struggle with the shame dynamic and what it meant for their relationship with God, with each other, and with nature. Furthermore, affect theorists contend that "shame exists only in terms of other affects." The shame affect "disturbs the normal, expected flow of the patterns for the positive affects interest or enjoyment." Thus, Nathanson states,

> The affect program for shame-humiliation is triggered in those common situations when an impediment occurs but whatever had been a competent stimulus for interest or enjoyment *remains* a competent stimulus for those affects. In other words, shame affect is a programmed response to an impediment to preexisting affect when there is every reason for that preexisting affect to continue! Shame affect is a highly painful mechanism that operates to pull the organism away from whatever might interest it or make it content. Shame is painful in direct proportion to the degree of positive affect it limits. As Tomkins has stated, shame will occur whenever desire outruns fulfillment. To the extent we humans seek pleasure we must experience shame.[19]

Nathanson quotes from a Robert Frost lecture he attended to describe a hypothetical paradisal world without shame as "A world where ask is get/And knock is open wide."[20]

Shame theorist Michael Lewis has gone so far as to say that "shame, more than sex or aggression, is responsible for guiding our psychic course." Shame is responsible for "depression or antisocial behavior. Our internal struggles are not battles between instincts and reality, but conflicts that typically involve the understanding and negotiating of shame, its elicitors and its frequency."[21]

Interestingly enough, the inherited physiological patterns that Sylvan calls "affects"—not the least of which include shame—seem in essence to be properly included in the family of phenomena that Carl Jung refers to as "archetypes." Thus, in 1952, more than a decade before Tomkins's *Affect, Imagery and Consciousness, The Negative Affects,* Jung wrote:

The archetypes are formal factors responsible for the organization of unconscious psychic processes: they are "patterns of behaviour." At the same time they have a "specific charge" and develop numinous effects which express themselves as *affects*. The affect produces a partial *abaissement du niveau mental,* for although it raises a particular content to a supernormal degree of luminosity, it does so by withdrawing so much energy from other possible contents of consciousness that they become darkened and eventually unconscious. Owing to the restriction of consciousness produced by the affect so long as it lasts, there is a corresponding lowering of orientation which in its turn gives the unconscious a favourable opportunity to slip into the space vacated. Thus we regularly find that unexpected or otherwise inhibited unconscious contents break through and find expression in the affect. Such contents are very often of an inferior or primitive nature and thus betray their archetypal origin.[22]

Tompkins and others conclude that the feeling we know as guilt (as well as remorse, embarrassment, and humiliation) is one of many subparts of the negative affect of shame. Guilt springs from shame. Researchers have not located a distinct physiological mechanism, "an innate affect, that would explain guilt in any way other than its relation to shame." Thus, although guilt

feels different from shame; nevertheless, it appears that guilt involves, at the very least, shame about action. Usually this action is one that has violated some rule or law or that has caused harm to another person. Guilt, however, seems to contain some degree of fear of retaliation on the part of whoever has been wronged by our action, so we might say that it involves a coassembly of the affects shame and fear. Empirically, we know that guilt often involves both the shame that lies latent in hidden action and the fear of retribution.[23]

Thus, another distinction one might make between the experience of guilt and shame is that guilt involves and evokes talion dread—an eye for an eye, a tooth for a tooth. "I hurt him, what I did was wrong, so now he will surely hurt me."[24]

Shame, "which involves more self-consciousness and self-imaging in general, is likely to involve an increase in feedback from all perceptual modalities."[25] The feeling of shame is experienced in the body and has a "special affinity for stirring autonomic stimulation, including blushing, sweating, increased heart rate." Thus shame involves more "body awareness" than does guilt, as well as "visual and auditory (verbal) imaging of the 'me' from the 'other person's point of view.'"[26] "In general, then, guilt involves less experience of the self than does shame. Shame is about the self; guilt involves activity of the self, with less perceptual feedback from the self's activity."[27] Shame causes what has been called an "implosion of the self":

> The body gestures and attitude include head bowed, eyes closed, body curved in on itself, making the person as small as possible. At the same time that it seeks to disappear, the self may be dealing with an excess of autonomic stimulation, blushing or sweating or diffuse rage, experienced as a "flood" of sensations. Shame is thus regarded by adults as a primitive reaction, in which body functions have gone out of control.[28]

Shame has also been called a "wordless" state.[29] It might be called the "feeling which dares not speak its name." In general, people are more willing to admit to feelings of guilt than shame. Guilty feelings imply basic trust in one's world, its laws, rules, and taboos, and in the persons who are the interpreters of these laws. But in shame there is doubt and mistrust of everything, particularly the self. As Helen Lynd puts it, "shame may be said to go deeper than guilt; it is worse to be inferior and isolated than to be wrong, to be an outcast in one's own eyes than to be condemned by society."[30] Shame is profoundly isolating. Shame confronts us with "our aloneness in the world."[31] Donald Capps makes the following observation about the isolating effect of shame, and the disinclination of most of us to talk about shame issues using the vocabulary of shame:

> Shame experiences are difficult to talk about, to communicate to others, and they are difficult for others to hear and listen to. They are difficult to communicate to another for two reasons. One is that to tell another person about a shame experience produces more shame; a shame experience becomes more, not less, shameful to the extent it is more widely known. Thus, whereas relating a guilty action to another may be cathartic, for such disclosure does not add to one's sense of guilt, the relating of a shame

> experience actually contributes to one's sense of shame. . . . The
> other reason shame experiences are difficult to communicate is
> that, in telling the story, one re-experiences the shame and the
> pain that goes along with it. It is virtually impossible to relate a
> shame experience as though it were over and done with. . . .
> [W]e relive shame experiences as we recall and describe them,
> and to relive the experience is to relive the pain that made the ex-
> perience a shameful one in the first place.[32]

I would have to take issue, based upon my own experience as a pastor
and the clinical observations and work of psychotherapists including
Helen Lynd, Helen Lewis, Andrew Morrison, and Leon Wurmser,
with Capps's suggestion that discussion of shame issues makes matters worse for the sufferer. Perhaps direct discussion of shame is in
the short run painfully shaming, but in the long run it is both cathartic
and healing, even salvific.

Shame can altogether sever one's human relationships:

> A person may feel forced to renounce the very striving to belong
> itself and resignedly accept an alienating existence. No matter
> how strong his or her inner yearning to belong may be, dignity
> as a human being matters more, and a shamed person may with-
> draw from a relationship in order to maintain that dignity.[33]

On one hand, it has been said that "the greatest pain of shame may
be the isolation it causes. If sufficiently isolated, estranged, one may
question one's own existence."[34] Thus, shame presents us with a
Hobson's choice: painful isolation and retention of one's dignity, or
willingness to tolerate the sense of looking a fool in one's community
of accountability.

In a culture that so highly values popularity and conformity, individuality is all too often not valued or affirmed. "To avoid shame, one
must avoid being different, or *seen* as different. The awareness of difference itself tranlates into feeling lesser deficient."[35] This might im-
pact one's ability to act upon one's creative impulses, one's ability to
assert and express one's own identity in the world. It will lead to the
prominence of what D. W. Winnicott calls the "False Self"—i.e., the
compliant self that hides and protects the "True Self."[36]

Shame is about *exposure:* exposure of private or inferior body
parts, inferiority, confusion, and weakness. Experience of embarrass-

ment, which is usually viewed as a fleeting and less severe subspecies of shame,[37] is illustrative, for it too involves exposure of matters that are private and nobody else's business. A couple is embarrassed if a cleaning person enters their hotel room when they are making love, even if they are a married couple of twenty years and have an indisputable right to be doing this. One is embarrassed by a slip of the tongue that might seem to expose a private thought, opinion, or fantasy. For example, I once sat with colleagues in a social situation, intending to refer to myself as the interim *rector* of a church. I mistakenly referred to myself instead as the interim *rectum*. Possible psychic reasons for this slip of the tongue were not lost on my listeners!

Other inner states that are properly viewed as subtypes of shame include discouragement, self-consciousness, shyness, humiliation, and guilt.[38] Thus, a seminarian wrote:

> I find myself revisiting, in ways that I acknowledge to be completely unnecessary, past traumas. . . . Often these memories are embarrassing ones. A romantic possibility about which I had built up great hopes, dashed by my natural awkwardness, comes immediately to mind. An opportunity to stand up and teach in front of my community at which I was totally unprepared and made a fool of myself. Accidentally saying something completely inappropriate in front of a large group. It is interesting to me that it is usually the embarrassing moments that flood back unwanted at odd intervals. . . . I am aware that these traumas stayed on some level imprinted on my mind. When I think of them I experience the pain all over again, like it was yesterday, though it seems totally unnecessary.

In shame experiences, many people describe feelings of freezing, numbness, leadenness. Another common response to the experience of shame is the desire to run away and/or hide.[39]

Shame is an innate affect, and all people experience it and its subspecies embarrassment and humiliation. For some individuals, however, it is a "dominant characteristic, a deeply engrained habitual mode of reacting to self and others. Such people may be described as shame-bound, shame-ridden, shame-prone or toxically or chronically shamed. They live permanently diminished, distrustful, unhappy and uncomfortable lives. . . ."[40]

It has been argued that shame is the affect which is the root source of many negative inner states, including: "depression, alienation, self-doubt, isolating loneliness, paranoid and schizoid phenomena, compulsive disorders, rageful acting out, splitting of the self, perfectionism, addictions, a deep sense of inferiority, inadequacy or failure, the so-called borderline conditions and disorders of narcissism."[41] John Bradshaw, a public personality who has helped bring consideration of shame issues out of hiding, has written that "the most paradoxical aspect of neurotic shame is that it is the core motivator of the superachieved and the underachieved, the Star and the Scapegoat, the 'Righteous' and the wretched, the powerful and the pathetic."[42] What these experiences have in common when we penetrate them is that they are all experiences of the godless place, the vortex.

Gerhard Piers, in his classic psychoanalytic description of shame, states, "Behind the feeling of shame stands . . . the fear of contempt which, on an even deeper level of the unconscious, spells fear of abandonment."[43] Franz Alexander agreed that that experience of shame is, in essence, vulnerability to the threat of rejection—rooted in separation anxiety and the fear of loss of love.[44]

Shame experiences are difficult to hear and to relate. Capps writes that listening to shame experiences

> tends to render the listener impotent, feeling as though nothing one can say will help. With guilt, the listener is usually able to provide some reassurance: "You didn't really mean it"; "It was a learning experience"; "To those who are truly sorry, God promises forgiveness, and the opportunity to make amends." How do you make amends for a shame experience? The primary victim of shame is the self. . . .
>
> Bereft of the usual reassurances that have some chance of working with those who are experiencing guilt, the listener usually tries to minimize the experience. . . .[45]

Some have seen a primordial relationship between shame and death. Carl Schneider points out these examples from common parlance: " 'I was so ashamed, I could have died'; 'I could have sunk into the ground and disappeared'; and 'I was mortified.'"[46] The etymology of the word *mortification* directly connects the feeling to death. Indeed, as Schneider and others have pointed out, there are compelling anthropological reports of cultures in which "people literally die of shame. Cannon, Mead, Benedict, and others inform us of societies in which 'deaths . . . are regarded as due to shame.'"[47] Thus, if the unconscious, irrational fear implied in guilt is talion dread and mutilation—i.e., castration—"the unconscious threat implied in shame anxiety is abandonment."[48]

Helen Lewis discusses shame as the experience of "the momentary loss of self . . . a disruption of consciousness and loss of control" in shame that is associated with death. She gives us this clinical example:

> P: When I find somebody looking at me I could die.
> T: Could die?
> P: Well, not literally (slight laugh) that's when I sort of have the feeling I could crawl through a hole. . . .[49]

Indeed, one component of shame may be a "blackout." In a clinical example proffered by Vicki Underland-Rosow, a woman said, "When I experience shame I feel as though I am looking at the world through shattered glass. Nothing is clear. I cannot hear anything that is said. Colors blur. My mind goes blank."[50] Underland-Rosow notes that "It is foolish to expect a person experiencing shame to remember anything said to him or her. Talking to a person experiencing shame is like talking to a drunk."[51] Michael Lewis observes that in shame there is a

> fusion of subject and object. . . . The self system is caught in a bind in which the ability to act or to continue acting becomes extremely difficult. Shame disrupts ongoing activity as the self focuses completely on itself, and the result is confusion. . . . Shame is the complete closure of the subject-object circle. . . . In guilt, although the self is the subject, the object is external to the self.[52]

Helen Lynd holds that some individual personalities develop along a "guilt axis" and others along a "shame axis." In her analysis, she draws heavily upon the work of Erik Erikson, whose unconscious inner stages of human development include one he calls "autonomy vs. shame and doubt." This, Erikson says, is the developmental challenge to be negotiated in the period associated with toilet training. The problems of this developmental stage revolve upon issues of "holding on and letting go." Erikson states:

> Shame is an emotion insufficiently studied, because in our civilization it is so early and easily absorbed by guilt. Shame supposes that one is completely exposed and conscious of being looked at: in one word, self-conscious. One is visible and not ready to be visible; which is why we dream of shame as a situation in which we are stared at in a condition of incomplete dress, in night attire, "with one's pants down." Shame is early expressed in an impulse to bury one's face, to sink, right then and there, into the ground. But this, I think, is essentially rage turned against the self. He who is ashamed would like to force the world not to look at him, not to notice his exposure. He would like to destroy the eyes of the world. Instead he must wish for his own invisibility.[53]

"Doubt," says Erikson, "is the brother of shame." While shame is about being exposed, his clinical observations led him to conclude that doubt

> has much to do with having a front and a back—and especially a "behind." For this reverse area of the body, with its aggressive and libidinal focus in the sphincters and in the buttocks, cannot be seen by the child, and yet it can be dominated by the will of others.[54]

The individual's sense of independence and autonomy is threatened when he or she feels that someone else can dominate the back of the body and "designate as evil those products of the bowels which were felt to be all right when they were being passed."[55] This can lead to compulsive, obsessive, paranoaic doubts in later periods of adulthood. The positive potentiality of this stage is basic trust, as opposed to shame and doubt. Erikson relates this basic trust

> to the institution of religion. The lasting need of the individual to have his will reaffirmed and delineated within an adult order of things which at the same time reaffirms and delineates the will of others has an institutional safeguard in the *principle of law and order.*[56]

If doubt is a by-product of shame, then trust opposes and overrides shame. In shame, there is an inherent lack of trust in those upon whom one is dependent for love, for physical sustenance and maintenance, for affirmation of oneself. Professor and public intellectual Martha Nussbaum writes that

> a good development will allow the gradual relaxing of omnipotence in favor of trust, as the infant learns not to be ashamed of neediness and to take a positive delight in the playful and creative "subtle interplay" of two imperfect beings.[57]

Shame, on the other hand, is an essential failure of trust in the goodness of oneself and others, and ultimately it is distrust in the goodness of God and life, distrust that we are the apple of God's eye, distrust that God is with us in the midst of suffering and adversity. Shame may be seen as a failure to trust in the essential acceptingness and lovingness of life itself. In short, shame is a failure of the experience of grace. It is the godless place. (Chapters 8 and 9 discuss this concept in detail.)

Erikson designates the next stage of unconscious human development as "initiative vs. guilt." This stage corresponds roughly to Freud's Oedipal period:

> Infantile sexuality and incest taboo, castration complex and superego all unite here to bring about that specifically human crisis during which the child must turn from an exclusive, pregenital attachment to his parents to the slow process of becoming a parent, a carrier of tradition. Here the most fateful split and transformation in the emotional powerhouse occurs, a split between potential human glory and potential total destruction. For here the child becomes forever divided in himself.[58]

The negative potentiality of this phase is that in adulthood, the individual will constantly suffer from conflict over exercise of initiative "expressed either in hysterical denial, which causes the repression of the wish or the abrogation of its executive organ by paralysis, inhibition or impotence; or in overcompensatory showing off. . . ."[59] This stage is a volatile one because "of the inner powerhouse of rage which must be submerged . . . as some of the fondest hopes and the wildest fantasies are repressed and inhibited."[60]

Shame is experienced

> whenever our most basic expectations of a significant other are suddenly exposed as wrong. To have someone we value unexpectedly betray our trust opens the self inside of us and exposes it to view. "What a fool I was to trust him!"[61]

In shame, there is no sense of being in control. We are "swallowed up in the sense of something that overwhelms us from without and 'takes us' unawares. We are taken by surprise, caught off guard, or off base . . . made a fool of."[62] Lynd sees the feeling of unexpectedness as "one of the central contrasts between shame and guilt":

> This unexpectedness is more than suddenness in time; it is also astonishment at seeing different parts of ourselves, conscious and unconscious, acknowledged and unacknowledged, suddenly coming together, and coming together with aspects of the world we have not recognized. . . . In situations in which we feel guilty, choice, foresight, awareness in regard to a specific act are at least possible. Being taken unpleasantly by surprise, the impossibility of ordered behavior, the sudden sense of exposure, of being unable to deal with what is happening, characterize shame. It is as if a self of which we are not aware makes us unable to grasp the situation and to control what we do. In shame, says Erikson, one is conscious of being—when one is unprepared—exposed, looked at, all around.[63]

Exposure of misplaced assumptions about one's situation is often shameful: "happiness, love, anticipation of a response that is not there, something personally momentous received as inconsequential. The greater the expectation, the more acute the shame. . . ."[64]

To be rejected, betrayed, or jilted in a marriage or love affair often provokes a shame reaction that feels like annihilation, because the lover is someone to whom one has exposed one's body and soul with the expectation that the lover can be trusted to hold this. As Helen Lewis notes, "At least in our culture, shame is probably a universal reaction to unrequited or thwarted love."[65]

Lynd goes on to make the very astute point that the shame-inducing phenomenon of "finding oneself in a position of incongruity, not ed as the person one thought one was, not feeling at ld one thought one knew, can occur repeatedly through-ss of identity through loss of job, loss of marriage or hip, social upheavals, retirement, the so-called empty-...t syndrome—any change in how one understands and lives one's sexual identity, even the mere fact of aging, has the potential to induce shame.

In his now classic book *Stigma,* Erving Goffman somewhat ironically refers to persons living without stigma of any kind as "normals." However, few enjoy the status of being normals. In the first place, to be a completely normative person means being a male. This immediately eliminates more than half of the population. Moreover,

> [t]here is only one complete unblushing male in America: a young, married, white, urban, northern, heterosexual Protestant father of college education, fully employed, of good complexion, weight, and height, and a recent record in sports. Every American male tends to look out upon the world from this perspective. . . . Any male who fails to qualify in any of these ways is likely to view himself—during moments at least—as unworthy, incomplete, and inferior.[67]

Entering adolescence with a developing female body (*any* female body, but particularly one that does not precisely fit the ideal), growing up in American culture with a racial or ethnic identity other than Caucasian, discovering oneself to have a gay or lesbian psychosexual identity—all are potentially shame inducing.

Of course, even those few who have been in Goffman's group of normals are destined to eventually experience stigma and its attendant shame if for no other reason than aging. The aging process, with its inevitable increase in dependency and physical frailty, and its loss of vitality, mental ability, sexual prowess, and attractiveness is often experienced as shameful, particularly in the youth-oriented culture of the United States. In his book *Still Here,* Ram Dass describes a shaming wake-up call he received at age sixty-two while riding a train between Connecticut and New York. The conductor came along to take his ticket:

> "I'll have to buy one from you," I said.
> "What kind will it be?" he asked.

"Do I have a choice?"

"Regular or senior citizen?"

Now, although I was bald, covered with age spots and battling high blood pressure and gout, it had never ever occurred to me—not once—that I could be called a senior citizen. . . . As the coach rattled on, I felt troubled and anxious, weighed down by my new label. Was the saving worth the cost? The role seemed so constricting—senior citizen! Old fogey![68]

Thus, the issue becomes not whether one experiences the shame of stigma "but rather how many varieties he has had his own experience with."[69]

Indeed, shame is a "life-cycle" phenomenon, with each stage of life containing its own shame-inducing potential; it occurs with some predictability at all of life's developmental crisis points.[70] In infancy and young childhood, shame is induced by powerlessness and dependence, among other things. In adolescence, it may be induced by the rapid changes in the body and by newly aroused genital desire, sometimes painfully apparent in boys. In young adulthood, it may be induced by the realization that one will never be the famous concert pianist or CEO one had hoped to be, by failed relationships, by what Shakespeare calls "the slings and arrows of outrageous fortune." In later years, it is experienced in the decline in physical attractiveness, sexual prowess, body function, and a return to dependence and powerlessness.[71]

Kaufman draws the evocative image of an "internal shame spiral." An event occurs—for example, trying to "act close to someone and feeling rebuffed"—and one looks inward. The experience becomes internalized, often including mental pictures. "The precipitating event is relived internally over and over, causing the sense of shame to deepen, to absorb other neutral experiences that happened before as well as those that may come later, until finally the self is engulfed."[72] There is a spiraling tornado effect in which everything gets swept up. I have often heard severely depressed people paralyzed in raging litanies of self-disparagement: they are no good; they are bad to the core, unloved and unlovable, rotten, mean, cruel, selfish.

Shame can also be experienced when unflattering or foolish aspects of people with whom we are strongly identified are exposed. We may feel shame about or on behalf of parents, siblings, spouses, and children.

Many theorists now believe that the experience of shame is a universal human propensity; it is not an abnormal affect. However, what has been disputed is the exact childhood origins of shame.[73] Possible psychic origins of toxic shame will be discussed in detail in Chapter 7. The point that I want to make at this juncture is, as Lynd puts it, "The particular aspects of self especially vulnerable to exposure differ in different cultures."[74] For example, in our culture, shame is related to the uncovering of nakedness. The amount of uncovering that might arouse shame has differed, however, even in Western culture, as one can see simply by comparing the acceptable dress codes of women today with that at the beginning of the twentieth century.

Furthermore, in other cultures the experience of shame may be evoked under completely different circumstances from our own. For example, Eastern cultures are sometimes referred to as "we cultures" because personal self-esteem is inextricably fused with the honor and reputation of the family. Thus, Alan Roland, a New York psychoanalyst who has lived in Eastern cultures and done psychotherapy with many Asian people, notes that "How one reflects on the family, and how one's contributions and behavior are or are not valued by other family members, as well as the very reputation of the family, itself, becomes central to we-self-esteem."[75]

Shame in Eastern cultures such as Japan and India occurs around the we-self. "The standards most important to the we-self are to avoid friction and maintain harmonious relationships. These are core self values."[76] Thus, according to Michael Lewis, Japanese persons typically experience shame when there is a failure in their sensitivity to others' feelings and needs.[77]

Thus, the propensity for shame seems to exist universally in humankind; it is only how and when it gets triggered that is not universal. One writer put it this way:

> Although the circumstances likely to precipitate shame are diverse, since diverse cultures produce diverse norms, phenomenologically the experience of shame and its outer manifestations are pretty much the same the world over: blushing, lowering of the eyes or other avoidance of eye contact, lowering of the head so that the face cannot be seen. Subjective descriptions of the experience also indicate that the inward effects are substantially the same: we feel that the ground is opening up and that we will disappear into the abyss (or we wish to); there is a desire for

flight away from the source of shame, accompanied by a feeling of paralysis, as though we were unable to move at all; our mental acuity diminishes, leaving us with a feeling that where there used to be a working mind there is now a slow-moving ooze— paralysis of the intellect; we sometimes have the sensation of intense heat from what I have called the "existential blush," which registers in some strange place which is not just psyche and not just soma but both at once, as though a hellish flame had located the precise juncture of bodyself and soulself, the infinitesimal stem from which our life sprung.[78]

* * *

Having expended a considerable amount of space expounding upon the horrors of shame, it is nevertheless a fact that much good can come from it. A great deal of powerful religious experience originates and emerges from the awful muck and mire of shame. If we stand honestly in the godless vortex of shame, with as little resort as possible to the shame defenses, we can emerge as more authentic, more creative, more compassionate, more mature, and better integrated. This is the growth that comes from grace. This is the very essence of religious transformation. Standing courageously in the shame vortex—allowing ourselves to admit to feeling small, inadequate, finite, and human—eventually leads to awe and a deeper connection with the one who *is* God, in whom we find our true home.

Chapter 4

The Revelatory Potential of Shame

The scarlet letter was her passport into regions where other women dared not tread. Shame, Despair, Solitude! These had been her teachers—stern and wild ones—and they had made her strong, but taught her much amiss.

Nathaniel Hawthorne, *The Scarlet Letter*

When we hear or read the word *shame* we tend immediately to understand that it is a negative and destructive human emotion, something we need to work to expunge. However, I contend that shame is part of the human condition, and we should not only try to learn to live with it but to learn from it. When shame overtakes our entire personality, of course, we do need and should seek healing, but even then the process of healing can teach us much about ourselves, about others, and about our relationship with others and with God. Shame holds many gifts for the development of authentic spirituality and personality.

The pioneering work of Helen Lynd was the first to discuss the revelatory, transformative potential of shame.[1] Accepting Erikson's formulation of the two formative stages—"autonomy versus shame and doubt" and "initiative versus guilt"—Lynd builds her distinction between personalities based primarily on the "shame axis" and those based primarily on the "guilt axis." Lynd agrees with Erikson that shame is an earlier experience than guilt:

Shame is doubt, including diffused anxiety, an overall ashamedness, a consciousness of the whole self, a feeling that life is happening to the individual. Anxiety is peculiarly associated with shame. In every potential crisis of development anxiety is possible, and each new conflict may revive latent anxiety. But anxiety has special relation to the conflict between shame and doubt and the developing sense of . . . autonomy.[2]

And again, "in shame there is doubt, a questioning of trust."[3]

Shame and guilt are in no sense polar opposites, and they "enter into the attitudes and behavior of most people, and often into the same situation." However, there are large differences in the balance and influences of the two from individual to individual, and whether a person lives more on the guilt or the shame axis impacts upon how he or she processes, understands, and acts upon life experiences. Lynd's illustrative presentation of some contrasts between the perspectives along the guilt access and those along the shame axis warrants reproduction in full:[4]

Guilt Axis	Shame Axis
Concerned with each separate, discrete act	Concerned with the overall self
Involves transgression of a specific code, violation of a specific taboo	Involves falling short, failure to reach an ideal
Involves an additive process; advance to healthy personality by deleting wrong acts and substituting right ones for them	Involves a total response that includes insight, something more than can be reached by addition
Involves competition, measurement on a scale, performing the acts prescribed as desirable	Involves acting in terms of the pervasive qualitative demands of oneself, more rigorous than external codes; each act partakes of the quality of the whole
Exposure of a specific misdemeanor, with emphasis on to whom exposed; exposure of something that should be hidden in a closet	Exposure of the quick of the self, most of all to oneself; exposure of something that can never be hidden in a closet, is in the depths of the earth or in the open sunlight
Concern about violation of social codes of cleanliness, politeness, and so on	Concern about unalterable features of one's body, way of moving, clumsiness, and so on

Feeling of wrongdoing for a specific harmful act toward someone one loves	Feeling that one may have loved the wrong person, or may be inadequate for the person one loves
Being a good, loyal friend, husband, wife, partner	Having an overflowing feeling for friend, husband, wife, children which makes goodness and loyalty a part of the whole experience with no need for separate emphasis
Trust built on the conception of no betrayal, no disloyal act, as a preliminary to giving affection	Trust, that is a process of discovery which gradually eliminates fear of exposure, which is not the result of an act of will but unfolds with the unfolding experience
Feelings of anger, jealousy, meanness for certain socially recognized causes	Inwardly deep feelings of anger, jealousy, meanness in outwardly slight situations known to oneself only
Emphasis on decision-making; any decision is better than none	Ability to live with some indecisiveness (multiple possibilities) even though it means living with some anxiety
Feeling of guilt toward someone who has denounced one for adequate or inadequate cause	Feeling of shame toward someone who trusts one if one is not meeting that trust
Emphasis on content of experience in work, leisure, personal relations	Emphasis on quality of experience, not only on content
Surmounting of guilt leads to righteousness	Transcending of shame may lead to sense of identity, freedom

Lynd's basic thesis, drawn from this comparison and from Erikson's analysis of stages of development, suggests to her "that a sense of identity cannot be reached along the guilt axis alone, that more is needed than discarding specific wrong acts and substituting right acts for them." She rhetorically asks, "Can confronting experiences of shame full in the face be one more clue to the discovery of what this something more is?"[5] Lynd devotes most of her book to demonstrating that this indeed is the case.

Identity based primarily on the guilt axis is identity formed in terms of what Lynd calls "the prohibiting superego." Individuals whose identity is formed along this axis "tend to find continuity in their lives either by means of basic emphasis on what others have taught them they should do and—more especially—should not do."[6] Individuals whose identity is formed more along the shame axis tend to look for their own lines of direction.

Lynd postulates that identity based more on the shame axis than the guilt axis "may go deeper and be more of a continuous process of creation" than identity based on the guilt axis. This is because the guilt axis leads individuals to find meaning and purpose in their lives based upon what others have taught them they should do and not do. This fits precisely with the spiritual/theological premise that has already been proposed: shame is at the root of many, if not most, religious conversions and transformations. Guilt alone does not put an individual in the vortex, the godless place, and does not typically lead to deep transformation. A person whose identity is focused on the guilt axis may "at relatively small emotional expense fulfill the requirements society makes of him":

> Shame, while touched off by a specific, often outwardly trivial occurrence initially felt as revealing one's own inadequacies, may also confront one with unrecognized desires of one's own and the inadequacy of society in giving expression to these desires. There is a natural tendency to seek cover from such experiences since the culture has little place for revelations of the inmost self or of the central dynamics of the society. But it is the whole purpose of oneself and of one's society that invites reexamination in the light of these experiences. Selective fulfilling of social roles when it occurs then becomes part of the continuing process rather than a series of isolable acts. Stubborn and minute control is replaced by the unfolding of the spirit. In a society more directly and variously expressive of human desires the guilt axis and the shame axis, role fulfillment and personal fulfillment, might more nearly coincide.[7]

Most important, confrontation of shame experience

> requires an ability to risk, if necessary, to endure disappoint-
> ment, frustration and ridicule. Commitment to any position or to
> any loyalty, like commitment to another person, involves the
> risk of being wrong and the risk of being ridiculous. It is *rela-*
> *tively* easy to take even difficult action if one is sure that one is
> right, that one has grasped the truth of a situation; it is relatively
> easy to entertain multiple possibilities of truth and of right ac-
> tion if one remains a spectator on the sidelines. Far more diffi-
> cult than either is to give everything one is in supporting all the
> truth one can see at any given time, with full awareness that
> there are other possibilities and that further knowledge may en-
> large and revise the hypotheses on which one has risked every-
> thing. Estrangement with life and with history—self-discovery
> and further discovery of the world—has always involved just
> such risks.[8]

One might even see guilt as a defense to shame. Guilt does not
reach as deeply into the experienced self as does shame. When we say
we feel guilty for acts or omissions, it may often be the case that we
are defending against the more difficult and self-revelatory experience of shame. Since guilt is a subpart of the shame affect and springs
from the shame affect, we may sometimes permit ourselves to go
only so deeply into the affect, i.e., to the experience of guilt, the product of the prohibiting superego, rather than the experience of essential flawedness.

At this point, Lynd's thinking seems to coalesce with D. W.
Winnicott's. The latter came to a conclusion similar to Lynd's, albeit
by a different route. For present purposes, it is sufficient to note Winnicott believed that although children might be taught rules and codes
to be obeyed, real morality was an inborn, internal morality to be
found and nurtured within each developing individual. For example,
he stated that "what is commonly called religion arises out of human
nature, whereas there are some who think of human nature as rescued
from savagery by a revelation from outside human nature."[9] He cautions parents that children can be taught "beliefs that have meaning
for yourself and that belong to the small cultural or religious area that
you happen to be born into or to choose as an alternative to the one
you were born into." However, the parent will succeed only "to the

extent that the child has a capacity to believe in anything at all."[10] This capacity depends not upon the rules that are taught but rather upon the "experience of the person as a developing baby and child in the matter of care."[11] In one of his many beguiling, enigmatic, and memorable statements, Winnicott noted: "Probably the greatest suffering in the human world is the suffering of the normal or healthy or mature person."[12] This underlines Winnicott's contention that a person who is governed by True Self experience is more likely to question the rules that are handed to him or her by society. This person's morality is, as Union Seminary Professor Ann Ulanov once said in a course lecture, "portable," but this comes at a price, and the price is that of painful grappling with the rules of his or her culture and willingness to bear the ostracism—sometimes punishment—that is often attendant upon breaking them.

We are brought back to Winnicott's concept of True Self/False Self which was touched on earlier. Winnicott's False Self develops "when the maternal caretaker is not sufficiently able to sense or respond to the needs of the infant. The infant is forced to attune itself to the mother's 'gestures' and to adapt itself to her much too early."[13] The person becomes merely "compliant" at the expense of development of his or her creative potential. Winnicott recognizes that the ability to compromise is an achievement: the False Self allows a person to fit in and to behave appropriately in social situations. However, in health, "the compromise ceases to become allowable when the issues become crucial. When this happens the True Self is able to override the compliant self."[14]

Thus, for example, Huckleberry Finn felt discomfort—"guilt"— because he did not report the runaway slave, Jim.[15] The false compliant self dictated that he do so. The moral code of his culture was that Jim was Miss Watson's property. He felt even more guilty when Jim spoke about buying or stealing his children, who belonged to someone else. However, Huckleberry Finn did not act on his guilt. Instead, he dealt with the conflict he felt between the only rules he had been taught—the "morality" of his cultural milieu—and a personal internal sense that turning Jim over was not something he could do. He would have felt shame had he done this, as distinguished from the guilt he felt for disregarding the moral code he had been taught—i.e., that Jim was Miss Watson's property and should be returned to her.

An obvious parallel example from Christian scripture of persons living on the "guilt axis" is the Pharisees who were dedicated to the traditions of the elders, and to meticulous observance of Jewish law. Paul himself boasted of his former zeal for ancestral traditions (Galatians 1:14). Pharisaic piety "included not only loyalty to the traditions but also punctilious observance of the laws" of Israel.[16] Paul exhorted Christian righteousness by faith, not adherence to the letter of Jewish law, "for the letter kills, but the Spirit gives life" (2 Corinthians 3:6). Further,

> For all who rely on works of the law are under a curse. . . . Now it is evident that no man is justified before God by the law; for "The one who is righteous will live by faith." But the law does not rest on faith. . . . Christ redeemed us from the curse of the law by becoming a curse for us—for it is written, "Cursed is everyone who hangs on a tree"—in order that in Christ Jesus the blessing of Abraham might come to the Gentiles, so that we might receive the promise of the Spirit through faith. (Galatians 3:10-14)

In the context of the current discussion, one could say that Paul saw the life, death, and resurrection of Jesus Christ as supplanting life on the "guilt axis"; Jesus' shameful death and elevation to the Godhead means that life on the guilt axis is not adequate:

> Therefore, since we are justified by faith, we have peace with God through our Lord Jesus Christ, through him we have obtained access to this grace in which we stand; and we boast in our hope of sharing the glory of God. And not only that, but we also rejoice in our sufferings, knowing that suffering produces endurance, and endurance produces character, and character produces hope, and hope does not disappoint us, because God's love has been poured into our hearts through the Holy Spirit which has been given to us. (Romans 5:1-5)

Martin Luther interpreted Paul as a theological opponent of Judaism. He contrasted "justification by works of law"—i.e., life on the "guilt axis"—with "justification by faith" in his indictment of Roman Catholic legalism. Modern scholars have taken issue with this interpretation.[17] Be that as it may, as Erikson notes, Martin Luther's "basic contribution was a living reformulation of faith. . . . The relation of faith and law is, of course, an eternal human problem, whether it appears in questions of church and state, mysticism and daily morality, or existential aloneness and political commitment."[18]

Certainly the crucifixion and later resurrection of the one whom Christians experience as the second person of the Godhead must confront us with the transformative possibility of shame. As Christians living in the twenty-first century we may do our best to sanitize and domesticate the Christ event, but we do so to our own loss, for it is in the scandal and the shame of the cross that its central mythic meaning emerges. The earliest Christians were frequently called to task about the fact that, as an oracle of Apollo recorded by Porphyry wrote, they were "persisting in . . . vain delusions, lamenting in song a god who died in delusions, who was condemned by judges whose verdict was just, and executed in the prime of life by the worst of deaths, a death bound with iron."[19] This oracle, originally in Greek, which was confirmed by no lesser pagans than Pliny, Tacitus, and Caecilius, confirmed that

> the one whom Christians claim as their God is a "dead God"—a contradiction in itself. . . . And if that were not enough, . . . he had been condemned to the worst form of death: he had to endure being fastened to the cross with nails.[20]

For people of the ancient world (Greeks, Romans, barbarians, and Jews), the cross was not just "any kind of death. . . . It was an utterly offensive affair, 'obscene' in the original sense of the word."[21] The shame and scandal of the cross seems to have put early Christians somewhat on the defensive: Justin describes the offense caused by the Christian message to the ancient world as "madness": "They say that our *madness* consists in the fact that we put a *crucified man* in the second place after the unchangeable and eternal God, the Creator of the world."[22]

Yet early Christians undoubtedly experienced a numinosity—transformative potential—in the horror of the shame of the cross. Thus, in the early second century, Melito's *Homily on the Passion* declared:

> He who hung the earth [in its place] hangs there, he who fixed the heavens is fixed there, he who made all things fast is made

fast upon the tree, *the Master has been insulted, God has been murdered,* the King of Israel has been slain by an Israelitish hand. O strange murder, strange crime! The master has been treated in unseemly fashion, his body naked, and not even deemed worthy of a covering, that [his nakedness] might not be seen. Therefore the lights [of heaven] turned away, and the day darkened, that it might hide him who was stripped upon the cross. (emphasis added)[23]

Surely it cannot be accidental that the manner of Jesus' death was the ultimate shameful death. Jesus stood in the vortex of shame, alone and with persons to whom he had ministered all through his life and in his last hours. He endured this shame without resort to shame defenses (Chapter 5) that most of us use to extract us from the shame vortex—the place that feels godless. We would do well to see Christ's resurrection as transformation of the archetypally constellated shame experience. The clinical work of Helen Lynd, Helen Lewis, and others confirms that "shame raises consciousness"; it is "the partner of self-awareness," and thus it can lead to transformation:

Its very occurrence arises from the fact that we are valuing animals. What is considered to be shameful varies greatly from age to age and from one culture to another. What is to be valued and what is to evoke shame is still much at issue in our society. But it is a serious mistake to confuse the need for altering specific values, social structures and lifestyles with a program that would eliminate the very capacity to feel shame over *anything*. To extirpate shame is to cripple our humanity.[24]

Shame makes us "self"-conscious and "self"-aware. It may assume pathological dimensions, but always it is a principal source of identity and, as such, it can be a gift, if confronted head-on: "Above all else, shame reveals the self inside the person, thereby exposing it to view. To feel shame is to feel seen in a painfully diminished sense."[25]

Helen Lynd makes the astute observation that

shame involves a quality of the unexpected; if in any way we feel it coming we feel powerless to avert it. This is in part because of the difficulty we have in admitting to ourselves either shame or the circumstances that give rise to shame. Whatever part voluntary action may have in the experience of shame is swallowed up in the sense of something that overwhelms us from without and "takes us" unawares. We are taken by surprise, caught off guard, or off base, caught unawares, made a fool of. It is as if we were suddenly invaded from the rear where we cannot see, are unprotected, and can be overpowered.[26]

The potential for shame to lead to an expanded sense of self-identity is due, at least in part, to the fact that shame is often experienced as a "sudden awareness of incongruity" between what a situation actually is and what one thought it was. Shame is, most fundamentally, a feeling of exposure of one's innermost parts, or of one's private parts. It is an exposure of self to the eyes of others and provides at the same time an unwelcome view of self to self.

Shame interrupts unquestioning, unconscious unawareness. Moreover, one of the central theses of Lynd's groundbreaking book is that

> it is possible that experiences of shame if confronted full in the face may throw an unexpected light on who one is and point the way toward who one may become. Fully faced, shame may become not primarily something to be covered, but a positive experience of revelation.[27]

To know oneself can be painful. "There is much that, left to ourselves, we would just as soon overlook."[28]

The revelatory potential of shame has profound religious and spiritual implications. It means that confrontation of shame can expand our relationship with our selves, with one another, and with God. As will be discussed, this revelatory, transformative potential of shame is implicit in scripture, and particularly in the message of the New Testament.

Chapter 5

Defenses Against Shame

> The expense of spirit in a waste of shame
> Is lust in action; and till action, lust
> Is perjur'd, murderous, bloody, full of blame,
> Savage, extreme, rude, cruel, not to trust;
> Enjoy'd no sooner but despised straight; . . .
>
> Shakespeare, "Sonnet 129"

All of us, to some degree, employ defenses that protect against the experience of shame. In fact, they often even protect us from identifying our experiences as shame experiences: admitting to feelings of shame is itself shaming.

Shame defenses help us flee from our true selves, from intimacy with one another, and from God. Deployment of shame defenses might temporarily help avoid the experience of shame. It takes us out of the shame vortex and makes us less permeable to God.

Many theorists have attempted to catalog defenses against shame. Perhaps the most helpful of these undertakings has been John Patton's. In his book *Is Human Forgiveness Possible?* Patton states that in his experience in pastoral counseling,

> although most people talk about guilt, theirs or someone else's, their most profound experience is with shame. Guilt can more nearly be dealt with according to rational principle, whereas shame is inevitably relational and personal.[1]

There is more personal power in the experience of guilt; we feel guilt for our acts or omissions, and this gives us a sense of control over future decisions. Shame makes us feel helpless.[2]

Patton says that an "act which calls for forgiveness usually causes guilt in the injuring person and shame in the person injured by that act."[3] Although I would certainly agree that shame often results from injury by another, I do not agree that the perpetrator of the injurious act never feels shame; he or she does feel shame which is fused with guilt. The shame affect is often ignited by trivial actions or occurrences, which may not be evil in and of themselves but are experienced as shameful because they go against cultural mores. To use a biblical example, Matthew tells us that "Pharisees and scribes" confronted Jesus with the allegation that his disciples "do not wash their hands before they eat" (Matthew 15:1-2). One might see this as an attempt to shame Jesus and his followers for a breach in their tradition, but in this case it was not successful because Jesus refused to be shamed, saying, "It is not what goes into the mouth that defiles a person, but it is what comes out of the mouth that defiles" (Matthew 15:10-11).

Patton says that the primary ways in which people defend themselves against the painful experience of shame are rage, exercise of power, and righteousness. Following is a brief description of these defenses, along with some others that have been identified.

Most people who have written about shame name rage as a powerful and primitive defense against the experience of shame. Rage may be directed against the shamed self or against the perceived source of one's shame.[4] Writing from the therapeutic perspective of an analyst, and relying upon extensive clinical material, Helen Lewis discusses the dangers of "undischarged" shame—i.e., shame feelings and experiences that have not been acknowledged as such. One way in which undischarged shame is manifested is through rage. The therapist is very likely to receive the fury of undischarged shame since the therapeutic process is often experienced as shaming. There the client sits, in a situation markedly unmutual, paying large sums of money to reveal shadow aspects of his or her psyche, discussing narcissistically painful subjects. The therapist, who cannot help being witness to the patient's shame experiences, may automatically be an object of the patient's humiliated fury, which may be either bypassed or unacknowledged. It is a repetition of past relationships with parental or other figures who witnessed humiliations. It is, however, not only a repetition of the past

> but a concurrent phenomenon of the present artificial, therapeutic relationship. It cannot be totally analyzed away by showing its resemblance to the past, and the question, "Why be ashamed

of being in treatment?" makes it easier to endure treatment, but can also increase the patient's shame of being ashamed, thereby leaving a residue of unanalyzed symptom-source.[5]

It is not unusual for us to react to shame-provoking injuries with anger; think of the old adage: "Hell hath no fury like a woman scorned." In past times and in other cultures to this day, finding one's wife in flagrante delicto with another man has been deemed a legitimate defense to murder one or both of them. A Latino man in a much-publicized recent murder case entered his longtime lover's house and, finding her dressed in a wedding gown preparing to marry another man, killed her on the spot. It emerged at his trial that he had known nothing of her plans to marry someone else and had very recently had sexual relations with her. His trial testimony as to his feelings had all of the earmarks of a profound shame reaction. As Helen Lynd would say, circumstances were different than he had believed them to be; he experienced a radical sense of betrayal and misplaced assumptions about himself and his place in his lover's life and affections. He said, "I felt betrayed and confused. . . . I felt like the universe was falling. I felt myself blacking out and falling and as I was falling I saw a white flash and a body falling."[6] Here we have an all-too-real-life description of the kind of blackout and rage that profound shame can cause.

Kohut uses the term *narcissistic rage* to denote this specific type of rage. He says that those who "are in the grip of narcissist rage show total lack of empathy toward the offender." Thus, there arises

> the unmodifiable wish to blot out the offense which was perpetrated against the grandiose self and the unforgiving fury which arises. . . . The empathic observer will understand the deeper significance of the often seemingly minor irritant which has provoked an attack of narcissistic rage and will not be taken aback by the seemingly disproportionate severity of the reaction.[7]

Kohut's contributions to the psychology of shame are invaluable from the depth psychological perspective, and will be discussed more fully in Chapter 7.

James Gilligan, who has written extensively on violence, believes that individual and collective violence inevitably have their origins in shame. For example, he argues that Nazi scapegoating of Jews was the consequence of "'status-envies' generated by economic inequities." The group that most strongly supported Hitler was the lower-middle class, which had already suffered humiliation in the wake of World War I.[8] How timely is this theory of shame as an important root of violence in this era when terrorists living in the rubble of Afghanistan summoned enough rage to hatch a plot to bring down the World Trade Center, the Pentagon, four commercial jets loaded with passengers, and violently murder thousands of people living in the "only remaining superpower," a nation possessing an embarrassment of riches. Others have also posited shame as "a hidden cause of much contemporary cultural damage."[9]

Another defense to shame is the assertion of *power.* Patton contends that "the striving for power" over others is often

> a direct attempt to compensate for the sense of inferiority in relation to another and the shame that it produces. To the extent one is successful in gaining power over others, one becomes increasingly less vulnerable to further shame.[10]

In addition, power is "used to compensate for shame which was internalized earlier in life."[11] Patton quotes as follows from Gershen Kaufman's book *Shame: The Power of Caring:*

> To the degree that one can now feel powerful in relation to others, through gaining power over them, one has reversed roles from the way it was in early life. . . .The power strategy may or may not include longings for vengeance and the active seeking of revenge. But it does encompass instances in which security is to be won through control and self-esteem is to be amassed through power.[12]

Patton notes that Rollo May has identified five types of power: exploitative, manipulative, competitive, nutrient, and integrative. Patton opines that the first three types of power—exploitative, manipulative, and competitive—are often used to defend against shame. Exploitative power

> "is exercised by those who have been radically rejected. . . . Exploitive power always presupposes violence or the threat of violence. In this kind of power there is . . . no choice or sponta-

neity at all on the part of the victims." Manipulative power is power *over* another person. It is the power to persuade, outwit or induce behavior by means of guilt or implied obligation. Here too there is very little spontaneity and freedom of choice left to the person defending with it or to the person defending against it. Competitive power is power *against* another. "In its negative form, it consists of one person going up not because of anything he does or any merit he has, but because his opponent goes down."[13]

It seems plausible to suggest that the honor/shame dynamic which has already been discussed as being so prominent in the ancient Middle East was, most essentially, a manifestation and a cultural institutionalization of the power defense. Individuals gained power and prestige—call it honor—over others as a shield, protection, and defense against the shame experience. It is just this defense that the Jesus of the gospel narratives so often resisted. For example, at the time of the commencement of his ministry, Satan tried to tempt Jesus to take power and possession over "all of the kingdoms of the world and their splendor" (Matthew 4:8), but Jesus resisted this temptation. Furthermore, Jesus consistently refused to collude with the religious and secular authorities of his day, even though doing so might well have placed him in a greater position of worldly power and would almost certainly have averted his violent execution.

One paradoxical manifestation of the power defense to shame experience is behavior that many would see as shameless. Some theorists have contended that "shameless" behavior is the absence of shame. However, as Leon Wurmser says:

> Shamelessness is no simple regression to a stage before the establishment of a shame barrier. . . . Superficial shamelessness about betrayal, sexual provocation, and exhibitionism, coupled with brazen abuse of another person, undaunted by fear of ridicule and mockery, constitutes a defiant display of "power" in displaced form. The weakness about which the person is ashamed refers to tender feelings, to kindness, to warmth; these emotions represent subjugation and must be avoided at all costs.[14]

I believe that a tragic example of the use of exploitative power in our time is seen in the ongoing pedophilia scandal that has gripped the Roman Catholic Church. Priests used their power over children in a manner many would see as shameless. Yet as Eugene Kennedy makes clear in *The Unhealed Wound: The Church and Human Sexuality,*[15] it is the very shame associated with human sexuality, a repressing of sexual impulses at an early age, setting men "at odds with sexuality and themselves," which causes this "sexual wound to weep"[16]—with the result that some priests use immature and vulnerable children for sexual gratification. Human sexuality is a very potent source of shame and shame defenses. Sexual shame springs directly from the conflict between body and spirit, which is the most basic source of all shame.

The defense of *righteousness* is often used by someone who has been shamed but is able to find ways to conclude that he or she has been wronged, and is therefore the one who is "right." Righteousness is a way of assigning guilt in a given situation to someone else. As Patton relates, this defense is much supported by institutional religion. Patton observes that

> The church has a long history of attempting to determine who is right in a particular human situation such as divorce or conflict between parents and children. Psychologically, however, righteousness functions in another way. If one cannot be loved, then he or she can find satisfaction in being right or righteous. "You may have rejected me, but I know that I am right."[17]

Patton gives as an example a woman whose husband unexpectedly abandoned her. The woman, "Emmie," was left with her shame, but she did not call it shame. The way that she defended against her feelings of shame was by constant reminders to herself and others of the "fact" that she was in the right—she was the injured party who had done no wrong. As Patton states, one problem with the defense of righteousness is that it makes real forgiveness of others difficult.

In the well-known passage from Luke in which a penitent woman enters a dinner party at the home of the Pharisee Simon and proceeds to weep at Jesus' feet, pouring costly ointment on him, Simon remonstrates in his heart that Jesus should not be allowing this sinful woman to touch him. Simon is a righteous man: he is obedient to the Hebrew law. He shows *contempt* for the penitent woman, and contempt is very much an outgrowth of the defenses of righteousness and rage. Contempt is a form of projection of shame.[18] However, Simon's righteousness and contempt is preventing the entry of grace.

Ironically enough given the recorded teachings and ministry of Jesus, the institutional Church chronically resorts to righteousness. One might see the Roman Catholic Church's response to the latest pedophilia scandals as resorting to the righteousness defense. Instead of looking to the fundamental root causes of this virtual epidemic of sexual shame, the Church now simply rushes to punish and cast out the "guilty" as if that will solve the underlying problem. The Church refuses to look at the unhealed wound of its theology and teachings on the subject of human sexuality—the denial, the repression and fear—that is clearly the root cause of these many tragedies.[19] The Church says, in essence, "those who have done these terrible acts must be punished and excluded, and although we are sorry we did not punish and exclude them before, our institution is righteous and inviolate." The Church and its hierarchy defend against their own shame by the use of righteousness, denying all of the evidence of the pain of the unhealed sexual wound that the Church's own teachings have inflicted on its bishops, cardinals, priests, sisters, and laypeople. Its teachings and its righteous stance have arisen from the primary source of all shame: the body and its desires and condition are seen as being at war with the spirit.

Patton's enumeration of shame defenses is excellent as far as it goes. However, he omits some important defenses that other theorists have emphasized.

The *withdrawal* defense has already been alluded to in the context of the isolating effect of shame. It is this defense that becomes activated when we make the conscious or unconscious determination we would rather be isolated and lonely than risk appearing foolish or being rejected.

Using the defense of *perfectionism,* one is always striving to avoid shame by being perfect, selfless, and beyond reproach in every respect. This is a "society-friendly" defense. It makes for good students, good employees, compliant children, good neighbors—i.e., overall "solid citizens." Perfectionism coincides very well with the Judeo-Christian ethic, with its emphasis on "moral" behavior.[20]

The *perfectionism* defense is a manifestation of the Winnicottian False Self. Martha Nussbaum, in a discussion of Winnicott's case study of "Mr. B" (a man who as a child felt loved only when he was "good") aptly writes that "shame . . . causes the real, vulnerable self to hide, the robotic and inauthentic 'false self' to come to the fore."[21] The defense of perfectionism is inherently unsatisfying, and it cannot succeed because perfection is a state no human can reach:

> The quest for perfection itself is self-limiting and hopelessly doomed both to fail and to plunge the individual back into the very mire of defectiveness from which he so longed to escape. One can never attain that perfection, and awareness of failure to do so reawakens that already-present sense of shame.[22]

Perfectionism is, in essence, a disowning of parts of the self and is implicated in "creating the personal shadow" which holds our shame.[23] See Chapter 6 for further discussion of shame as "shadow" in the Jungian sense.

In the defense of *defeatism,* one simply gives up to shame. This defense can be activated any number of ways. One may sink into a state of deep depression, spiraling ever deeper into the vortex of everything that is wrong with oneself. A study of college students that was conducted indicated blame of character (i.e., shame) is directly related to clinical depression, whereas blame of behavior (i.e., guilt) does not give rise to depressive symptoms. In Freud's seminal essay "Mourning and Melancholia,"[24] he discussed how depression arises from the tendency to turn anger in on the self, with consequent and inordinately low self-esteem. Another possible consequence of the defense of defeatism is addiction to drugs, alcohol, sex, or food. One could also simply give up and not even attempt to fulfill one's creative, life-giving potential.

Using the *transfer of blame* defense, a person is not interested in trying to find ways to repair or deal with whatever the mess is in his or her life but only in transferring blame to someone else. "When blaming generalizes as a strategy, we have the familiar pattern of 'scapegoating.'"[25] Someone else is found to bear the shame and the blame. In Jungian terms, this defense is projection of one's own shadow material on others. It furnishes an explanation for the success of the most demonic aspects of Hitler's Third Reich: a Germany that had been humiliated and shamed by the Allied nations at the conclusion of World War I transferred blame to "the Jews" for all of its defeats and humiliations. Those who cannot confront their own homosexual feelings—i.e., they feel shame about them—attack and scapegoat openly gay and lesbian people.

Andrew Morrison and others have cogently argued for the inclusion of *envy* as a defense to shame.[26] I think that the contention has merit and that envy is a by-product of shame. Shame results from the "invidious comparison" of self with another, or with an ego ideal. It is just this kind of comparison that often gives rise to envy.

Melanie Klein viewed envy as a need to devalue, spoil, and render powerless the good object.[27] Ann Belford Ulanov has noted that when there is envy, something good, something positive, can always be found. Envy attempts to destroy the good "because it originates outside oneself and remains outside one's control."[28] As Morrison puts it,

> [f]or envy of the powerful object to flourish, that object must be compared with a shame-ridden, incompetent self. . . . [E]nvy also serves as a *protection* against the experience of shame, at least with respect to another object. The subject's attention shifts from the self's shame to the object's power and thus displaces preoccupation from the meager state of the self to the powerful state of the object. In addition, insofar as envy undermines the importance of the object, it may also lead to reduction of shame with regard to the formerly omnipotent other.[29]

Jesus did not fall back into any of these shame defenses. He stood courageously in the midst of shame and confronted it repeatedly in his life, ministry, and death. Perhaps we see him standing most courageously and intentionally in the shame vortex in the gospel accounts of his trial, during which he refused to be goaded by the mockery, the interrogation, and the humiliation heaped upon him by Pilate and his own people. All of the defenses of shame have at least one thing in common: they take us out of the vortex, out of the place of tension between isolation and individuation and unity—the tension between the instinctual and the *imago dei*—and they make transformation impossible. Only by standing in the vortex and admitting and confronting the tension that is the experience of shame can we achieve transformation.

Chapter 6

Methodology in the Use
of Depth Psychology in Theological
Study and Ministry

O for God's sake
they are connected underneath

From Muriel Rukeyser, *Islands*

As an ordained person active in parish ministry, I approach the
question of the etiology, significance, and ramifications of shame
from a Christian faith perspective. I assume the actual existence of
God whose being undergirds all of human life and seeks ways to draw
us into relationship with it. However, having said this, I also maintain
that the insights of depth psychology must inform this study. As Morton Kelsey has written, "the masters of the devotional life and depth
psychologists need each other."[1]

The ministry of an Episcopal priest, as set forth in the ordinal of the
1979 *Book of Common Prayer,* is to "work as a pastor, priest and
teacher," to "preach the Gospel," and to take one's "share in the councils of the Church."[2]

I believe that the roles of "pastor, priest and teacher," "preaching
the Gospel," and "sharing in the councils of the Church" are greatly
enhanced by understandings gleaned from depth psychology.

By this I do not mean to suggest that in pastoral care and counseling situations a priest or minister should be in the habit of explicitly
expounding theories of depth psychology. Nor should one preach the
gospel in the explicit terms of depth psychology, administer the sacraments with explicit reference to theories of depth psychology, or
expound theories of depth psychology at denominational conventions and conferences; quite the contrary. People who come to church
to participate in worship services, and those who come for pastoral

care and counseling, expect their ministers to have theological insight and to speak the language of the Christian faith tradition. For a minister to habitually use the explicit language of depth psychology in ecclesiastical settings is not particularly helpful. It tends to elicit dazed looks at best and hostility at worst. Most people are not conversant in this language and may feel that a minister who uses it is deliberately obfuscating matters.

Furthermore, it is important for ordained people to claim their particular authority as stewards of God's mysteries, as living symbols of the Church which Christians hold to be the Body of Christ in the world. This symbolic role is very different from the healing role of therapists, and it sometimes evokes different concerns and questions from those for whom we are caring. Clergy are expected to bring theological and spiritual perspectives to their work. They are called upon to hold questions about God, faith, guilt, morality, their feelings about the institutional Church, their experience of divinity, and, of course, the experience of shame. Ann Belford Ulanov has written extensively on this. Clergy, she states,

> stand publicly for the existence of this mysterious heart of Being and its interest in us, its reaching out to us, to bring us home, no matter how far we have been away, or how far we have fallen into disarray and negligence. Just as mental health professionals must acknowledge the existence of Spirit and their own relation or non-relation to it to do their clinical work responsibly, so clergy much acknowledge psychic reality to which their function of symbolizing the mercy of God must connect if they are to fulfill their ministry.
>
> Clergy represent the connection of Spirit; the connection must include people's psychological life along with our political and social life, our ethical conduct, how we manage money, deal with citizens different from ourselves and receive their dealings with us.[3]

However, our relationship with God and, indeed, aspects of Godself can profitably be explored through the mechanisms of the human psyche as they are understood through the idiom of depth psychology, and these burgeoning understandings must inform the work of the Church and its ministers. Pastoral theology and depth psychology can be seen as interpenetrating, interlocking disciplines, mutually informing each other.

I have searched for a metaphor that would describe how I see the understandings of depth psychology as informing the work of the institutional Church and its representatives. Kathleen O'Connor referred to psychology and religion as different "lenses" in looking for understanding and meaning.[4] What comes to my mind are the 3-D glasses which are sometimes provided so that movies and certain photographic images can be seen in three-dimensional form. Yes, an image can be seen in two dimensions, but in three-dimensional form the image seems to come toward us, entering our space, when we are wearing the glasses. In fact, like scripture and faith itself, a film or an image made for viewing with 3-D glasses is somewhat fuzzy when viewed without the glasses. In images made for 3-D viewing, "'layering' becomes a literal component of the design, in which different levels of the composition exist at different perceptual levels, in a 'real' three dimensional space."[5] The layers become discernible with the use of 3-D glasses, which work by separating each eye's perception of certain colors. For ministers and other theologians, depth psychology can be a kind of 3-D lens that adds a new layer to viewing scripture and our experience of God. We can look at scripture and spiritual experience without the lens that depth psychology provides, but we miss the depth and clarity that depth psychology can add.

Another, analogous metaphor also comes to mind. In recent years a graphic phenomenon has emerged using what are referred to as "3-D stereograms." Three-dimensional stereogram art is a fascinating product of the computer age, whereby software programs fracture 3-D images. Through "three-dimensional viewing"—accomplished with practice by "looking through" an illustration as though viewing something about ten feet away instead of right in front of the eyes—a remarkable 3-D image emerges that otherwise was undetectable.[6] When one looks only casually at the stereograms, one sees only a two-dimensional abstract mass of color—"wallpaper." The 3-D image is discernible only by learning how to see it, how to allow the eyes to be focused on an invisible object more distant than the printed page. This three-dimensional viewing is analogous to what understanding of depth psychology can do for pastors. It gives us the ability to view scripture and the religious life through a three-dimensional understanding. We not only see length and width but can also actually experience a third dimension, which is depth. The fourth dimension is transcendent and must remain unapproachable.

Depth psychology is an important tool in understanding our motivations, intentions, and desires. Religious truths and knowledge of God are filtered through the human senses and the human body; they are filtered through our own life experiences and frames of reference. The greatest religious geniuses have always known that spiritual maturity and understanding depends upon self-knowledge. Thus, we find Christ in the Gospel of Thomas: "If you bring forth what is within you, what you bring forth will save you. If you do not bring forth what is within you, what you do not bring forth will destroy you."[7] Likewise, elsewhere in the Gospel of Thomas, Christ says: "Let him who seeks continue seeking until he finds. When he finds, he will become troubled. When he becomes troubled, he will be astonished, and he will rule over all things."[8] St. Teresa wrote in her autobiography in the sixteenth century that

> the matter of self-knowledge must never be neglected. No soul on this road is such a giant that it does not often need to become a child at the breast again. (This must never be forgotten: I may repeat it again and again, for it is of great importance.) For there is no state of prayer, however sublime, in which it is not necessary to go back to the beginning.[9]

Perhaps no one has written more movingly about the extreme forms of psychic disease and their implications for religious life than Anton Boisen. Boisen himself had been diagnosed with schizophrenia (then known as dementia praecox) and was hospitalized for psychotic episodes six times between 1895 and 1937.[10] During that same period, Boisen founded the clinical pastoral education movement that has been so important a part of the training of chaplains and ordained ministers in the United States. Central to his work was the premise that "certain forms of mental illness, particularly those characterized by anxiety and conviction of sin, are not evils. They are instead manifestations of the power that makes for health. They are analogous to fever or inflammation in the body."[11] Boisen saw his own experience of mental illness as the psyche's attempt at "reorganization" in accordance with God's purpose for him. Boisen wrote:

I am thus very sure that the experience which plunged me into this new field of labor was mental illness of the most profound and unmistakable variety. I am equally sure that it was for me a problem solving religious experience.[12]

It is significant that Boisen was particularly convinced mental illness contained the power that made for health and creative endeavor. Boisen believed that much mental illness (including his own) arose from dealing with one's sexual needs and desires as they conflicted with societal norms and standards of conduct. In reading his autobiographical work, one cannot escape the conclusion that he suffered from severe personal shame, no doubt fostered by his parents' Victorian conviction that he was oversexed, beginning in his early childhood. This was an opinion that Boisen does not seem to have ever seriously questioned, even in old age.[13] The shame this conviction must have produced, particularly in a man who never married but instead carried a lifelong unrequited love (obsession would probably be a more accurate word) for a woman whom he met as a young man, can only be imagined.

In his book *Exploration of the Inner World,* Boisen wrote that "to be plunged as a patient into a hospital for the insane may be a tragedy or it may be an opportunity. For me it was an opportunity."[14] Furthermore, Boisen noted, "The Christian church has long recognized the significance of the inner conflict, and the classical description of such conflicts is that which Paul of Tarsus gives us in the seventh chapter of Romans."[15] Boisen believed there to be a "relationship between the mystical and the pathological which is to be explained by the fact . . . that religious concern is invariably associated with the attempt to grapple with the vital issues of life."[16] Pastoral theologian Daniel Day Williams said that "the struggle with the neurosis may become the focal point of the wrestle of the soul with God. We know that this happens. We need to know much more about why and how it happens."[17]

In Boisen's *Out of the Depths,* he wrote that "Mental disorder is the price humanity has to pay for having the power of choice and the capacity for growth."[18] He lamented the general failure of the Church to minister to the mentally ill and was "convinced that in so far as we attain any true understanding of the [mentally ill], . . . so far shall we be able to see the meaning and end of human life."[19]

The tools that St. Teresa and her contemporaries had for achieving self-knowledge were very different from the tools that people of the twenty-first century have. Understanding of the human psyche in our particular cultural location requires some basic knowledge of the idiom of depth psychology. In the early twentieth century, Sigmund Freud picked up various strands of thought and experience, from the "cure of souls" by clergy, to the clinical study of hypnosis, to interest in parapsychological phenomena such as clairvoyance and purported communications with the dead, to "animal magnetism," which was first introduced by Franz Anton Mesmer in the late eighteenth century. Freud may be credited with developing the first "scientific" account of the unconscious.[20]

Regardless of contemporary opinions about the merits of his particular theories, the fact remains that Freud's work advanced the idea of the reality of the dynamic unconscious. As one prominent student of Western thought put it, Freudian psychoanalysis and its many outgrowths began the process of freeing the modern mind from its

> naïve unconsciousness . . . as it brought to light the archaeological depths of the psyche, disclosed the intelligibility of dreams, fantasy and psycho-pathological symptoms, . . . demonstrated the importance of infantile experience in conditioning adult life, . . . unveiled the psychological relevance of mythology and symbolism, recognized the psychic structural components of the ego, superego, and id, revealed the mechanisms of resistance, repression, and projection, and brought forth a host of other insights laying open the mind's character and internal dynamics.[21]

Depth psychologists since Freud have advanced ideas that have plumbed deeply into the outermost limits of the human psyche to explore and attempt to understand feelings, impulses, emotional experiences, mental illness, and motivation. Most of these people, including (to name just a few) Alfred Adler, Otto Rank, Sandor Ferenczi, W. R. D. Fairbairn, Melanie Klein, Donald Winnicott, Margaret Mahler, John Bowlby, Otto Kernberg, and Heinz Kohut, have not proceeded from a religious worldview. As a matter of fact, many of them (beginning with Freud himself) have been avowedly areligious or avidly antireligious. Others, such as Christopher Bollas, Michael Balint, W. R. Bion, and Marion Milner, have written in terms that often seem profoundly spiritual but have not appropriated explicitly religious referents. A very notable exception was Carl Jung, who broke with Freud because of the former's insistence on the existence of a specifically religious/spiritual impulse in humankind.

However, regardless of whether depth psychologists have maintained explicitly religious points of view, their ideas about the operation of the human psyche have often had profound religious, spiritual, and theological implications, just as Darwin's *On the Origin of Species* has had profound implications for Judeao-Christian use and understanding of scripture.

One may well ask whether it is legitimate to appropriate the work of secular clinicians and scholars of the psyche to develop new understandings of who God is and how God makes itself known to human beings. I believe that it is just as appropriate as the use of any other contemporary idioms—some might say "scientific" understandings—in the development of new theologies for a new day. God is always making all things new, and perhaps most especially human understandings of who God is and how God acts in human history, and in the material world, in relationships between and among people, and in the human psyche. Theology differs from great art in that the latter is beautiful and moving from age to age, whereas theologies are always works in process. Yesterday's theology, as satisfying as it might have been in its time, must always be subject to rethinking and reimagining. The only thing that is absolute is God itself. Daniel Day Williams put it this way:

> The work of interpreting Christian faith is never finished. . . . It is God who is the absolute truth, not theology. . . . In seeking the integrity of the Christian witness as it bears upon the significance of the pastor's task, we recognize that we need all possible scientific and humanistic understanding of human beings and the way they live with one another. . . . Our Christian ministry participates in the deepest mystery of all, the life of the soul before God. We need both the light of faith and the patiently acquired light of empirical understanding if we are to serve God as ministers of the Church.[22]

Williams is unequivocal in his assertion of the need for pastoral work to be informed by understandings derived from other disciplines:

The pastor who seeks to help a paranoid by sympathy alone or by offering only the consolation of prayer and religious assurance is not really feeding the hungry person or giving the cup of cold water. *Love requires intelligence in action. . . . Those who emphasize personal relationship and acceptance often forget the discipline and preparation which have gone into the experience of the counselor or pastor who has developed the habits, insights and skills which open the way to fruitful personal meeting. The Christian understanding of salvation, we conclude, requires a continuing dialogue between Christian believers and the sciences of man. It excludes dogmatism on either side.* (emphasis added)[23]

Theology alone does not provide sufficient guidance in dealing with human problems:

> What the psychologist knows about the child's relation to the mother becomes suddenly illuminating for understanding why a particular person cannot understand the mercy of God. By the same token, psychology by itself is never enough, for we are led straight back to the question of who man is and what his life is all about.[24]

Pastoral theologians, pastoral counselors, pastoral caregivers, and depth psychologists need the 3-D glasses provided by one another's disciplines. I, as a pastor, priest, and teacher working in chaplaincy and in the institutional Church, am much helped if I can find a footing in depth psychology. Without this footing, I might easily drift into clichés and abstractions which, due to their dull familiarity, are all but meaningless standing alone. These often repeated abstractions are formulaic "church-speak." Before I entered seminary, I assumed that others, and particularly clergy, understood exactly what these phrases meant. I was thus surprised to discover that even clergy have trouble articulating meaning for statements such as those which follow:

> "Christ died for our sins."
> "We are washed in the blood of the lamb."
> "When you suffer, remember that Christ suffered too and this will make you feel better."

"God gave himself for us, a perfect sacrifice for the whole
world."
"If you beleive in Jesus Christ you will be saved."
"Jesus was both fully God and fully human."
"The Christian God is Trinitarian—Father, Son, and Holy Spirit."

Without the 3-D lens of depth psychology, these theological statements have little meaning. Nobody really understands them, and in
the Church they have come to function rather like elevator music.
Making such theological statements on their own tends only to stop the
conversation, because Christians feel that they are supposed to immediately understand their meaning. I am not suggesting here that these
statements of faith should be eliminated from our liturgy or that they do
not have deep psychic and mythic meaning. What I mean to say is that
a basis in depth psychology helps enflesh such faith statements with
meaning. It grounds us. It honors our humanity, while helping us to
confront the awesome otherness of God.

Ana Maria Rizzuto's groundbreaking work examined the origins,
development, and use of God images by applying theoretical insights
derived from depth psychologists to empirical clinical material, demonstrating that the "mature person re-encounters the God of his childhood"—as developed through the significant caretakers in the person's
development—"in later years at every corner of life: birth, marriage,
death."[25] We will see in Chapter 7 how problems in the relationship
between child and caretaker can create toxic shame in a developing
individual.

It must be said that the field of psychology and religion is always
reexamining itself. As Kathleen O'Connor, a psychotherapist and
professor of psychology and religion, put it, we find ourselves working against a "background of debates" about such basic issues as "the
epistemological status of both psychology as a science and religious
experience as a way of knowing. . . ."[26] O'Connor notes:

The twentieth century opened with a trust and optimism in science, reason, enlightenment and modernity. At its end we witnessed a profound undermining of confidence in the adequacy
of these means to describe and interpret human experience and
reality. "Psychology" emerged in the context of modernistic
culture with great promise that objective knowledge could ulti-

mately be achieved through the deployment of reason and specific scientific methods. Within recent decades, however, it has become increasingly clear that the empiricist foundations of "psychology" as a science are deeply flawed.[27]

Thus,

> it is possible to view "psychology" and "religion" as different ways of knowing, as different lenses through which we view human experience, and different knowledges and systems of understanding, different language and symbolic systems that are created (and re-created) in what is essentially a shared human task—the construction (and reconstruction) of meanings that ground and sustain human existence, in ways that avoid absolutism on the one hand and pure relativism on the other. It is the dynamic quality and interplay between "certainty-uncertainty" in psychology's quest, and between "belief-unbelief" in the religious odyssey that I find so irresistable yet so problematic.[28]

Freud himself, who seldom admitted to being engaged in other than a strictly empirical science, in his old age once referred to his instinct theory as "our mythology," adding, "instincts are mythical entities, magnificent in their indefiniteness."[29]

The proposition that religion and depth psychology should be interpenetrating, interlocking disciplines is strangely abhorrent to some.[30] Psychologists and theologians (including clergy who minister within the institutional church) have traditionally regarded each other across a chasm of great suspicion, which is rather remarkable given the fact that the "science" of psychology clearly has its ancestry and original roots in theology and the "cure of souls."[31] In his classic book *The Individual and His Religion,* Gordon Allport noted that:

> [F]or the most part psychotherapists employ implements borrowed from the clergy. The reason is simple enough: until recent times the church alone dealt with troubles of personality. The borrowed devices include listening, encouragement, advice, and the relationship of transference wherein the applicant finds security in dependence upon his counselor. Historically, the church has employed the Sacrament of Penance, and although

the ritual of confession is certainly different from the ritual of the analyst's couch, the element of similarity is still apparent.[32]

Traditionally, psychiatry has seen spirituality as having pathological implications. As Stanislov Grof puts it,

> Although not clearly spelled out, it is somehow implicit in the current psychiatric system of thought that mental health is associated with atheism, materialism, and the world view of mechanistic science. Thus, spiritual experiences, religious beliefs and involvement in spiritual practices would generally support a psychopathological diagnosis.[33]

Allport in 1950 observed that since the Victorian age when William James delivered *The Varieties of Religious Experience,* "religion and sex seem to have reversed their positions." Thus,

> William James could bring himself to devote barely two pages to the role of sex in human life which he labeled euphemistically as "the instinct of love." Yet no taboos held him back from directing the torrent of his genius into the *Varieties of Religious Experience.* On religion he spoke freely and with unexcelled brilliance. Today, by contrast, psychologists write with the frankness of Freud or Kinsey on the sexual passions . . . but blush and grow silent when the religious passions come into view. Scarcely any modern textbook writers in psychology devote as much as two shamefaced pages to the subject—even though religion, like sex, is an almost universal interest of the human race.[34]

Carl Jung, who may be credited with being the first twentieth-century depth psychologist to ascribe a specifically religious impulse in the psyche,[35] said,

> I have been accused of "deifying the soul." Not I but [Godself] has deified it! *I* did not attribute a religious function to the soul, I merely produced the facts which prove that the soul is *naturaliter religiosa,* i.e., produces a religious function.[36]

Further,

> It would be blasphemy to assert that God can manifest . . . every-
> where save only in the human soul. . . . It would be going too far
> perhaps to speak of an affinity; but at all events the soul must
> contain in itself the faculty of relationship to God, i.e., the corre-
> spondence, otherwise a connection could never come about.[37]

In response to the sometimes heard argument that the field of psychology and religion "psychologizes" God and/or "reduces" God to
an element in the human psyche, I note first that to say God is present
in the human psyche is certainly not to deny God's presence elsewhere or to deny that God is transcendent and unknowable as well as
immanent. Moreover, to say that God is present in the human psyche
is really not anything new. The immanence of God in the psyche has
been known to mystics of every religious tradition in all times and
places.[38] In Deuteronomy, Moses declared to the ancient Israelites
that God's word is not "far away . . . No, the word is very near you; it
is in your mouth and in your heart for you to observe" (Deuteronomy
30:14). Jesus himself said (at least in some translations): "For, in fact,
the Kingdom of God is within you" (Luke 17:21).[39]

But how do we "observe" it? Occasionally the experience overwhelms us with a direct and powerful experience of ultimate reality.[40] Or we may suffer from more or less painful spiritual struggles
that hide behind psychic symptoms of depression, neurosis, sometimes psychosis. Oftentimes, as we have seen, shame is at the root
of these illnesses. This is not to suggest that the symptoms are not real
or that they do not have to be dealt with, often with the help of professionals in the mental health field (i.e., psychologists, analysts, psy-
chiatrists, social workers). Nor is it to say that the suffering itself is
always or primarily a manifestation of God. The bits and pieces,
shards and fragments, of an individual's psyche may be so far flung
and unintegrated that he or she may need to do substantial integrative
work before even beginning to have any sense of God's grace or presence in the psyche.[41] However, there may well be times in which
mental disease is a way in which God claims attention in the psyche
and in life. This is so because even an intimation of the infinite God
cannot be suddenly held in the container of the tiny human psyche. "It
is a fearful thing to come into the hands of the living God" (Hebrews
10:31).

Scripture is full of stories of people who have been brought to their knees by that encounter. They are confronted and overwhelmed with the enormity of God and their contrasting smallness and finiteness. This is the ontological basis of the shame experience, the "awe" side of shame which comes from realizing that although we may be *of God*, we are not God, and that we are tiny, fragile, finite creatures. Indeed, this awe aspect of the shame experience seems to the root of, or impetus for, much religious transformation. One thinks, for example, of Moses, confronting the terror of the burning bush before him; of the prophets Isaiah, Jeremiah, and Ezekiel; of Peter who fell to his knees when he first perceived that Jesus was the Christ; of the woman who entered the dinner party of Simon the Pharisee and proceeded to fall at Jesus' feet and wash them with her tears; of Paul, who fell from his horse and was struck blind upon encountering the risen Christ. It takes considerable stretching, and the psychic pain that goes with it, to integrate and make sense of such experiences as these individuals from scripture did. Sometimes the struggle with a neurosis may be the way for the soul to enter into deeper relationship with God. [42] The "stone that the builders rejected" can, in such case, become "the cornerstone" (Luke 20:17).

Biblical characters are, in the words of Wayne Rollins, "bearers of archetypal truths about the human condition that are alive and at work in the conscious and unconscious haunts of the human psyche or mind."[43] "Psychological biblical criticism," as it is now sometimes called,[44] provides a new hermeneutics for understanding scripture and, through that understanding, deepens and enhances religious meaning. Psychology and theology have common roots. Paul Tillich wrote that the two realms cannot be neatly separated: "here a system of theological doctrines and there congeries of psychological insights." To the contrary, as Tillich wrote, "The relationship is not one of existing alongside each other; it is a relationship of mutual interpenetration."[45] This interpenetration of psychology and spirituality "is necessary if religion is to work. There is no way of standing on one's own center without outside support."[46]

Depth psychology and spirituality at their best both deal with the following issues: first, intrapsychic experience or the individual's inner life and experience; second, relationships between and among individuals, and between individuals and their world; and third, experience that is felt and understood as experience of something transcending the personal (sometimes known as God). Depth psychology "calls its working area psychic experience or human behavior; [theology] is concerned with the relationship of mystery and truth of . . . eternal symbols . . . to the human situation."[47] The two disciplines "share a concentration on the hidden depths of human experience and a determination to probe these depths."[48]

The joint study of psychology and religion provides invaluable tools for ministers, theologians, and laypeople who are intentionally seeking to be engaged in the spiritual life. First, it furnishes a way of understanding spiritual experience from a psychological perspective. How might God be using the structures of the psyche to establish and maintain relationships with human beings? Second, it provides pastoral caregivers with a more informed understanding of the human psyche and unconscious processes, as well as ideas about how these processes might be related to mystical-spiritual experience. Third, it provides a vital new entrance point for theology about the doctrines of the Triune God (Creator, Redeemer, and Sustainer), about creation and humanity in particular. Fourth, it provides new theoretical insights into psychological experiences and mechanisms, particularly experience and understanding of God. Fifth, it provides important insights into the psychological power of religious rituals and practices—e.g., the sacraments and sacramental rights of the Church. Sixth, it provides a fruitful hermeneutic for opening and enlivening scripture in preaching in a postmodern world in which many people can no longer accept much of its historical factuality. Last, it provides new insights into issues and problems faced by ecclesiastical institutions—from local parishes of all sizes, to dioceses and presbyteries, to the universal "one Holy Catholic and apostolic Church."

It is important for developing theologies on the principle doctrines of the Church—humanity, God, Christ, the Holy Spirit, salvation, atonement, eschatology—to be informed by or at least cognizant of theories of depth psychology. The reality of the psyche and its structures and processes must be acknowledged and given their due in the theological and spiritual discourse of our time. In an age of ever-increasing psychological sophistication and understanding, theology ignores these realities at the cost of becoming dead and irrelevant.

Consider a hypothetical example. Much to his horror, a middle-aged, married-with-children successful businessman has fallen in love with the gifted young male minister who now serves his parish. The businessman had only begun to attend church after his children were born "to set an example." Most of his life had passed with little thought given to spiritual matters; instead, he had spent it in worldly pursuits, building a family, establishing himself in his business and community. Soon after the new minister arrived, this businessman accepted an invitation to serve on his church's governing board. As time passed, he spent increasing amounts of time talking with the minister about his life and his feelings. He was horrified, ashamed, disoriented, and confused by his new feelings. He began to be distracted in his work and family life. Finally, he tearfully confessed his feelings to the minister.

What happens next?

Do the minister and businessman begin an affair that eventually leads to a scandalous termination of the pastor's ministry and possibly an end to the businessman's marriage? Does the minister, acting out of fear, indignantly tell the businessman that his feelings are unacceptable, and suggest to him that if he cannot bury them he should consider leaving the parish? Does the minister immediately refer the businessman to a therapist and begin to ignore and shun him? Does the minister punch the businessman in the nose? Does the businessman, feeling shamed and humiliated, begin to act out aggressively in the parish, poisoning good and productive energy and undermining ministry? All of these are scenarios that could be enacted in situations such as this one.

If the minister has had any meaningful exposure to depth psychology, he might see this matter in three dimensions. The businessman's feelings undoubtedly have profound spiritual as well as psychological dimensions. They are insistently addressing him. Something important and exciting is happening; it can be seen as an opportunity, a message from God. From a Jungian perspective, it is likely that the businessman is *projecting* his unlived spiritual side onto the minister. His life has been too one sided. He is being called to live more fully by a part of himself that he has pushed down all of his life as he zealously pursued a good livelihood, a house in the best neighborhood, a solid reputation. The businessman may experience sexual desire for the minister, and he feels shame on account of this. If the minister has the 3-D perspective, he may be able to help the businessman discover a part of himself that has been buried. The businessman might be called to expand, to become less fixed in the material world, to grow himself, to discover a part of himself that he never knew existed. He is being called to greater wholeness, and it might not fit with his one-sided image of himself as businessman, father, and husband. He has fallen in love with his own spiritual side, which he has identified with the minister who witnessed to and affirmed its reality in their conversations and work together.

This is the 3-D perspective. It takes account of both the psychological and the spiritual—the man might need to explore issues of his childhood and his sexuality, and/or there might be difficult issues in his marriage that need addressing—but there is a transcendent perspective too. The two perspectives interpenetrate each other and operate in tandem. The transcendent carries ineffable power, hope, and the potential for grace—something new—to enter into the psychological situation. The psychological perspective is primarily about adjustment, but the transcendent perspective carries the hope of transformation through the conscious enduring of psychic conflict until the knot loosens and can be untangled.

Depth psychology is an important, contemporary secular way of understanding human motives, desire, psychopathology. It provides informed and meaningful explanations for contemporary people which is analogous to the understanding that first century-people in Palestine had of the "demons" we read so much of in scripture. We need the 3-D lens of depth psychology to enhance the image, to bring the image out to us, to give it flesh and liveliness. Perhaps modern depth psychology is not as scientific as Freud had held it out to be, but truth can be found in many of the theories—a truth that resonates deeply in the hearts of those who study it and those who benefit by it in personal therapy and analysis.

As Ann and Barry Ulanov have stated, depth psychologists and their clients, and those interested in religious experience, from the perspective of priests, spiritual directors, and persons having such experiences, "share a concentration on the hidden depths of human experience and a determination to probe these depths. They go beyond their differences . . . in their common experience which we think is best called *primordial experience*."[49] The Ulanovs describe primordial experience as the place in which

> we encounter directly the original strata of human life; we meet all that has gone before us that remains instinct in the human

psyche. . . . [I]t is the most basic and important level of human experience, though much of our conscious life is devoted to eluding and repressing it.[50]

Elsewhere, Ann Ulanov wrote that

to put psyche together with Spirit means that a vital place of connecting to God lies in our immediate experience of Spirit touching us through our conscious thoughts and feelings, as well as our dreams, symptoms and complexes that come through our unconscious.[51]

We are embodied creatures. In my view, God has made us for relationship with Godself, and this is the most fundamental goal of human life. In the often-quoted cry of St. Augustine, written more than 1,500 years before the advent of depth psychology, he stated it this way: "You stir . . . [us] to take pleasure in praising you, because you have made us for yourself, and our heart is restless until it rests in you."[52] Paraphrasing the view of Karl Barth, Paul Ricouer puts it this way: "The origin of faith lies in the solicitation of man by the object of faith."[53]

Perhaps the most fundamental question that the joint study of psychology and religion asks is, "Exactly *how* does God 'stir' us?" It is a premise of this book that the innate and unique human potential for shame is one important mechanism used by God to draw us closer: shame of being born in a manger; shame in being executed half naked on a tree, in public view. We feel shame for that which we experience as scandalous. It reveals to us both awe and dread. As will be discussed, shame may be viewed most fundamentally as a consequence of the tension between our creatureliness and all of the implications of our creatureliness—including hunger, thirst, sexual longing, infirmity, aging, and death—and the sense that we humans have of also being made of Spirit. The vortex of that tension is the place where God feels absent. It is the godless place that opens us up to God.

The great fourteenth-century mystic and spiritual director Julian of Norwich saw no contradiction between our instinctual animal nature and our longing for relationship with God. Indeed, she saw the longing for God as arising out of the same substance as our creatureliness. She experienced God as telling her this:

> I am he, the great supreme goodness of every kind of thing; I am
> he who makes you to love; I am he who make you to long; I am
> he, the endless fulfilling of all true desires. For where the soul is
> highest, noblest, most honourable, still it is lowest, meekest and
> mildest.
>
> And so from this foundation in substance we have all the
> powers of our sensuality by the gift of nature.[54]

Clearly Julian understood that our longing and love derives from the
very places where we feel ourselves lowest, most depraved, most *un-
godlike*—i.e., from the perspective of this book, most ashamed and
most shamed. Without explicitly using the word *shame,* Julian articulates the tension between the dual human consciousness of creatureliness and spirit, of finitude and eternity. She understands that we can
achieve our greatest human potential by standing in the tension between our humanity and the *imago dei.* For our businessman who is
in love with his priest, it is in admitting his sexual desire while seeing
the projection of his God piece on him. It is standing in the vortex
which feels like the godless place but which in fact is a God-filled
place, a place where the experience of grace can enter in.

Rudolph Otto in his classic book *The Idea of the Holy* argued that human beings have a disposition for numinous experiences and that some
people even have a talent for them. Erich Fromm admitted that "there is
no one without a religious need."[55]

John McDargh approached the question of religiosity from object
relations theory, which has proved so fertile in the interdisciplinary
field of psychology and religion. He asks the fundamental question,
that I am also interested in: "How is it that human beings are consti-
tuted by their development [in the phrasing of Psalm 27:8-9] to 'seek
the face of God?' Something in our fundamental nature, something in
our heart, compels us to face the faceless universe."[56] But exactly
what is that "something" in our nature? McDargh answers this question with close scholarly analysis of the religious implications of the
groundbreaking object relations theories of W. R. D. Fairbairn, Donald Winnicott, Harry Guntrip, Ana-Maria Rizzuto, William Meissner, and others. McDargh sees it as self-evident that, as a species, human beings are "notably religious."[57]

Israeli psychologist and professor Mashe Halevi Spero wrote the
following in *Religious Objects As Psychological Structures:*

[T]he entire enterprise of outlining the "psychological" under-pinning of religious experience . . . may actually provide rela-tively accurate perspectives on what is *in essence* a halakhic [religious] reality. Psychological assertions are therefore *quite* relevant and elemental to religious experience, and not as if from without but from within.[58]

Gordon Allport observed that "all of human life revolves around desire" and, quoting K. Dunlap, "there seem to be no desires that are not, or have not at some time been, items in religion."[59] Humankind has understood its longing for relationship with the real and living God in many ways throughout history. Scripture talks about it: "As the deer longs for flowing streams, so my soul longs for you, O God . . ." (Psalm 42). The mystics of old penned some of the most beautiful prose and poetry ever written about the human desire for re-lationship with God. (See, for example, Teresa of Avila's *Interior Castle* or John of the Cross's *Living Flame of Love*.) Scholars of our own age such as William James have done phenomenological studies about the experience of encounter with the transcendent. Now, fi-nally, we are in a place and time where we can begin to utilize the work and observations of modern post-Freudian depth psychology to begin to try to understand the psychological mechanisms of faith and religious experience. We put on our 3-D glasses in order to bring per-spective and grounding to religious experience, so that we can make greater meaning of it. We who minister in the institutional Church can apply principles of depth psychology to bring new and fresh meaning to scripture in our preaching; to understand and empathize with parishioners in pastoral care and counseling situations; to ex-plore with our parishioners the psychic/mythic meaning of the sacra-ments and the theological statements of the Church (e.g., "Christ died for our sins"); to participate in the counsels of the institutional Church in such a way as to help it incorporate some of its shadow ele-ments—the places that go underground and get distorted and made even more malevolent because of the Church's traditional overidenti-fication with "purity" and God itself. We can find in our psychic pro-cesses—even those that the church has long characterized as broken, disordered, and sinful—reason to see different ways that God works in us and draws us into relationship with Godself. This is very hope-ful, very positive, very affirming of our humanity.

THE MINISTER'S PERSPECTIVE

I have already alluded to the symbolism that the ordained representative of the institutional Church carries, which differs markedly from the healing role of mental health professionals. What are the implications of this in terms of how we relate to people as professionals?

Psychologist Paul Pruyser spent much of his professional life puzzling over the appropriate relationship between psychotherapy and pastoral care. Ultimately, he recommended a *perspectival approach* to client/patient care, in which caregiver (psychiatrist, psychologist, social worker, minister) would approach the patient from his or her own particular perspective. "There is no *limit* on the topics any team member can address."[60] As Deborah van Deusen Hunsinger puts it, the pastoral caregiver can and should make use of "bilingual competencies"—i.e., the language and understanding of pastoral caregiving and that of depth psychology.[61]

Clergy have certain prerogatives that other professionals do not ordinarily have. First, we typically have opportunities to witness our parishioners' interactions and relationships with others, including family members. Parish clergy have some degree of social contact with their parishioners, such as at church functions and in the larger community. The boundaries between priest and parishioner are a great deal less rigid and absolute than those between psychotherapist and client. As well, we have what Paul Pruyser refers to as the rights of "access and initiative."[62] If concerned about someone, a clergy member can appear at his or her home, at the jail where the individual is in custody, at his or her hospital bed. Clergy can call the person on the phone just to check in. We have at our disposal the rites and rituals of the Church, including the sacraments, anointing of the sick and laying on of hands, reading and discussing comforting passages of scripture, as well as having the authority to bless and absolve of sins on behalf of the Church (depending of course on denominational affiliation). Last but not least, we can be expected to offer prayer with and for the sufferer. By reason of our vocational association with the Church, we may carry a projection of the Holy which can, if not abused, be comforting and consoling.

Psychotherapy obviously has an important place in making meaning of psychic suffering. Psychotherapists are in possession of many useful tools, including a fixed psychotherapeutic time and space that is utilized week after week, sometimes for years, in which to work through complex and thorny issues and, of course, a body of knowledge and an arsenal of techniques and strategies. Psychotherapists have the opportunity to work with clients for as long as it takes to find some peace and healing. The same is not true of the parish clergy. Ministers in parishes might be trained to use psychotherapeutic methods for providing pastoral care and spot counseling, but it is not advisable for them to do therapy because it is misleading and can lead to boundary violations and role confusion. Indeed, the Church Insurance Company, which insures the counseling work of clergy in the Protestant Episcopal Church, has directed that priests in a parish setting must refer an individual to professional counseling after six sessions have been held around a given life issue.[63] However, although psychology "knows the healing power of love, [it] finds itself unable to do much about it."[64] When all is said and done, a psychotherapist is not in a position to "supply the love his patient needs, nor to receive the love his patient wants to give."[65]

A parish pastor has the unique privilege, opportunity, and burden of standing in front of a particular faith community week after week, preaching the gospel and celebrating the sacraments of the church. He or she does this knowing much about the lives of those sitting in the pews. Leading worship, preaching, and pastoral care are all part of the fabric of pastoral work in a parish setting.[66] If we are attentive, we hear shame in our parishioners' anguish over loss of jobs, loss of relationships, failures in child rearing, addictions of all kinds, the aging process, even illness as it saps away strength and ultimately life itself.

Can we provide the sense of "deep calling to deep" (Psalm 42) that people need in times when they want their shame to be heard, even as they couch it in expressions of rage, contempt, depression, or righteousness? This depends in no small part on the honesty with which we ourselves confront our own demons, our own shame issues. Daniel Day Williams had the sense that something was missing from the vows we take when we are ordained:

> Perhaps someday there will be recognition in appropriate language in the form for ordination of ministers of the need for self understanding of their own psychological needs, hostilities and fears. . . . When the minister has begun to be released from false

pretenses, from unacknowledged anxieties, and is learning the joy of entering freely into the comradeship of the search for the meaning of life with another person, the high potentialities for his becoming a channel of grace may be realized. It is not only the precious good of psychological health for its own sake which is the goal here, but the release of constructive and healing power. And let us add one more quite necessary point. Health is a mysterious entity, especially when we seek it for the mind. It is surely more than adjustment. The constructively healthy personalities have for the most part known radical inner struggle. We are not asking for personalities neatly grooved. We are asking only how the struggles we have may lead to creating understanding rather than despair.[67]

In short, pastors need depth psychology not only for assessing their parishioners' pastoral needs but also in assisting the pastors themselves in coming to terms with their own shame issues. This personal coming to terms is the first and perhaps most fundamental step we need to take—it must be reckoned as part of our vocational call—if we have any hope of being fully present channels of grace for those to whom we minister.

In Chapter 7, I discuss theories as to the psychological etiology of shame in human beings. As I began to comprehend the ubiquity of the psychological phenomenon of shame in human life, I felt compelled to construct an understanding of its theological and spiritual significance, as well as its transformative potential—both informed by the psychological realities. This will be the subject of Chapters 8 and 9. Putting the two perspective together creates the three-dimensional image that can enliven and ground our understanding of faith experience, as well as bring something new, fresh, and hopeful to it.

Chapter 7

Toward an Understanding of Shame from Perspectives of Depth Psychology

Shame is the Shawl of Pink
In which we wrap the Soul
To keep it from infesting Eyes—
The elemental Veil
Which helpless nature drops
When pushed upon a scene
Repugnant to her probity
Shame is the tint divine.

Emily Dickinson, #1412, c. 1877

This chapter examines the work of certain twentieth-century theorists in the field of depth psychology who have concerned themselves most with shame-related issues. Looking at shame from the perspective of different theories of depth psychology gives us a context and a grounding in our humanity for entering into deeper and more authentic relationship with God. The understandings of depth psychology on the subject of shame, in providing us with a perspective that differs from the stock religious perspective, can give us courage to face shame, which cripples us in our longing and pursuit of abundant life. I attempt in this chapter to summarize the work of some psychological theorists who have worked most clearly—although not always explicitly—with shame issues. As we come to ever deeper psychological understandings of the etiology of shame in human beings, we put on the 3-D glasses which bring into relief the significance of the religious stories and symbols that feed us and transform us. The psychological understandings lead us to honor our humanity even as they help connect us to our divinity.

FREUD'S REFERENCES TO SHAME

I begin this discussion of the intrapsychic development of shame with Sigmund Freud, the father of modern depth psychology. Freud's explicit references to shame are limited. There are a total of only thirty-six indexed uses of the word *shame* in *The Standard Edition of the Complete Psychological Works of Sigmund Freud*. Many uses of the word are parenthetical, as the concept of shame is somewhat underdeveloped in Freud's work. Still, I think it is important to look at what he has to say about it in order to provide a backdrop and context for the work on shame that followed.

Shame for Freud seems often to involve exposure—the "fear of other people knowing" about something one reproaches oneself for. "I reproach myself on account of an event—I am afraid other people know about it—therefore I feel ashamed in front of other people."[1]

For example, Freud uses the word *shame* often in connection with the common dream of being in a public place totally or half undressed,[2] or in connection with feelings associated with actually being seen in a state of undress.[3] Freud, who of course wrote in German, notes that "through a long series of generations the genitals have been for us the *'pudenta,'* objects of shame, and even (as a result of further successful sexual repression) of disgust."[4] The word *shame* derives from the German *Scham,* which has as its root meaning "genitals, pudenta, private parts."[5] Freud states that when men began to walk upright, their "genitals, which were previously concealed" became "visible and in need of protection, and so provoked feelings of shame in him."[6]

Freud also uses the word *shame* in connection with the feeling we may have when we have been caught in a "slip of the tongue" which has some obvious significance, because it exposes something embarrassing about our actual feelings or thoughts.[7]

Freud often and without any real explanation states that shame is one of the affects that inhibits the expression of the sexual instinct.[8] He also contends that feelings of shame cause the direct expression of sexuality in female children to be earlier and more completely inhibited than that of male children, presumably because of the humiliation that a female child experiences when she discovers she is without a penis.[9] In his "New Introductory Lectures on Psychoanalysis," Freud is explicit about this: "Shame, which is considered to be a feminine characteristic *par excellence* but is far more a matter of convention than might be supposed, has as its purpose, we believe, concealment of genital deficiency."[10]

The word *guilt* appears 127 indexed times in Freud's work according to my count—almost four times as often as shame. This is not surprising, given the centrality of the concepts of the Oedipus complex to his sexual theory, including talion dread and fear of castration. Freud believed that religion and human civilization in general began with the killing by a primal horde of prehistoric sons of the patriarch, who had exercised sexual domination and control over the clan's women. The sons killed and then devoured their father out of a sense of rage, but later their triumph became mixed with remorse, for they loved their father and needed to identify with him even as they hated him.[11] This event, says Freud, became the prototype for the dynamic of all father/son relationships, with the successful negotiation of the Oedipus complex being an all-important prerequisite for normal development. Thus, in "Civilization and Its Discontents," Freud states the following:

> if the human sense of guilt goes back to the killing of the primal father, that was after all a case of "remorse." Are we to assume that at that time a conscience as a sense of guilt were not, as we have presupposed, in existence before the deed? If not, where, in this case, did the remorse come from? There is no doubt that this case should explain the secret of the sense of guilt to us. . . . And I believe it does. The remorse was the result of the primordial ambivalence of feeling towards the father. His sons hated him, but they loved him, too. After their hatred had been satisfied by their act of aggression, their love came to the fore in the remorse for the deed. It set up the super-ego by identification with the father; it gave that agency the father's power, as though as a punishment for the deed of aggression they had carried out against him, and it created the restrictions which were intended to prevent a repetition of the deed. And since the inclination to aggressiveness against the father was repeated in the following generations, the sense of guilt, too, persisted, and it was suppressed and carried over to the super-ego. . . . Whether one has killed one's father or has abstained from doing so is not really the decisive thing. One is bound to feel guilty in either case, for

the sense of guilt is an expression of the conflict due to ambivalence, of the eternal struggle between Eros and the instinct of
destruction or death.[12]

Thus, for Freud the superego, the mechanism by which the standards of the parents and their culture are incorporated into the individual, and specifically the child's fear of punishment by the parents
for transgression, is the initial source of the feeling of guilt. There are
two stages in the development of superego guilt or "conscience":
first, the fear of outside authority; and second, the fear of the harsh
superego itself once the authority's rules and standards are internalized. For Freud, "psychopathology is the overdeveloped sense of
guilt, resulting from the overdeveloped superego."[13]

From a review of Freud's uses of the word *shame,* it seems that he
did not really focus on the phenomenon of shame per se. He uses the
word almost in passing, as if to refer to a response to a situation that
he deems self-explanatory and self-evident. Freud never defines
shame, nor does he really explore the question of the etiology of
shame. Helen Lewis, Michael Lewis, and others have contended that
this lack is due to a failure of Freud and his interpreters (until quite recently) to explore the concept of the ego-ideal which they claim is
central to the experience of shame. One reason for this neglect, in
turn, "may have been the relatively late acknowledgment in Freudian
psychoanalytic writings of the importance of the concept of the self,
as distinguished from the ego."[14]

Another interesting twist on the question of why the subject of
shame per se was not much considered by Freud is Andrew Morrison's argument[15] that in Freud's mind consideration of this subject
might have veered too close to Alfred Adler's work. Adler linked
shame to the "masculine protest," to "organ inferiority," the so-called
"inferiority complex," and "the extreme bashfulness of many nervous
people."[16]

Despite the dearth of express references to shame in Freud's work,
there is one place in which he describes the phenomenon of shame
without calling it by that name. In "Mourning and Melancholia," he
compares the phenomena of "mourning" and "melancholia." Mourning is "the reaction to the loss of a loved person, or to the loss of some
abstraction that has taken the place of one." The features of melancholia, on the other hand, are as follows:

a profoundly painful dejection, abrogation of interest in the outside world, loss of the capacity to love, inhibitions of all activity,
and a lowering of the self-regarding feelings to a degree that
finds utterance in self-reproaches, and self-revilings, and culmi-
nates in a delusional expectation of punishment. This picture
becomes a little more intelligible when we consider that, with
one exception, the same traits are met with in grief. The fall in
self-esteem is absent in grief; but otherwise the features are the
same.[17]

Freud notes that in mourning, one suffers the loss of a love-object;
it thus becomes necessary to engage in the painful work of withdrawing the attachment of the libido from the lost object. He contends that melancholia must also "in some way" be "related to an unconscious loss of a love-object, in contradistinction to mourning, in
which there is nothing about the loss which is unconscious."[18] However, while in mourning the loss is conscious,

the inhibition of the melancholic seems puzzling to us because
we cannot see what absorbs him so entirely. Now the melancholic displays something else which is lacking in grief—an extraordinary fall in his self-esteem, an impoverishment of his ego
on a grand scale. *In grief the world becomes poor and empty; in
melancholia it is the ego itself. The patient represents to us as
worthless, incapable of any effort and morally despicable; he
reproaches himself, vilifies himself and expects to be cast out
and chastised. He abases himself before everyone.* (emphasis
added)[19]

Freud's description of the condition then known as "melancholia"
and now usually known as depression is clearly one type of shame
symptomology.

In melancholia, "the ego debases and rages against itself."[20] The
self-reproaches of the melancholic "are reproaches against a loved
object which have been shifted on to the patient's own ego."[21] Stated
further in the piece, "it is because everything derogatory that they say
of themselves at bottom relates to someone else that they are not
ashamed and do not hide their heads."[22] Freud concludes:

The self-torments of melancholiacs, which are without doubt pleasurable, signify, just like the corresponding phenomenon in the obsessional neurosis, a gratification of sadistic tendencies and of hate, both of which relate to an object and in this way have both been turned round upon the self.[23]

Morrison agrees that many cases of depression "reflect helplessness, shattered self-esteem, and ego (or self-) deflation"; that "many of the attributes associated with depression are the very same qualities and feelings that generate shame and low self-esteem"; that shame is an "important ingredient," even a "stimulus" to depression; and that in both shame and depression there is a state of "helplessness to alter the compromised state of the self."[24]

In his "Outline of Psychoanalysis" (1938), Freud provides another clue to his thinking on the subject of shame. He states that on humankind's "path to cultural development," there is the necessity for "holding back aggressiveness" leading to "illness (mortification)."[25] "Mortification"—the German is *Krankung,* which literally means "to make sick"—like melancholia, is a product of the superego.[26] So too is the shame that Freud talks about as inhibiting the expression of sexuality. As Helen Lewis aptly observes, several of Freud's patients were coping with the shame of unrequited love and/or personal betrayal. However, Freud would have it that the suffering of these people was based upon the frustration of their sexual needs vis-à-vis their love-objects. I must part company with Freud to the extent that he would suggest shame (as distinguished from guilt) is a product of the superego. It may be accurate to say that Freud never developed a theory of shame as being distinct from guilt. Later theorists hold more of the keys to the etiology of shame.

In his paper "On Narcissism" (1914), however, although Freud does not make explicit reference to the phenomenon of shame, as noted by Morrison, it was in this paper that he "first evolved the ego ideal construct."[27] Freud states the following in that paper:

It would not surprise us if we were to find a special psychical agency which performs the task of seeing that narcissistic satisfaction from the ego ideal is ensured and which, with this end in view, constantly watches the actual ego and measures it by that ideal.[28]

As Morrison further notes, "since shame is experienced in relationship to the self, libidinal energy associated with the shame experience is closely tied to narcissism and its vicissitudes."[29]

A MAP OF THE LANDSCAPE AFTER FREUD

Having summarized Freud's allusions to shame, I will now reflect upon the work of some later depth psychologists who have made the most helpful contributions to our thinking on the etiology of toxic shame in human beings.

As I surveyed the work of theorists in this field, a picture emerged of different levels or layers of understanding of the etiology of shame. Each layer offers its own truth. So far, in describing the phenomenology of shame, I have been examining the skin of it, which is visible to us all. But studying shame is like looking at a series of clear overlays or transparencies such as those found in physiology books. As one goes deeper, as one flips the transparencies, one sees the skeleton, then the muscles, the organs, the circulatory system, the nervous system, the lymph system—i.e., the "guts" of what makes shame happen. As one flips the transparencies, one goes to ever deeper layers: from Karen Horney, whose "pride system" is essentially cultural, to Alice Miller, who attributes shame to the "poisonous pedagogy" of families of origin, to the intrapsychic metapsychology of Heinz Kohut, to the archetypal level of Carl Jung and then, finally, to the *tremendum,* where there are no words, where one can only stand in awe and gape at the abyss with inarticulate dread. Each layer contains its own truth. Each layer expands the understanding of the origins and possible meanings and potentialities of shame.

Taken together, these layers of understanding enable us to peer into the experience of shame. Jesus said, "the truth will make you free" (John 8:32). The bases, etiologies, and pervasiveness of shame in human life are truths that we need to know in order to attain the freedom of which Jesus speaks. Without these truths, we are bound by shame and cannot be transformed by it.

KAREN HORNEY'S "PRIDE SYSTEM"

Helen Lewis observes that shame is a "narcissistic reaction, evoked by a lapse from the ego-ideal."[30] She sees theorists represented by persons such as Karen Horney as moving toward the development of a working concept of the self/ego ideal as a major factor in the study of mental illness.

Horney developed a pragmatic theory of neurosis which has as its center the "pride system."[31] The pride system seeks to organize the self around an unrealistic, artificially constructed *self-idealizing* process, as distinguished from a healthy and realistic *self-realizing* process. Horney differed from Freud in that she was not so much interested in discussing innate biological drives and instincts as motivations for human behavior as about responses that we make as a result of our culture and our upbringing. Horney was interested in the impulse of human beings to glorify themselves, to have positive self-regard, and to desire others to hold us in positive regard.

Horney's pride system is a compensation for feelings of worthlessness and inadequacy—i.e., injuries to the narcissistic structure—by the development of idealized images of ourselves that generate neurotic pride, neurotic claims, tyrannical "shoulds," and self-hate. Horney contends that we are motivated by a "search for glory," by which we seek to actualize an idealized self.[32] The search for glory can be manifested in a relentless pursuit of perfection, in neurotic ambition, or, failing these, in a drive toward vindictive triumph.

The pride system can also give rise to neurotic claims, such as needing to believe that one is entitled to benefits and privileges without corresponding effort as well as belief that one is exempt from illness, aging, and death. [33]

The pride system's "tyranny of the shoulds" impairs spontaneity in feelings and actions as well as authentic morality. There is a coercive character to morality generated by the tyranny of the shoulds—what Lynd would call an orientation toward the guilt axis, and what Winnicott would call False Self living.

For Horney, the central conflict in the neurotic person is between the real self and the idealized self. She sees three basic styles of negotiation of that conflict; they are instructive in understanding some of the basic ways in which we contend with feelings of shame.

The first style is the *expansive* solution. This consists of three sub-types. The first is the *narcissistic* type, in which a person imagines that he or she is the idealized self and seems to adore it:

> He has (consciously) no doubts; he *is* the anointed, the man of destiny, the prophet, the great giver, the benefactor of mankind. All of this contains a grain of truth. He often is gifted beyond average, early and easily won distinctions, and sometimes was the favored and admired child.[34]

The second subtype of the expansive solution is the *perfectionist* who identifies himself or herself with his or her standards. "This type feels superior because of his high standards, moral and intellectual, and on this basis looks down on others."[35]

The third is the *arrogant vindictive* subtype. His or her main motivation is the need for vindictive triumph over others. While Horney cautions that the need for vindictive triumph is a "regular ingredient in any search for glory," in the arrogant vindictive type it assumes overwhelming priority and intensity. This makes a person extremely competitive and unable to "tolerate anyone who knows or achieves more than he does, wields more power, or in any way questions his superiority."[36] There is a pervasive attitude of distrust of others.

The second basic style of negotiating the conflict between the real self and the idealized self is the *self-effacing* solution. This person approaches life in a manner opposite to that of a person who employs the expansive solution. The self-effacing individual

> tends to subordinate himself to others, to be dependent upon them, to appease them. . . . In sharp contrast to the expansive type, he lives with a diffuse sense of failure (to measure up to his shoulds) and hence tends to feel guilty, inferior, or contempt-ible.[37]

Many people suffering from depression openly speak of themselves in this way which, indeed, also recalls Freud's description of the melancholiac in his paper "Mourning and Melancholia." Moreover, the person who employs the self-effacing solution may "provoke others to treat him badly, and thus transfer the inner scene to the outside. In this way too he becomes the noble victim suffering under an ignoble and cruel world."[38] The self-effacing type is the classic doormat.

The third basic way for negotiating the conflict between the real self and the idealized self is *resignation.* Resignation can take three different forms. One is *withdrawal and disengagement* from activities. A second is *open rebellion*—taking an "I-don't-give-a-damn-about-anything" attitude. Such a person may leave home, quit his or her job, and become militantly aggressive toward everyone. The third subtype of resignation, and probably the most prevalent in U.S. culture, is *shallow living.*[39] The emphasis here is on enjoying oneself and living on the surface. A person may pursue "prestige or opportunistic success" with no real values or morals. Or a person may be a "well-adapted automaton" with no deep or authentic feelings about anything. The personality is flat and without affect. He or she may be wealthy, traveling around the world and frequenting clubs and cocktail parties, or this individual may be middle class, spending all of his or her free time playing cards, gossiping, or watching television. Such people have overadapted to culture. They may seem healthy on the surface but in fact are always needing to "push down a gnawing feeling of futility by means of distracting pleasures."[40] They are not obviously disturbed by conflicts and may display no particular symptoms, such as anxiety or depression. They do not experience the "something wrongness"—i.e., shame—of which William James speaks.[41] Consequently, they do not experience a personal relationship with a living God. They may attend church, but their experience of religion, like everything else in their lives, is shallow.

Horney does not make much explicit use of the word *shame* in her work, but the pride system she outlines and the strategies she describes as supporting it are surely the symptoms and defenses of shame. Recall that the entire pride system is constructed around basic feelings of worthlessness and inadequacy. The existence in one's mind's eye of an idealized self, and the elaborate mechanisms that the individual in Horney's system utilizes to deal with the disparity between the idealized self and the real self all arise from and have their underpinnings in shame. One experiences shame because one's real self is not in fact the ideal self, and there is an implicit judgment that the real self is not worth having and holding and presenting to the world.

Horney's work contains simple and undeniable truth. It is, indeed, disarming in the truth that it describes. However, I find that Horney's theory is missing the depth which would explain and account for how and why this pride system, the search for glory, the self-idealizing process—all part of the so-called comprehensive neurotic solution—emerges in the first place. She describes the phenomenon, the mechanisms, and the defenses of shame in Technicolor, and her description is certainly enlightening as far as it goes, but it fails to account for the pride system (or what we might call the defensive shame system) in terms of human biology or human growth and development. And so we move on in our examination of theorists who have looked closely at shame-related issues.

ALICE MILLER AND "POISONOUS PEDAGOGY"

Alice Miller, similar to Karen Horney, wrote from her perspective as an experienced psychoanalyst. Miller wrote about the abuse that many, if not most, children of Western culture suffer by reason of what she terms "poisonous pedagogy."[42] Poisonous pedagogy teaches that adults are the masters of the dependent child. The child's will must be "broken" as soon as possible. The parents are always right and determine in a "godlike fashion what is right and what is wrong." Children are not deserving of respect, and it is only the parents' feelings that matter.[43] Miller develops the argument throughout her work that the prevalence of poisonous pedagogy has resulted in many of us learning to hide our own feelings, needs, and memories in order to meet our parents' expectations and win their "love."

In its extreme forms, poisonous pedagogy has resulted in many children being physically abused, and such people often grow up to be violent themselves. Violent acts are "often done in the name of 'patriotism' or religious beliefs."[44] People raised under poisonous pedagogy who appear to be successful are plagued by feelings of emptiness and alienation. The worst of it is that a "vicious circle of contempt" is set up in which the feelings of helplessness, powerlessness, and unlovability are passed on to and perpetuated in the next generation. "Disregard for those who are smaller and weaker is thus the best defense against a breakthrough of one's own feelings of helplessness: it is an expression of this split-off weakness." Parents use "their 'grown-upness' to avenge themselves unconsciously on their child for their own earlier humiliation. They encounter their own humiliating past in the child's eyes, and they ward it off with the power they now have."[45]

Clearly, Miller is talking about the development and perpetuation through poisonous pedagogy and the vicious circle of contempt of the shame-based personality from generation to generation. Miller, also similar to Horney, is concerned with the development of personality which contains the implicit assumption that one's true and real self, one's actual feelings and desires, are not worthy or lovable. Therefore, individuals must strive to conform themselves, their desires, the very structure of their lives to meet the ideal image of the good and acceptable person they were raised with. We find in these persons what Michael Lewis terms a "global"[46] evaluation of the totality of the self as "bad" and unworthy of love or respect.

Miller comes a bit closer to the root of the shame problem than does Horney. Horney sets out an elaborate phenomenological comprehensive neurotic solution to the disparity between the ideal self and the real self, but she is not much preoccupied with the etiology of this conflict. Miller takes it as far as a description of the poisonous pedagogy and vicious circle of contempt which passes shame on from generation to generation. All of this is probably helpful from a clinical point of view. Miller says that

> it is one of the turning points in therapy when the patient comes to the emotional insight that all the love she has captured with so much effort and self-denial was not meant for her as she really was, that the admiration for her beauty and achievements was aimed at this beauty and not at the child herself. In therapy, the small and lonely child that is hidden behind her achievements wakes up and asks: "What would have happened if I had appeared before you sad, needy, angry, furious? Where would your love have been then? . . . Does this mean that it was not really me you loved, but only what I pretended to be? The well-behaved, reliably empathic, understanding, and convenient child, who in fact was never a child at all?"[47]

Miller has much to offer, but in the end she too leaves me unsatisfied. She comes closer to the core of the problem but does not reach it. To say that we feel shame because of the way we are raised and because of our cultures is to beg the question. Human beings and their cultures and pedagogy do not spring whole cloth from the earth, nor can they be instantly changed just because we do not like what we see. Culture and pedagogy, poisonous or pristine, emerge and evolve out of the depths of the human psyche. So we will try to go deeper into the etiology of shame than to say that "they"—i.e., culture or our parents and grandparents—caused shame. The next deepest place to go in exploring the etiology of shame is to the depths of the human psyche.

HEINZ KOHUT'S SELF-PSYCHOLOGY

Heinz Kohut is the depth psychology theorist who developed the most nuanced and explicit ideas as to the intrapsychic etiology of shame in human persons. Kohut was responsible for a major theoretical development within psychoanalysis referred to as self-psychology. Andrew Morrison has written that "Just as guilt is the central negative affect in classical (conflict/drive) theory . . . *shame* occupies that position in problems of narcissism, in the psychology of the self and its deficits."[48] I agree.

While Freud emphasized the Oedipal struggle, for Kohut the pre-Oedipal experience is decisive. Freud saw the real beginning of one's personhood unfolding in the Oedipal conflict. The issue for Kohut was much more basic—i.e., the formation of the self as "an independent center of initiative, an independent recipient of impressions."[49] For Kohut, pre-Oedipal self-formation is more basic than the Oedipal conflict because

> for those who are struggling to become a self, actual conflicts with others, such as those encountered in the Oedipal stage, are often conspicuous by their absence, or relatively unimportant. Certainly they do not assume the decisive role in the child's development that Freud ascribed to them, for such conflicts assume that the child has a self that is sufficiently strong that it may risk itself in conflict or negotiation with others.[50]

For Freud neurotic structures result from unresolved libidenal desires for parents, while for Kohut, the primary neuroses are self-pathologies which result "from inadequately formed or poorly established selves."[51] As has been noted, Freud had "emphasized the guilt feelings that result from ambivalent desires felt toward parental objects," whereas Kohut stressed the feelings of shame that he saw resulting from "poor parental mirroring of ideals and ambitions."[52] Kohut referred to Freud's Oedipal personality as the Guilty Self, and to the pre-Oedipal, narcissistic personality as the Tragic Self.[53] "The Tragic Self knows very little guilt, but is well acquainted with feelings of deep shame, which are immobilizing and debilitating."[54]

Freud had set it out that narcissism—primary love of self—was an immature way station that needed to be passed and renounced in favor of mature object love. Kohut, on the other hand, understands narcissism to be a normal part of life, present from birth to death, and not to be relinquished in favor of object love. Narcissism has a natural course of development that takes place in a whole and functioning self. Kohut contends that narcissism, which he defines as the libidinal investment in the self, needs to be an integrated part of the personality. In narcissistic personality disturbances,

> the principal source of discomfort is . . . the result of the psyche's inability to regulate self-esteem and to maintain it at normal levels; and the specific (pathogenic) experiences of the personality which are correlated to this central psychological defect lie within the narcissistic realm and fall into a spectrum which extends from anxious grandiosity and excitement, on the one hand, to mild embarrassment and self-consciousness, or severe shame, hypochondria, and depression, on the other.[55]

In his important essay "Forms and Transformations of Narcissism,"[56] Kohut contends that the narcissistic experience begins with the infant's blissful state, which is inevitably upset by unavoidable failures, delays, and shortcomings in maternal care. The infant replaces the previous perfection with two systems: by attempting to imbue an admired outside "other"—the idealized parent imago—with the previous perfection; and by establishing a grandiose and exhibitionistic image of the self—the grandiose self (originally referred to by Kohut as "the narcissistic self").

The Idealized Imago

Although the idealization of the parent imago

> is a direct continuation of the child's original narcissism, the cognitive image of the idealized parent changes with the maturation of the child's cognitive equipment. During an important transitional period when gratification and frustration are gradually recognized as coming from an external source, the object alternatingly emerges from and resubmerges into the self. When separated from the self, however, the child's experience of the object is total at each point of development, and the seemingly objective classification into "part" and "whole" objects rests on the adult observer's value judgment.[57]

Attachment to the perfect other restores the child's sense of wholeness and bliss. The idealized imago allows the child to have the fantasy of a perfect other with whom union is sought. Union with this perfect being brings contentment, strength, and wholeness. This is the story of the wish to merge with the perfect other who possesses kindness, wisdom, strength, and a capacity to sooth, settle, and help maintain emotional balance.

I cannot resist the mention here of a relatively recent film that could be referred to as illustrative of any number of psychological phenomena: *A.I.* (2001). In this film, the prototype child robot "David" was programmed with the capacity to love a particular parental figure. Specifically, David was programmed to love Monica—"Mommy"— whose only biological child was in a coma. When Monica's biological child unexpectedly revives, problems develop and David is cast out of the family and abandoned. *A.I.* is the story of David's relentless need to find and reconnect with Mommy. The mommy of the film was, for David, the perfect being, the person he absolutely had to be with in order to feel alive. For David, Mommy possessed kindness, wisdom, strength, and a complete capacity to soothe, settle, and maintain emotional balance.

Children and adults connect on a deep level with David's longing to be with the idealized parental imago, to merge with her, to be soothed and comforted and cared for by her. The David of the film was emotionally arrested at that place. He could not live without the idealized parental imago. The subconscious mental process that goes on regarding the idealized figure is as follows: "You are perfect, but I am part of you."

As a child matures, every perceived deviation of the idealized imago from perfection "leads to a corresponding internal preservation of the externally lost quality of the object."[58] The idealized imago and the process of transforming the idealized imago through internalization lead to a healthy ability to admire others and an ability for enthusiasm. Kohut uses the term *transmuting internalization* to denote the process by which idealization is gradually withdrawn from the child's caretaker and internalized:

> These internalizations create new structures that assume the psychological functions previously performed by the idealized object, devoid of the personal qualities of the object. Fractionated withdrawal of idealization occurs when the child's disappointments are gradual and of manageable degree. Kohut calls this gradual disillusionment "optimal frustration."[59]

It is not a very far stretch to see that religious persons can and do use God, or God in Christ, as an idealized imago which possesses kindness, wisdom, strength, and a capacity to soothe, settle, and maintain emotional balance through prayer, contemplation, and worship.[60]

In its pathological forms, i.e., when the parent refuses to permit a degree of idealization, a person might develop a compelling need for merger with powerful objects, or, in psychosis, might even develop delusional ideations of powerful persecutors.[61]

The Grandiose Self

Next, Kohut considers the line of development of the narcissistic or grandiose self. Narcissism is not just invested in the idealized imago; some is retained for investment in the self:

> Just as the overvaluation of the "other" is a phase-appropriate step in the maturation of narcissism, so too is the overvaluation of the self. Whereas the idealized parental imago gazes in awe at the object of its idealization, the narcissistic self wishes to be *viewed* with awe and admiration. . . . The idealized parental imago contributes to our ideals; the narcissistic [grandiose] self contributes to our ambitions.[62]

Kohut saw healthy and realistic dreams, goals, and ambitions as deriving from the devolution of the childhood system of grandiose fantasies, which seek affirmation for the grandeur and perfection of the self by an important "other." The sole meaning of the "other" is in serving as a witness to and affirmant of the child's grandiose exhibitionistic needs. In an often-quoted descriptive summation of the needs of the child's grandiose self, Kohut writes, "After psychological separation has taken place the child needs the *gleam in the mother's eye* in order to maintain the narcissistic libidinal suffusion which now concerns, in their sequence, the leading functions and activities of the various maturational phases (emphasis added)."[63] And—not to get ahead of myself, for this will be discussed more in the chapters that follow—just as we need to be "the gleam in the mother's eye" during young childhood, so too in adulthood, with the God we worship, we want to be known and loved for who we are. Thus, for example, the psalmist in Psalm 17:6-8 cries out:

I call upon you for you will answer me, O God;
    incline your ear to me, hear my words.
Wonderously show me your steadfast love,
    O Savior of those who take refuge from their adversaries
    at your right hand.
Guard me as the apple of your eye;
    Hide me in the shadow of your wings. (emphasis added)

In the lovely priestly blessing of Numbers 6:24-26, the members of the worshiping community are wished a sense of God's loving mirroring:

The Lord bless you and keep you:
The Lord make his face to shine upon you, and be gracious to you:
The Lord lift up his countenance upon you, and give you peace.

The child's grandiose self manifests in exhibitionism. Anyone who has parented a young child, or otherwise spent much time with young children, will be struck by the child's frequent cries: "Look at me!" or "Look at what I made!" or "Look at what I did!" or "I am going to be a famous soccer player, and artist, and the president of the United States!"

Kohut provides us with this psychological and physiological description of shame:

> The exhibitionistic surface of the body-self, the skin . . . shows . . . not the pleasant warmth of successful exhibitionism, but heat and blushing side by side with pallor. It is this disorganized mixture of massive discharge (tension decrease) and blockage (tension increase) in the area of exhibitionistic libido, that is experienced as shame.[64]

Thandeka says that this means that

> the parts of the self that have not been consistently, lovingly and empathetically affirmed because they are different from what the caretaker expected are "split off" from the child's operative, conscious activities with others or separated from it through repression.[65]

Whether one grows up to be relatively healthy or unhealthy emotionally depends upon how and the extent to which this grandiose exhibitionism "has been integrated into the realistic purposes of the ego."[66] If the early narcissistic exhibitionistic fantasies are not deflated by "sudden and premature experiences of rejection and traumatic disappointment" but instead are

> gradually integrated into the ego's reality-oriented organization, then the ego will be able to make adaptive use of the sense of power. The grandiosity eventually becomes integrated into the ego as the healthy enjoyment of activities and successes, accompanied by a feeling of confidence.[67]

One might imagine two three-year-old children who, upon returning home from nursery school, present their respective mothers with the perennial macaroni collage made on construction paper, complete with an abundance of dripping white Elmer's Glue-All. Each child proudly says, "Mommy, look at what I made today! I want to be an artist when I grow up." One mother says, "Oh, how beautiful! What a fine job you did on this. What a great artist you are!" She displays the collage in a prominent place in the house. The other mother says, "Ugh. What a mess. You didn't need to use so much glue. And how unoriginal! Why can't these teachers think of better projects for you kids to do?"

The maturation and transformation of the grandiose self is, in large part, dependent upon the primary caretaker's *mirroring.* Andrew Morrison puts it this way:

> When Kohut spoke of mirroring, he was referring to that empathic capacity of the attuned and loving mother to understand, reflect, and respond to the infant's subjective, self-affirming quality of contentment and satisfaction. In this context, then, mirroring is a supportive and affirming gesture, as opposed to the coolly indifferent, objectifying, or distorting image of the mirror of objective self awareness.[68]

In young childhood, it is important for the gleam in the primary caretaker's eye to mirror "the child's exhibitionistic display" and for the primary caretaker otherwise to participate in and respond favorably to the "child's narcissistic-exhibitionistic enjoyment" in order to "confirm the child's self-esteem and, by gradually increasing selectivity of these responses, begin to channel it into realistic directions."[69]

One of the primary consequences of failure in appropriate mirroring and the childhood working through of the grandiose self is a propensity for shame and humiliation. Narcissistic shame can be manifested in crude fantasies of a grandiose self, which remain outside of awareness through a "vertical split," or by the forces of repression which convert the shame to depression vis-à-vis a "horizontal split":[70]

> The vertical split is responsible for the vast contradictions in thought and action that can exist in one person. . . . The humiliation, shame and fear of overexcitement that are usually associated with the grandiose self reside in the split-off sector because they are so much at variance with the rest of the personality.[71]

For Kohut, one likely consequence of narcissistic shame is *narcissistic rage,* which has already been alluded to as one of the defenses of shame. Kohut saw shame and rage as the "two principal experiential and behavioral manifestations of disturbed narcissistic equilibrium."[72]

"Forms and Transformations of Narcissism" marked the beginning of the conceptualization of what Kohut later called the *bipolar self*.[73] Ambitions (which develop out of the material of the grandiose self) represent one pole, and ideals (arising out of integration of the idealized self) represent the other pole. Kohut suggests that experientially, an individual is "led by ideals and pushed by ambitions."[74]

In that seminal article, Kohut set forth his basic ideas about the origins of debilitating shame. He contended that shame "arises when the ego is unable to provide a proper discharge for the exhibitionistic demands of the narcissistic self."[75] Kohut continues his discussion of the origins of shame as follows:

> Indeed, in almost all clinically significant instances of shame propensity the personality is characterized by a defective idealization of the superego and by a concentration of the narcissistic libido upon the narcissistic self; and it is therefore the ambitious, success-driven person with a poorly integrated grandiose-self concept and intense exhibitionistic-narcissistic tensions who is most prone to experience shame. If the pressures from the narcissistic self are intense and the ego is unable to control them, the personality will respond with shame to failures of any kind. . . .
>
> Under optimal circumstances, therefore, the ego ideal and the goal structure of the ego are the personality's best protection against narcissistic vulnerability and shame propensity.[76]

Simply put, Kohut's ideas regarding the etiology of a shame-based personality turn upon the failure of the primary caretaker to convey a basic sense of "all rightness" to the young child. The child's original sense of bliss and union with the source of life itself must necessarily give way to an understanding of himself or herself as a separate being set apart and adrift in creation. A failure of mirroring of the grandiose self causes these lessons to be learned too abruptly and too soon. One writer put it this way:

> A situation of trust has to be established while, on the one hand [the child's] feeling of being separate increases in him the awareness of his needs and, on the other, his anxiety whenever he feels small, impotent and cannot really make things happen the way he wishes. In the best of cases, with parental care, toler-

ance and support, the little child can accept this painful state of affairs. The omnipotence and magic powers are projected on to the parents, who by containing them eventually lead the young child to manage his feelings of inadequacy, guilt and shortcomings in a realistic way. Because a child is not aware that he will outgrow each one of the developmental stages, his shortcoming related to each of them tend to make him feel guilty and devalued, ashamed of his smallness, envious of his bigger and more powerful parents, and wish to grow up quickly.[77]

Thus, for Kohut "shame arises when the selfobjects do not respond with the expected mirroring, approval and admiration to the 'boundless exhibitionism' of the grandiose self."[78] If adequate mirroring does not occur, the result is that pervasive "something wrongness," of smallness, of deficiency and inadequacy in the face of life itself. In other words, a sense of shame will permeate and dominate the entire personality. Without adequate mirroring, narcissism—cathexis of self— is not able to have its due and the energy associated with it becomes unavailable for the living of abundant life. When a child's native temperament disappoints a parent, the ground is laid for the genesis of shame. When affirmation is not forthcoming at vulnerable moments, an awareness of the difference between the self and the other can translate into the "invidious comparison. That comparison is one of good versus bad, better versus worse."[79] The shame-based person constantly feels judged and condemned in the core of his or her being. He or she is seen and found wanting. He or she is exposed and what is inside is no good, or at least not good enough.

These feelings are normal—to a degree—because no person is God. Furthermore, no one can be perfectly mirrored because no primary caretaker is perfect. Even if one were, we all must discover sooner or later that our infantile sense of omnipotence is an illusion, that our primary caretaker may treat us as the center of the universe and as beautiful and perfect in every way, but that this is not a view shared by others; we are, after all, limited and finite. In short, we are not God. This is a shaming realization, even for the healthiest of us. I am reminded of a pastoral conversation with a man who had recurring difficulty being faithful in his marriage. He told me he found it painful that he could not have sexual intimacy with every woman he found attractive. He experienced this as a constant and humiliating affront: a reminder of the finiteness of his life.

The shame we feel at the core of our being is essentially a matter of degree. A certain type of shame has been called "ontological" or "inherent" shame. This is not deemed pathological but, to the contrary, is an inborn affect—part of what defines us as human. It arises out of the condition of our having to contend with the embodied human form with all of its demands, limitations, and finiteness.[80]

Shame moves from being purely destructive to being potentially transformative when we stop dwelling on our inadequacies and failings and we give ourselves over to a sense of awe at the enormity of that which contains us and hold us—that which we are a part of.

Kohutian Healing

The goal in therapeutic treatment is to bring people into contact with parts of themselves that had previously been disavowed. Revelation and owning of the disavowed parts, and healing of the vertical split, strengthen the ego because substantial energy is needed to maintain the disavowal. Then, the strengthened ego is in a better position to engage the archaic elements of the grandiose self that are below the repression barrier—the horizontal split. The second part of analysis is geared toward taking down the horizontal barrier (maintained by repression), so that the "reality ego" is provided with narcissistic energies. This tends to eliminate "low self-esteem, shame propensity, and hypochondria which had prevailed in this structure so long as it was deprived of narcissistic energies."[81]

Kohut's therapy sought

> the integration of the grandiose self, with its wish to be known as beautiful, wondrous, admirable and exalted, into the rest of the personality. The humiliating, crude, exhibitionistic narcissism that previously was disavowed modifies and is available to enhance self esteem.[82]

Kohut refers to those who provide specific psychological functions for the developing self as *selfobjects*. "These objects provide specific psychological functions for the developing self. As such, they are experienced as part of the self. . . ."[83] Objects that provide selfobject needs are not experienced as entities in their own rights but rather in terms of their need-fulfilling function. Thus, selfobjects are not considered separate from the self in terms of the psychological functions they provide.

In Kohutian analysis, a major goal is

> the establishment of empathic communication between the self and its selfobjects on mature adult levels instead of the level of repressed or split-off unmodified narcissistic needs. . . . Drawing upon his clinical observations, Kohut asserts that the need for selfobjects exists throughout life.[84]

However, through analysis "the *unmodified needs* for merger with an idealized selfobject and/or mirroring by an affirming selfobject are diminished."[85] The self becomes more able to relate to selfobjects at more mature levels. This understanding of a need to relate to selfobjects even in mature and healthy adulthood differs from the classical Freudian view which "works toward the Western value-laden goals of separation and independence."[86] Paramount in Kohut's work is the need for relationship rather than, as classical theory would have it, drive satisfaction. For Kohut, the analytic cure is about "the gradual establishment of empathic contact with mature self-objects rather than 'autonomy.'"[87]

Kohut refers to the reactivation of early narcissistic modes as "narcissistic transferences." The "mirror transference" represents the mobilization of the grandiose self and the "idealizing transference" represents the activation of the idealized parental imago.[88]

Kohut goes farther than other depth theorists to present a plausible theory as to why some people are so wracked with shame while others are more able to shrug off insult and humiliation with equanimity and even humor. Jimmy Durante made a profitable career joking about the size of his nose, but anyone who mocked the oversized nose of Cyrano de Bergerac risked being killed. Some people can pick themselves up and dust themselves off from the most shameful exposure and humiliation—witness the extraordinary recovery of the Clinton presidency following the Monica Lewinsky scandal, in which Clinton was exposed, shamed, and humiliated in the most intimate areas of his life before the entire country and around the world. Other people are laid low by the slightest setbacks and affronts.

There is a "shame continuum" in people. Shame experiences and personalities run the gamut from relatively mild to being so constant as to result in a "shame-bound" or "shame-based" personality.[89] Morrison contends that in order to experience shame at all, a person must have some modicum of ego strength: "When concerns of fragmentation predominate . . . patients do not have the luxury to register shame."[90]

A central task of human life is that of evolving a unique personal identity that provides direction, purpose, and meaning, as well as enables the individual to retain "a sense of inner worth in the face of the vicissitudes of life with which we must contend, not the least of which are anxiety, suffering and a lack of absolute control over our lives." The inevitable lack of absolute control means some vulnerability to shame. "Some experiencing of defeat, failure, or rejection is inescapable in life. It is this fundamental reality which make of shame a universal, inevitable occurrence as well as a potential obstacle in the development of a secure, self-affirming identity."[91]

Shame theorist Andrew Morrison agrees with the premise of this book that Kohut's intrapsychic metapsychology goes the farthest to explain the phenomenon of shame. However, Morrison feels that Kohut's view

> is too limited when he maintains that shame reflects only the breakthrough of unneutralized grandiosity and not failure to meet the goals and expectations of the ego-ideal, or the "experience near" *shape of the ideal self.* . . . Using Kohut's language, I believe that shame can also be experienced because of failure in relationship to the idealized parental imago.[92]

Morrison argues with some force that by reason of the fact that the self's initial pursuit of merger with the idealized parental imago is an aspect of narcissistic development, "shame over failure in the compensatory (or healthy) pursuit of ideals (as over any failure with regard to the idealized selfobject) is potentially as devastating as is the shame from overwhelming grandiosity."[93] Moreover, "failure of the parental selfobject to respond to the self's idealizing needs and quest for merger is a prominent source of shame vulnerability and a model for subsequent shame over the self's experience of its needs."[94] Morrison contends that shame experienced in connection with the failure of the idealized parental imago "tends to be less archaic and more differentiated than that experienced a result of overwhelming grandiosity"—reflecting Kohut's "developmental sequence from grandiosity to idealization."[95]

"Forms and Transformations of Narcissism"

In "Forms and Transformations of Narcissism," Kohut examines some positive transformations of narcissism. First, he looks at a possible relationship between narcissistic energy and creativity. In other words, he looks at the positive, creative, and generative uses for which narcissistic libido can be used—in contradistinction with feelings of shame which bleed and deplete the self and its creative expression by forever turning inward, turning the self inside out.

At this point, Kohut begins to sound distinctly spiritual, although his work lacks explicit religious referents. We begin to see an overlapping of depth psychology and religion. Kohut's spiritual life was and remains something of a mystery,[96] yet it becomes clear in "Forms and Transformations of Narcissism" that the very narcissism which in its archaic form gives rise to severe personality disorders, and which arise most fundamentally out of pathological shame, can be transformed into empathy, humor, wisdom, and cosmic narcissism. Beyond the obvious fact that creative activity can lead to fame and acclaim, "in creative work, narcissistic energies are employed that have been changed into . . . idealizing libido. . . ."[97] Kohut contends that "the creative individual, whether in art or science, is less psychologically separated from his surroundings than the noncreative one; the 'I-you' barrier is not as clearly defined."[98] In a typical person, the idealization component of narcissism survives in the state of being in love; if there is any idealizing libido left over it "may account for a brief spurt of artistic activity not uncommon during this state."[99] For very creative people, however,

> the spreading of the libidinal investment upon "collective alternates" and ultimately upon "the world" . . . appears to me as an indication of narcissistic experience of the world (an expanded self that includes the world) rather than as the manifestation of a "love affair" within an unqualified context of object love.[100]

Moreover,

> The creative individual is keenly aware of those aspects of his surroundings which are of significance to his work, and he invests them with narcissistic-idealizing libido. Like the air we

breathe, they are most clearly experienced at the moment of union with the self.[101]

The next transformation of narcissism that Kohut discusses is empathy: "the mode by which one gathers psychological data about
other people and, when they say what they think or feel, imagines
their inner experience even though it is not open to direct observation."[102] Kohut is well known for his exposition of the belief that empathy is a critical element of psychological observation and is therefore of special importance for the psychoanalyst. Kohut states that

> the groundwork for our ability to obtain access to another's
> mind is laid by the fact that in our earliest mental organization
> the feelings, actions and behavior of the mother had been in-
> cluded in our self. This *primary empathy* with the mother pre-
> pares us for the recognition that to a large extent the basic inner
> experiences of other people remain similar to our own.[103]

When we relate to others in an archaic, unintegrated narcissistic
mode, empathy is impossible. A psychoanalyst must have the ability
"to employ the transformed narcissistic cathexes in empathic observation."[104]

A third transformation of narcissistic energy is what Kohut calls "a
cosmic narcissism which has transcended the bounds of the individual."[105] Kohut sees this cosmic narcissism as "the ultimate attitude
toward life"—a "new expanded, transformed narcissism." This ultimate transformation of narcissism is based upon a total acceptance of
the finiteness of one's existence, of death:[106]

> Just as the child's *primary empathy* with the mother is the pre-
> cursor of the adult's ability to be empathic, so his *primary iden-
> tity* with her must be considered the precursor of an expansion
> of self, late in life, when the finiteness of individual existence is
> acknowledged. The original psychological universe, i.e., the
> primordial experience of the mother, is "remembered" by many
> people in the form of the occasionally occurring vague reverber-
> ations known by the term "oceanic feeling" (Freud, 1930, pp. 64-
> 73). The achievement—as the certainty of eventual death is
> fully realized—of a shift of the narcissistic cathexes from the
> self to a concept of participation in a supraindividual and time-

less existence must also be regarded as genetically predetermined by the child's primary identity with the mother. In contrast
to the oceanic feeling, however, which is experienced passively
(and usually fleetingly), the genuine shift of the cathexes toward
a cosmic narcissism is the enduring, creative result of the steadfast activities of an autonomous ego, and only very few are able
to attain it.[107]

Cosmic narcissism represents nothing less than a "genuine decathexis of the self" and can "only be achieved by an intact, well-func-
tioning ego; and it is accompanied by sadness as the cathexis is transferred from the cherished self to the supraindividual ideals and to the
world with which one identifies."[108] The achievement of cosmic narcissism "does not present a picture of grandiosity and elation" but
rather of "a quiet inner triumph with an admixture of undenied melancholy."[109] One reason that so few can or do approach cosmic narcissism is that it is achieved only when all of the defenses to shame
have fallen and the individual can endure being in the shame vortex
without those defenses. Going back to the hypothetical businessman
posited in Chapter 6, can he endure the feelings he is having without
acting out rage, without withdrawing, projecting, and scapegoating,
without becoming "righteous," without becoming depressed? Cosmic
narcissism brings into play the sense of awe we feel in the presence of
God. Feelings of inadequacy—a variety of shame—are replaced by a
sense of being part of, contained and held by, the *tremendum* that is
God itself.
Another transformation of narcissism discussed in "Forms and
Transformations of Narcissism" is wisdom. Attainment of wisdom
rests on "acceptance of the limitations of . . . physical, intellectual and
emotional powers."[110] I have set forth the basic thesis that ontological
shame is the inevitable consequence of the stress created by the tension between our consciousness and our finite creatureliness. Kohut
says that achievement of wisdom requires "relinquishment of narcissistic delusions, *including acceptance of the inevitability of death*"
(emphasis added).[111]
Pervasive, debilitating shame probably cannot exist alongside cosmic narcissism, empathy, or wisdom. Kohutian theory sees shame
propensity as the consequence of overconcentration of the narcissistic libido upon the narcissistic self. Narcissistic libido so concen-
trated is not available for transformation into cosmic narcissism or

wisdom. It is too busy always looking inward; court is always in session, with the internal prosecutor responding with the defenses of shame to any perceived failures, shortcomings, or slights. The defenses of shame require the expenditure of vast amounts of energy that thus become unavailable for creativity or for empathy, much less for wisdom or cosmic narcissism. The defenses of shame take the individual out of the vortex—the place of tension that feels like a godless place but is in fact a place where grace enters. Still, it may be the exquisite suffering with that very intensity which ultimately leads some individuals in desperation to seek transformation.

SHAME AS ARCHETYPAL EXPERIENCE:
A JUNGIAN PERSPECTIVE

As indicated, this chapter is an attempt to plumb ever deeper into the etiology and experience of shame in human life and in the human psyche. The next logical place to go after the examination of Kohut's intrapsychic metapsychological understanding of the psychic structure and origins of shame is the archetypal level that may be understood and articulated with reference to the theories of Carl Jung.

Jung himself rarely alluded to shame per se. The General Index to his *Collected Works*[112] reveals only five indexed references to the word *shame,* and the word is usually used along with the word *disgust* (i.e., "shame and disgust") to describe Freudian theory of resistance to sexual fantasy or shame connected with nakedness.

In view of lively contemporary interest in shame, some modern-day Jungians have very profitably plumbed his theories to develop understandings of the meaning of shame in psychic life.

In a 1988 article that appeared in the *Journal of Analytical Psychology,* Peer Hultberg's premise was that

> Shame is strongly connected with the shadow and the persona; in other words, with man as a social being. But it is also . . . intimately linked with the self and with a personal experience of self. At times it is a violent feeling which may last for a staggeringly long time and even after fifty years produce a wince and the wish in a person to sink deep down under the surface of the earth. . . . If, however, one is open to the problem of shame and

allows feelings of shame to emerge they can lead into great psychic depths.[113]

Shame has two distinct functions: "one serves social adaptation, and the other protects the self and the integrity of the individual. One ensures membership in human society through conformity, the other ensures that the collective does not violate the individual." Hultberg concludes that although shame plays a primary role in depression and other neurotic symptoms, it nevertheless can lead one to the authentic self.[114]

Hultberg associates the experience of "eternal shame" with hell itself: "overwhelming and all-consuming pain, encompassing both body and soul, implying utter physical destruction while yet one is being kept intensively alive and conscious."[115]

Mara Sidoli writes without citation that "Jung himself linked feelings of shame caused by the experience of one's own inadequacy and the shadow archetype."[116] As noted by Sandra Edelman, Sidoli might have been referring here to the following passage from Jung's *Aion:*

> The shadow is a moral problem that challenges the whole ego-personality, for no one can become conscious of the shadow without considerable moral effort. To become conscious of it involves recognizing the dark aspects of the personality as present and real. . . . Affects occur usually where adaptation is weakest, namely a certain degree of inferiority and the existence of a lower level of personality.[117]

That shame is an archetypal experience, as illustrated perhaps most clearly by the Genesis account of the expulsion of Adam and Eve from paradise[118] (see discussion in Chapter 8), cannot be seriously questioned.

Sandra Edelman is an author who has done the most to construct a distinctly Jungian approach to shame. In her 1998 book *Turning the Gorgon: A Meditation on Shame* she articulates and develops the following premise:

> In some shamecarriers, at some time before the ego is formed, the infant psyche encounters the daemonic aspect of the sacred, the dark side of the numen; this encounter imprints the infant's

archaic psyche with a sense not of "shame" but of its own defilement and consequent feeling of dread which, unless mitigated by a holding environment created by an empathic mother, becomes pervasive and chronic.[119]

Edelman's premise is based upon the heuristic assumption that

> beneath the explications of shame discussed in received theory, there is for *some of us* another deeper explication which can extend, not repudiate, what is already understood by clinicians. That deeper—probably *deepest*—layer takes us into the religious dimension, and it is there where we may find another way, still holding psychology by one hand, to grasp the nature of ontic shame.[120]

Edelman's use of depth psychology as a ground for examining religious experiences coincides with my own belief that even as we peer into the religious dimension to look at shame, we do well to "hold psychology by one hand."[121] This conveys the sense that depth psychology gives us something to grasp, something to hold onto, as we study depths that are fundamentally unfathomable. It gives us courage, a place to stand, a lifeline to help us avoid slipping and falling into an abyss from which it may be very difficult to escape.

In its extreme form, says Edelman, shame evokes "terror, awe, and the threat of annihilation, the obliteration of one's existence. Such a vocabulary points beyond the natural, human sphere to the realm of the supernatural, the non-human, the archetypal; in short, to the divine."[122] Shame has been likened to "a wound made from the inside by *an unseen hand*," and an "almost indescribable fear."[123] The punishment expected by the shame carrier "whether expected from within or without, contains an *uncanny elementary force*."[124] Interestingly, even secular depth theorists have observed that "shame is close to the feeling of awe." Helen Block Lewis adds that "It is the feeling-state to which one is more susceptible when one has fallen in love. The 'other' is a prominent and powerful force in the experience of shame."[125]

Edelman notes that such descriptions point beyond "the natural, human sphere to the realm of the supernatural, the non-human, the archetypal; in short, to the divine." At its most intense, shame is experienced as *dread*—what Rudolph Otto called "daemonic dread"—expounded upon by Edelman as follows:

We are in the proximity to the *mysterium tremendum,* that ultimate numinosity which is "hidden and esoteric . . . beyond conception or understanding, extraordinary and unfamiliar" (the *mysterium*) which causes a response of "fear that is more than fear proper . . . a terror fraught with an inward shuddering."[126]

And, quoting Paul Pruyser, Edelman says that the numinous mystery—the *mysterium tremendum*—"always invokes both shuddering and admiration. It attracts and repels at once. It elicits devotion and fear. It instills dread and trust. It is dangerous and comforting. It inspires awe and bliss."[127]

It is the daemonic sacred, the unknowable, which is the *tremendum* and which becomes the taboo area of the sacred. . . . In Pruyser's words, "The *tremendum* consists of 'all the sources of terror,' all the threats which exist or are sensed."[128]

The author of Hebrews notes, "It is a fearful thing to fall into the hands of the living God" (Hebrews 10:31). Paul Ricoeur has written that "the Sacred is perceived, in the archaic stage of the religious consciousness, as that which does not permit a man to stand, that which makes him die."[129]

Die? Is this too dramatic? I think not, if we understand this to mean become dead to a false way of living. Jesus indeed said,

Those who want to save their life will lose it, and those who lose their life for my sake, and for the sake of the gospel, will save it. . . . Those who are ashamed of me and of my words . . . of them the Son of Man will also be ashamed when he comes in the glory of his Father. (Mark 8:35-38)

When we view this saying with the 3-D lens that depth psychology provides, we might find Jesus urging us toward the cosmic narcissism of which Kohut speaks. This condition is, almost by definition, a relinquishment of toxic shame, a willingness and ability to trust, a dropping of the self-consciousness that erects unhelpful boundaries between and among us, and between us and God. This kind of "dying" means trusting that one will be held by something bigger, something that one feels oneself to be a part of. This is the mystical experience of union. The dark side of this awe—the fear and dread—can be a way station on the path to the experience of being held. Shuddering comes before admiration and awe. The dread and fear is the last barrier that is dropped in the shedding of toxic shame. It is just the other side of peace—but one can only go through it. Sometimes we never do get to the other side.

Rudolph Otto's most basic contribution was his assertion that the experience of the numinous

> is a primal element of our psychical nature that needs to be grasped purely in its uniqueness and cannot itself be explained by anything else. Like all other primal psychical elements, it *emerges* in due course in the developing life of human mind and spirit . . .[130]

Edelman poses the rhetorical question, "Without such an 'imprint' in the psyche, . . . how would we ever have evolved the idea of god, since there is nothing in ordinary sensory experience to suggest god's existence?"[131]

How indeed? Without the capacity for shame, experience of God would not be possible. Without the sense of "something wrongness," how would we ever really experience "rightness"?

Edelman reminds us that the Greeks had a goddess of shame, Aidos, who was the nursemaid of Athene. The ancient Greeks seemed to use the word *aidos* for something more nuanced than the way we use the word "shame," something linked to "one's relationship to the collective." It may be understood as "respect for public opinion, respect for honor, one of the primary necessary conditions for human existence; as a sense of duty; as consciousness of moral obligation; as 'a modest bashfulness, a quiet respectful awe within nature and toward nature.'"[132] For the ancient Greek,

> the highest good was the esteem of his fellows, . . . In such a society, anything which exposes a man to the contempt or ridicule of his fellows, which causes him to "lose face," is felt as unbearable. "Loss of face" always involved diminution of one's honor, which could be brought about by behaving in a way which deviated from fairly clear collective standards.[133]

Thus, in ancient Greece, *aidos* was both a sense of duty and respect for honor, and shame was a consequence of failing in either sphere in the eyes of one's friends. The battle cry of the men of *The Iliad* was the single word *"Aidos!"*[134] Any failures in this respect could mean removal from the collective.

Significantly, the goddess Aidos did not live on Olympia with the other deities but roamed the earth. Nevertheless, she "had an altar on the Athenian acropolis . . . and a reserved seat in the theater of Dionysos, indicating how close she was to the heart of the community."[135]

Aidos was an important bulwark in the structure of civilization. "It provided the constraints for the preservation . . . of all that was most cherished by the Greeks—honor, justice, beauty, courage, reason, balance . . ." The argument has been cogently made that *aidos* originated "as the reaction which the holy excites in a human being."[136] The goddess Athene was the protector of the city-state of Athens and was linked with the forces that would keep the body politic intact. Thus, it is not surprising that she would have had Aidos for a nursemaid. Edelman contends that Athene is "an archetypal embodiment not of the normative but of the transcendent function, that 'third thing' which arises out of the conflict between opposites and which at once contains the opposites and transcends them."[137]

If *aidos* is, most essentially, "reverence for one's self," Edelman contends that the opposite of reverence which Athene held in tension with *aidos* was the Gorgon—a "hellish" symbol of "tormented shame."[138] One of the three Gorgons of Greek myth was Medusa. Edelman notes that the best known version of the Medusa myth is that Medusa, who was mortal, violated Athene's temple by having sex there with Poseidon. For this offense Athene turned Medusa into a monster: any man who looked upon her face was thenceforth turned to stone. Athene helps Perseus to slay the Gorgon, after which Perseus presents her head to Athene, who put it on her shield, as both protection and defense: "It was meant not only to ward off evil but to lend its wearer the power of terrorizing, even petrifying, the enemy. It can both protect the wearer, and be destructive to the foe."[139] The Gorgon, with her "evil eye" and her "uncanny, unmanageable, dark, potentially death-dealing, terror inspiring energies, is an entity who points straight into what Paul Ricoeur has called the taboo area of the sacred." Moreover, the archetypal image of the Gorgon has effects which

> offer compelling parallels with the effects of deep shame: the
> sense of paralysis (petrification); the sense of exposure, of being

seen in a devastating way (the gaze of the Evil Eye); the terror of extinction; the psyche (head) as the seat of energy; the involvement of death. In this perspective, the Gorgon could be called the archetypal image of shame and dread, and the opposite of *aidos*.[140]

Edelman notes that many modern depth psychologists are in basic agreement that "it is the mother's capacity to intuit, embrace and 'metabolize' the infant's affects and chaos, which determines much of the infant psyche's developmental path. . . ." Here is where Edelman's ideas begin to coalesce with more conventional paths in depth psychology: Kohut himself wrote that the basic factor that elicits certain psychological illnesses, and in particular narcissistic disorders, is "the fear of the cold, unempathatic" selfobject. Kohut explicitly mentions Medusa in this connection:

> True, behind the head of the Medusa lies the supposedly castrated genital of the woman. But behind the dreadful genital of the woman lies the cold, unresponding, nonmirroring face of a mother (or of a psychotic father who has usurped the mother's self-object functions) who is unable to provide life-sustaining acceptance for her child because she is depressed or latently schizophrenic or afflicted with some other distortion of her personality.[141]

The terror that this evokes in the infant psyche is "the stuff of our worst nightmares"[142]—i.e., the "hell" referred to by Hultberg.

However, Edelman brings us right to the numinous by considering the personal mother and then turning to consider the archetypal energies that are "imprints" in the human psyche. The personal mother cannot be left out of the equation because her personality and mothering style will inevitably affect the inner archetypal world of the infant. Across cultures, we see the archetype of the terrible mother alongside that of the nurturing mother. Witness the bloodthirsty Kali, the alter ego of the life-producing Pavarti and the Hindu equivalent of the Gorgon. The daemonic will, according to Edelman, often is assigned to the feminine gender because of the human mother's physiological centrality in birth and nurturing, which in turn means that nature itself is usually seen as feminine. I am reminded too of the fierce projection of evil on women persecuted as "witches" in medieval Europe and later in the American colonies. Robin Briggs points out that these projections of archetypal evil must necessarily have been fueled by the "formative role played by infantile attachment to the mother, with all its ambiguities and the ferocious interplay between love and hate."[143]

When shame is so profound that it "penetrates into that dark place of paralysis and terror" it becomes dread. It is the anxiety that Winnicott calls the "threat of annihilation" which, in his view, "is a very real primitive anxiety, long antedating any anxiety that includes the word death in its description." Maternal failures are experienced "as threats to personal self-existence."[144] When a mother fails to be "good enough"—i.e., when she fails to positively respond to her infant's needs in a developmentally appropriate manner and time, the infant faces "unthinkable anxiety," an interruption of his "going on being"; all later experiences of anxiety are anxiety about the "breakdown that has already been experienced."[145]

Kohut aptly calls this experience "disintegration anxiety" and believes it to be "the deepest anxiety man can experience."[146] What is feared is "not physical extinction but loss of humanness: psychological death."[147] Clearly the attempt to describe disintegration anxiety is the attempt to describe the indescribable. This experience comes from the failure of response from an empathic selfobject. Without this we cannot psychologically survive because we are placed in a totally isolated psychological condition that is the sine qua non of shame. It might be said that without the empathic response—when we are continually met with cold indifference—the experience of profound shame is triggered. The disintegration anxiety that Kohut talks about is the experience of the abyss, the daemonic dread which Edelman describes.

Chapter 8

Toward a Theology of Shame

Just as I am, without one plea, but that thy blood was shed
for me, and that thou bid'st me come to thee, O Lamb of
God, I come, I come.

Just as I am, though tossed about with many a conflict,
many a doubt; fightings and fears within, without, O
Lamb of God, I come, I come.

Just as I am, poor, wretched, blind; sight, riches, healing of
the mind, yea, all I need, in thee to find, O Lamb of God,
I come, I come.

Hymn 693, Episcopal Hymnal, 1982

"WHERE CAN I FLEE FROM YOUR PRESENCE?"

This book began with a discussion of the prominent place of shame
in the Christ event, with the suggestion that the experience of shame
is archetypal and that the phenomenon must be fathomed if the enduring psychic importance of the Christ event is to be understood. In
his all too brief theological discussion of shame, Dietrich Bonhoeffer
remarked that "shame is overcome only in the fact of final shaming,
namely the becoming manifest of knowledge before God."[1] What
event could possibly be more of a "final shaming" than the crucifixion? What transformation of shame could be more explicit than the
resurrection of the one who had been shamed?

I have moved through a discussion of shame from a depth psychology perspective and in this chapter attempt to relate what has been
discussed to building a spiritual and theological understanding of
shame.

Sartre devotes considerable time discussing the phenomenon of shame feelings in his principal text of existentialism, *Being and Nothingness.* He describes shame as an "immediate shudder which runs through me from head to foot without any discursive preparation."[2] It is an "internal hemorrhage."[3] It is a profoundly painful experience of being exposed to, observed by, and judged by the Other. "I am ashamed of what I am. Shame therefore realizes an intimate relation of myself to myself. Through shame I have discovered an aspect of *my* being."[4] Shame means recognition. "I recognize that I *am* as the Other sees me."[5]

The psalmist in Psalm 139 says,

O Lord, you have searched me and known me.
You know when I sit down and when I rise up;
     you discern my thoughts from far away.
You search out my path and my lying down,
     and are acquainted with all my ways.
Even before a word is on my tongue,
     O Lord, you know it completely. . . .
Where can I go from your spirit?
Or where can I flee from your presence?
If I ascend to heaven, you are there.
If I make my bed in Sheol, you are there. . . .
For it was you who formed my inward parts;
     you knit me together in my mother's womb. . . .
My frame was not hidden from you when I was being made in secret,
     intricately woven in the depths of the earth.
Your eyes beheld my unformed substance.

The ancient Collect for Purity, which remains part of the standard Eucharistic celebration in the Episcopal *Book of Common Prayer,* likewise acknowledges God's omniscience regarding all of our thoughts:

Almighty God, to you all hearts are open, all desires known, and from you no secrets are hid: cleanse the thoughts of our hearts by the inspiration of your Holy Spirit, that we may perfectly love you, and worthily magnify your holy Name, through Christ our Lord.[6]

Nietzsche, too, is horrified, not comforted, by the prying eyes of an omniscient, omnipotent God. "The inescapability of the unblinking God who knows everything is degrading for Nietzsche: he feels powerless to defend himself against the most intimate of exposures."[7] Like Sartre, Nietzsche is appalled by the sense of being "trapped, utterly fixed by the eye of the Other."[8] As Carl Schneider points out, there is a clear religious context for Satre's revulsion at being observed:

> Our shame is not a feeling of being this or that guilty object but in general being an object; that is, of recognizing myself in this degraded, fixed and dependent being which I am for the Other. Shame is the feeling of an original *fall.*[9]

Sartre expressly alludes to the Genesis story of Adam and Eve's expulsion from paradise:

> I am guilty first when beneath the Other's look I experience my alienation and my nakedness as a fall from grace which I must assume. This is the meaning of the famous line from Scripture: "They knew that they were naked."[10]

"Shame before God" is "the recognition of my being an object before a subject which can never be an object."[11] A seminarian wrote of a recurrent dream that reflects a horror of being observed:

> I remember specifically the sound of a helicopter from when I was very young. We lived next to a large municipal park and there was a police helicopter that would fly over our house late at night sometimes with a spotlight searching for illegal activity. The sound of a helicopter or the beam of a spotlight to this day scare me. I dreamed for days about that helicopter and jumping off the roof to escape from it.

Helen Lewis has noted that one of the functions of shame is

> the protection against the loss of self-boundaries. . . . Shame functions as a sharp, in fact, painful, reminder that the fantasy experience of the "other" is vicarious. Shame brings into focal

awareness both the self and the "other," with the imagery that the "other" rejects the self. It thus helps to maintain the sense of separate identity, by making the self the focus of experience.[12]

This observation "parallels Erikson's observation that shame is the 'opposite' of autonomy."[13]

The obtrusive, prying eyes of the Other for both Nietzsche and Sartre represent an outrageous denial of freedom and privacy. Helen Lynd and her followers have asserted that the feeling of shame is revelatory, transforming, and leads to greater freedom, but Nietzsche and Sartre feel humiliated and trapped by a disrespectful, intrusive God "to whom all hearts are open, all desires known and from whom no secrets are hid"; a God who has "searched me and known me" and "discerns my thoughts from far away."

Martin Luther himself "described states of badness which in many forms pervade human existence from childhood."[14] He describes shame, for example, as "an emotion first experienced when the infant stands naked in space and feels belittled":

> He is put to sin and shame before God . . . this shame is now a thousand times greater, that a man must blush in the presence of God. For this means that there is no corner or hole in the whole of creation into which a man might creep, not even in hell, but he must let himself be exposed to the gaze of the whole creation, and stand in the open with all his shame, as a bad conscience feels when it is really struck.[15]

How we feel about a God who has searched us and known us, and who discerns our thoughts from far away, depends in no small part upon whether we experience God as benevolent. If God is not completely benevolent, then to have no secrets hidden from God is dangerous.[16] A well-known children's Christmas song about Santa Claus warns:

> He sees you when you're sleeping,
> He knows when you're awake.
> He knows if you've been bad or good,
> So be good for goodness sake!

Here is a grown-up version of this idea, written by C. S. Lewis:

> In the end the Face which is the delight or the terror of the universe must be turned upon each of us either with one expression or with the other, either conferring glory inexpressible or inflicting shame that can never be cured or disguised.[17]

Thus, C. S. Lewis's God is in some respects no more comforting than Nietzsche's; it is only a benevolent God if one has nothing to be ashamed of before God's eyes.

Nietzsche's solution is to kill God; he cannot endure the "horror of the all-reflecting mirror."[18] In Paul Tillich's sermon on Psalm 139 ("The Escape from God"), Tillich agrees with Nietzsche that God is inescapable. "He is God only *because* He is inescapable. And only that which is inescapable is God."[19]

> It is safe to say that a man who has never tried to flee God has never experienced the God Who really is God. When I speak of God, I do not refer to the many gods of our own making, the gods with whom we can live rather comfortably. For there is no reason to flee a god who is the perfect picture of everything that is good in man. . . . A god whom we can easily bear, a god from whom we do not have to hide, a god whom we do not hate in moments, a god whose destruction we never desire, is not God at all, and has no reality.[20]

The God that Nietzsche and Sartre, and even Tillich and Lewis, describe is not a cuddly teddy bear. It is, again in Sartre's words, one before whom we feel ourselves as objects yet it can never really be an object itself. Enormous, omniscient, inscrutable, all-seeing—how do the best sniveling human creatures bear up under this God's knowledge of us?

THE "SICK SOUL"

I believe that shame, this sense of being somehow flawed or at least feeble, inadequate, or finite, is an ontological part of what it means to be human. It seems, in any event, to be a precondition for deep religious experience. In William James's classic book *The Varieties of Religious Experience,* he wrote that despite differences in religious traditions, they all have in common (1) an uneasiness and (2) its solution:

1. The uneasiness, reduced to its simplest terms, is a sense that there is *something wrong about us* as we naturally stand.
2. The solution is a sense that *we are saved from the wrongness* by making proper connection with the higher powers.[21]

James is summarizing what this book refers to as the transformation of shame experience—emotional life on the shame axis. In fact, one might see *The Varieties of Religious Experience* as a phenomenological description of the religious conversions of individuals who have endured the shame vortex, the godless place.

When this transformation happens, it does not mean that one is suddenly freed from suffering. However, it does impart a sense of being held in the matrix of the infinite and eternal. It means that one can live emotionally and spiritually on a different plane, even as one attends as best as one can to the challenges, failures, joys, and losses of one's own life journey.

James saw two basic types of religious temperaments: the "healthy-minded" and the "sick soul." He gave the name of "healthy mindedness to the tendency which looks on all things and sees that they are good."[22] The healthy-minded temperament has a "constitutional incapacity for prolonged suffering" and "a tendency to see things optimistically . . . in which the individual's character is set."[23] In response to persons subject to a sense of "something wrong," the healthy-minded person would say something like, " 'Stuff and nonsense, get out into the open air!' or 'Cheer up, old fellow, you'll be all right erelong, if you will only drop your morbidness!' "[24] This temperament might tend to fall into the "shallow living" subtype of Karen Horney's pride system.

Julius Rubin in *Religious Melancholy and Protestant Experience in America* notes that James could barely hide his disdain for the mental hygiene movements of his time, exemplified by mind-cure movements and Mary Baker Eddy's Christian Science, which actually denied the real existence of evil.[25] Thus, in 1902 James wrote, in words that are startling for their continued relevance to the present day,

The advance of liberalism, so-called, in Christianity, during the past fifty years, may fairly be called a victory of the healthy-mindedness within the church over the morbidness with which the old hell-fire theology was more harmoniously related. We have now whole congregations whose preachers, far from magnifying our consciousness of sin, seem devoted rather to making little of it. They ignore, or even deny, eternal punishment, and insist on the dignity rather than the depravity of man. They look at the continual preoccupation of the old-fashioned Christian with the salvation of his soul as something sickly and reprehensible rather than admirable; and a sanguine and "muscular" attitude, which to our forefathers would have seemed purely heathen, has become in their eyes an ideal element of Christian character. I am not asking whether or not they are right, I am only pointing out the change.[26]

James left little question of his own opinion of the ultimate inefficacy of the unbridled optimism of healthy-mindedness when he wrote:

[T]here is no doubt that healthy-mindedness is inadequate as a positive philosophical doctrine, because the evil facts which it refuses positively to account for are a genuine portion of reality; and they may after all be the best key to life's significance, and possibly the only openers of our eyes to the deepest levels of truth.

The normal process of life contains moments as bad as any of those which insane melancholy is filled with, moments in which radical evil gets its innings and takes its solid turn. The lunatic's visions of horror are all drawn from the material of daily fact. Our civilization is founded on the shambles, and every individual existence goes out on a lonely spasm of helpless agony. If you protest, my friend, wait till you arrive there yourself![27]

The religion of the "sick soul" is one which is more prone to conviction of sin and sense of "something wrong about us as we naturally stand." James explored the depression and religious melancholy of Tolstoy and John Bunyan as described in the words of their own memoirs, arguing that "religious melancholy characterized the existential condition of God's unregenerate people."[28] James' description of the religious melancholic contains the following synthesis, which seems to get to the heart of the nature of such an individual:

> If the individual be of tender conscience and religiously quickened, the unhappiness will take the form of moral remorse and compunction, of feeling inwardly vile and wrong, and of standing in false relations to the author of one's being and the appointer of one's spiritual fate. This is the religious melancholy and "conviction of sin" that have played so large a part in the history of Protestant Christianity.[29]

James' "sick soul" is one who suffers from a deep and abiding sense of shame. I once sat in a journeyers group with a young man who was struggling with a call to the priesthood. Tears filled his eyes and his face became flushed as he said, "Lately I feel so filled with horror at the sins I have committed, the sins I commit every day, the people I have hurt in my life, even the thoughtless mistakes I make every day that hurt people's feelings." This is the attitude of James' "sick soul." This is a sense of essential flawedness, of something wrong at the core of one's being. This is shame.

THE PARADOX:
SHAME AS BORDERLINE PHENOMENON
BETWEEN UNION AND SEPARATION

As has already been discussed, shame is an archetypal human experience.[30] It has been said that "The very capacity for experiencing shame, the design of shame inscribed in the human soul—this is a sine qua non of humanity."[31]

The Genesis story of Adam and Eve's expulsion from the Garden of Eden is, at its core, a story of shame. It is the story of the beginning of humankind's dawning awareness of being different from the other beasts. It is the story of our longing to be at peace with our maker, of feeling ourselves somehow connected with God—made in God's image—yet always experiencing ourselves as falling short and being *exposed*—physically in the demands, desires, sufferings, and finiteness of the flesh, intellectually in our ignorance about the origins and meaning of our existence, and spiritually and emotionally in our existential loneliness.

Tillich calls the condition of the primordial couple before they ate of the Tree of Knowledge of good and evil the "state of dreaming innocence" where "freedom and destiny are in harmony."[32] The couple's temptation and disobedience of God represent the essential split and the existential dilemma that has always existed between the human spirit, which longs to be united with God, and the human body. Ernest Becker puts it this way:

> [Humankind] has a symbolic identity that brings him sharply out of nature. He is a symbolic self, a creature with a name, a life history. He is a creator with a mind that soars out to speculate about atoms and infinity. . . . This immense expansion, this dexterity, this ethereality, this self-consciousness gives to man literally the status of a small god in nature, as the Renaissance thinkers knew. . . . This is the paradox: [humankind] is out of nature and hopelessly in it; he is dual, up in the stars and yet housed in a heart-pumping, breath-grasping body that once belonged to a fish and still carries the gill-marks to prove it. His body is a material fleshy casing that is alien to him in many ways—the strangest and most repugnant way being that it aches and bleeds and will decay and die. [Humankind] is literally split in two: he has an awareness of his own splendid uniqueness in that he sticks out of nature with a towering majesty, and yet goes back into the ground a few feet in order blindly and dumbly to rot and disappear forever. It is a terrifying dilemma to be in and have to live with.[33]

Human beings inevitably must confront the frailty and finiteness of the body which stands in such tension with our sense of having something in the core of our being bearing God's image, and also we must constantly deal with the demands and pressures imposed by our instinctual nature—demands we sometimes do not experience as consistent with the God image imprinted on us. We need food and drink, shelter, clothing for our frail frames. We hunger for sexual intimacy. We want bodily creature comforts. Our instinctual nature moves us to set our face toward the world and often to compete with other human beings for resources, for money, for position and status, for jobs, for power, for sexual partners. We feel ashamed because of the existence of these needs and desires which are our creaturely inheritance and, paradoxically, we feel ashamed when we fail to "measure up" to our fellows in achieving and obtaining them.

Rudolph Otto also seems to have believed humankind's problem with its existence was based upon the issues attendant upon its creatureliness. Our sense of "profaneness" comes not necessarily from our actions but rather from our "very existence as creature before that which is supreme above all creatures."[34]

That human beings from the beginning of the end of their "dreaming innocence" were impelled to cover their bodies must strike us as significant from this perspective. Suddenly, the body is recognized as "a problem"—something that needs to be covered from the prying eyes of others. The body is an irrefutable confirmation that we are not spirit—or in any event not *just* spirit—but part of nature. Adam and Eve felt the paradigmatic experience in shame: a sense of exposure.

As we have seen, two of the most predictable and universal responses to feelings of shame are the urge to hide and conceal and the urge to flee the situation that has caused pain.[35] Adam and Eve responded to their feelings of shame in precisely those ways: first, in their attempt to hide from God (Genesis 3:8) and their concealment (i.e., of their genitals with fig leaves), and second, by ultimately fleeing from the Garden of Eden and from God, who had witnessed their shame. This, I think, is the ultimate meaning of the Adam and Eve story. It is really not about God's expulsion and banishment of the primal couple from the garden and/or from God's presence, but rather the couple's own shame experience and their need to separate themselves from the unity they had felt with nature itself and from God's presence.

It seems that from God's perspective, this experience of shame meant that the humans had "become like one of us, knowing good from evil" (Genesis 3:22). From the human perspective, however, it was this very consciousness that brought with it the recognition of our limitations, our nakedness before God. Mario Jacoby puts it this way:

> Humility and consciousness of the limits of the ego are some of the most difficult and important achievements along the path of psychic development. The ego must not identify with the supraordinate Self, for this would mean grandiosity and mental illness. . . . The growth of consciousness, symbolized by the eating

of the fruit of the tree of knowledge, leads to a loss of paradisal unitary reality. No longer does one enjoy blissful ignorance of the painful conflicts caused by the polarization of inner and outer, subject and object, ego and self.[36]

God provided coverings for Adam and Eve as they left Paradise. This strikes me as a touching demonstration of God's appreciation of and sensitivity to their shame feelings. It is reminiscent of the sensitivity needed from parents of prepubescent children who suddenly become modest about their bodies even—perhaps especially—in the presence of the very ones who years before had bathed, diapered, and dressed them.

Shame has not been a prominent topic in theological discourse. However, Bonhoeffer's *Ethics* contains a brief discussion of shame that, like this book, links it to the Adam and Eve story and sees shame as an experience of "disunion" from God.

> "Their eyes were opened" (Gen. 3:7). Man perceives himself in his disunion with God and with men. He perceives that he is naked. . . laid bare. Hence there arises shame. *Shame is man's ineffaceable recollection of his estrangement from the origin; it is grief for the estrangement, and the powerless longing to return to unity with the origin. . . . [M]an is ashamed of the loss of his unity with God and with other men.* Shame and remorse are generally mistaken for one another. Man feels remorse when he has been at fault, and he feels shame when he lacks something. Shame is more original than remorse. (emphasis added)[37]

However, Bonhoeffer goes on to observe, covering—in the Genesis story represented by the covering of the genitals—"keeps awake shame, and with it the memory of the disunion with the origin, and also because man, disunited as he is, must now withdraw himself and must live in concealment."[38] For Bonhoeffer, "covering" may or may not be literal. We feel shamed when we perceive what we lack. Adam and Eve felt original shame when they recognized that they lacked unity with God, and they covered their physical nakedness. Another kind of covering occurs when we lower our eyes when a stranger's eye meets our gaze, not because of remorse or guilt but because we are mindful of something we lack—"namely, the lost wholeness of life. . . ."[39] Simply put, "shame seeks a covering as a means of overcoming the disunion."[40] All too often, we use as coverings the defenses to shame discussed in Chapter 5.

This theme of tension between separation and union, between pulling apart and drawing close, between wanting to be part of the collective and wanting to be one's own most authentic and creative individual person is central in religious experience and, I believe, central to the meaning and paradoxes of shame. It is in our confrontation and negotiation of shame that this tension is favorably resolved. We need to come to terms with the fact that even when and if we find a sense of unity with God, this does not mean that we have found identity with God. Until we accept this reality, we continue to flail and flap around like fish out of water—out of our reality, trying to breathe an element that is not meant for us. In honest relating to our particular shame issues, we can achieve our most creative and authentic selves and, and the same time, experience ourselves in union with God, even coming to some measure of peace with the demands of our societies and able to make meaningful decisions about when to "go along to get along" and when to stand up and stand out, when to be part of the herd and when to risk expressing our individuality. In addition, honest relating to our own shame issues is a prerequisite for giving and receiving deep love, especially sexual love, fraught as it is with intimacy, exposure of body and soul, and risk of loss and rejection.

Shame *is* paradoxical: there are two distinct aspects to it. One aspect serves social adaptation and ensures membership in human society through conformity. We do not want to be the objects of scorn and ridicule. To give one example that may be crude but has the advantage of clarity, this is why we do not defecate in the street. This is also why we do not go out in public naked. The advent of human shame caused Adam and Eve to cover themselves. Every child born into human society needs to be taught the basic rules that will enable her or him to be a more or less accepted member of that society. Indeed, studies have demonstrated that the shame affect is evolutionarily adaptive in that it "serves the important function of appeasing observers of social transgressions, a function which reestablishes social harmony following the rule violations that inevitably disrupt social interaction."[41]

The other seemingly opposed attribute of shame is the aspect which ensures that the collective does not violate the individual's boundaries and personal integrity.[42] This is the aspect of shame that is revelatory of personal identity as discussed by Helen Lynd. In a similar vein, Alfred Adler saw shame as having both a "connecting effect" and a "separating effect," and he viewed it as having "great importance for human society: 'Shame is a product of the feeling of relatedness and as such impossible to exclude from the life of the human soul. Human society would be impossible without this affect.'"[43]

As noted by Gershen Kaufman, the need to *identify,* the wish to be like the parent and others in one's culture, is the motive that enables the transmission of culture. The need for identification continues throughout life and presses for expression, whether this be in relation to specific persons such as parents or mentors, or in relation to groups. A sense of kindred spirit, of common purpose, brings together those of us who identify with one another through whatever seems to unite us: religion, a cause, a hobby, a way of life.[44]

However, while identification gives us the important feeling that we belong, differentiation embraces no less a striving for separation and mastery. This is the instrument through which individuation occurs:

> Every individual needs to differentiate his or her own unique self, to discard those attitudes and practices acquired from others which do not suit or have served their purpose and are no longer wanted, and to develop those qualities which are most congruent with the real self inside. To differentiate is to say, "This is me—I am different."[45]

As Helen Lewis notes, "Implicit in the concept of the self is the idea of the boundaries of the self. By boundaries of the self is meant . . . the function of maintaining the separateness of the self."[46] Shame is a primary guardian of those boundaries, which, however, vary in permeability with different occasions. For example, when one is in love, physical and emotional boundaries may sometimes seem nonexistent; one feels quite permeable—even "merged" with the beloved. This is why a rupture or betrayal in a love relationship is often agonizing.

Carl Schneider's work is pertinent here. Schneider distinguishes between "discretion shame" and "disgrace shame."[47] Discretion shame is in essence modesty. It is about protective covering, boundaries, and the realm of privacy. It is about protection of our vulnerability and of our private thoughts, feelings, and activities. It is about having discretion about what we are going to share and with whom. Discretion shame "sustains the personal and social ordering of the world."[48] Boundaries are what give shape to the self and make the self complete and of a piece. In helping to set limits and boundaries, shame gives us a sense of who and what we are as well as who and what we are not.

Disgrace shame is, on the other hand, "a painful experience of the disintegration of one's world. A break occurs in the self's relationship with itself and others."[49] This very disorienting, painful self-consciousness is what gives disgrace shame its revelatory potential.

Apropos of this point, Jacoby describes a tribe in New Guinea that distinguishes between "skin shame" and "deep shame." To be found urinating or having sex in public generates skin shame but to insult the spirits of the ancestors provokes deep shame. "In the first case, shame is an emotional response to the violation of social norms"— the norms that hold society together, and each of us as acceptable members of it. "The second form of shame comes into play with the violation of an inner value system associated with the ego ideal."[50] The other powerful example that Jacoby gives of an apparent experience of deep shame is Peter's feelings when the cock crowed and he had denied Jesus three times. Peter remembered the words of Jesus and wept bitterly for his cowardice and betrayal. He was ashamed.[51]

Since Helen Lynd's groundbreaking work was published in 1958, some of the many authors that have delved into the issues of shame have suggested it is always and everywhere a bad thing. For example, Vicki Underland-Rosow takes issue with the idea that shame is, under any circumstances, good or adaptive, much less (as contended by John Bradshaw) a psychological foundation of any kind of spirituality. To the contrary, she states:

> Shame is antithetical to spirituality. Much institutional religion in our culture separates humans from themselves (their feelings, desires and thoughts), from each other, the universe and a Higher Power. Spirituality brings things together. Spirituality involves connections. Spirituality is often experienced as profound oneness with the universe. Shame involves separation, alienation. Spirituality has no need for disconnection: Most western religion demands separation and shame.[52]

This analysis assumes it is in the nature of things that human beings should experience a perpetual state of unity and connection with the source of being and with one another. It also assumes that authen-

tic spirituality does not include experience of brokenness, disloca-
tion, and fragmentation. If this were so, there would be no individuation, no creativity, no invention, no progress. In order to individuate
and come into their own as separate and authentic human beings,
people need to experience boundaries between themselves and God
and one another. Shame is one of those affects that enables this experience.

The advent of shame caused Adam and Eve to leave the paradisal
garden. Yes, this was the end of dreaming innocence. It was the end of
humankind's thoughtless unity with God and nature and an end too of
humankind's unthinking identification with God. However, it was
also the beginning of human creativity and invention. Eve ate of the
Tree of Knowledge. This was the beginning of shame. From this archetypal moment, human individuals began to experience boundaries. Leaving the garden set limits and gave shape, substance, and direction to human life. They went out of Eden and began to work, to
create, to invent—in short, to become individuals and to start the long
process of individuation, both as a species and as individual persons.
They lost their unthinking experience of unity with God and nature, but
they began the process of finding themselves as human creatures.
That unity which was lost is what individuals seek in a lifelong quest.
The negotiation of the suffering involved in grasping and seizing that
which was gained while still holding on to a piece of the unity that
was lost is the challenge of human existence.

This is a theme that recurs with remarkable persistence in the
shame literature, even in the writings of purely secular authors. Thus,
for example, Leon Wurmser sees shame as "the guardian of inner reality"; "shame guards the separate private self with its boundaries and
prevents intrusion and merger."[53] Shame has already been discussed
as an isolating phenomenon. This very quality means that shame creates boundaries, and sometimes desirable ones, between individuals.
Thus, notes Wurmser, the general phenomena of shame guards primary process thinking: "Would one not expect that we would need a
constantly vigilant guardian to protect the inner life from being overwhelmed by the spellbinding force of others?" Wurmser goes on:

> Specifically, I submit, then, that shame may be needed as a
> guard for the autonomy of the primary processes, the most inti-
> mate life we all have—our feelings, "the logic of the heart." On
> the other end of the developmental spectrum it means that

shame fences in that field of life that allows creativity to blossom and insight to arise. *In one sentence then: Shame protects privacy; it functions as a guardian against any outer power that might exploit the weakness in the essential realms of the self and interfere with one's own inner logic.* (emphasis added)[54]

Bonhoeffer arrives at much the same conclusion. While on one hand he contends that "the covering of shame conceals everything nascent that proceeds from man's yearning for the reattainment of the unity which he has lost," on the other hand he acknowledges that

> the secrecy of shame remains outspread over the creative power of man which comes to him in the self-sought union of the disunited. It is the memory of the disunion from the Creator, and the robbery from the Creator, which is here disclosed. This is true of the coming into being of human life, just as it is true of the coming into being of a work of art, or a scientific discovery, and indeed of any creative work which arises from the union of man with the world of things. Only when life is born, when the work is perfected, is the secret broken through by jubilant open joy. But the secret of its coming into being it bears within itself forever.
>
> The dialectic of concealment and exposure is only a sign of shame. Yet shame is not overcome by it; it is rather confirmed by it. Shame can be overcome only when the original unity is restored, . . . Shame is overcome only in the enduring of an act of final shaming, namely the becoming manifest of knowledge before God.[55]

In his book *Escape from Freedom,* Erich Fromm puts it this way:

> The social history of man started with his emerging from a state of oneness with the natural world to an awareness of himself as an entity separate from surrounding nature and men. Yet this awareness remained very dim over long periods of history. The individual continued to be tied to the natural and social world from which he emerged; while being partly aware of himself as a separate entity, he felt also part of the world around him. The growing process of emergence of the individual from his original ties, a process which we may call "individuation," seems to

have reached its peak in modern history in the centuries between the reformation and the present.[56]

Fromm draws direct parallels between the emergence of humankind's awareness of itself as separate and apart from surrounding nature and the person's individuation:

> In the life history of an individual we find the same process. A child is born when it is no longer one with its mother and becomes a biological entity separate from her. Yet, while this biological separation is the beginning of individual human existence, the child remains functionally one with the mother for a considerable period.
>
> To the degree to which an individual, figuratively speaking, has not yet completely severed the umbilical cord which fastens him to the outside world, he lacks freedom; but these ties give him security and a feeling of belonging and of being rooted somewhere. . . . They are organic in the sense that they are a part of normal human development; they imply a lack of individuality, but they also give security and orientation to the individual. They are the ties that connect the child with its mother, the member of a primitive community with his clan and nature, or the medieval man with the Church and his social caste.[57]

This honest negotiation of shame issues may, I believe, be the single most important psychic meaning of the life, death, and resurrection of Christ. In a conversation about this book with a respected and experienced clergy colleague, she suddenly exclaimed, "We in the Church are always talking about sin and guilt, but maybe Christianity is really about redemption from and in shame!" That day I felt I had made my first convert to an understanding of the centrality of shame in the psychic power of Christianity.

THE COMPETING URGES TOWARD UNION AND INDIVIDUATION

Contemporary scholarship has only recently begun to plumb the rich depths of shame, and to see the centrality of shame in Christian theology and practice. Clearly, this awareness has been sparked and cross-fertilized by the work of depth psychology and particularly by Heinz Kohut. For example, in his book *The Depleted Self,* Donald Capps uses Kohut's work and that of some of his interpreters to build and articulate the premise that "Christian theology has well-developed theologies of guilt, while the majority of its constituency is struggling with debilitating, demoralizing and even dehumanizing effects of shame."[58]

Stephen Pattison, a theologian and priest of the Church of England, has recently published a thorough and formidable indictment of Christianity's role in promoting and capitalizing on shame while failing to recognize shame's pathological and debilitating elements and consequences. Pattison writes:

> The emphasis on guilt and the dangers of "selfishness" means that little attention . . . has been paid within the religious community to the depradations and prevalence of shame. Christians may even be encouraged to renounce the desire and need to be mirrored in such a way as to attain a proper sense of selfhood, thus denying the benevolence and necessity of divine mirroring which is suggested by, for example, the words of the Aaronic blessing.[59]

This book began with a synopsis of the shameful aspects of the life and death of Jesus of Nazareth which form a leitmotif, if a largely implicit one, of the gospel narratives. In the words of Isaiah (53:7-11):

> He was oppressed, and he was afflicted,
>   yet he did not open his mouth;
> like a lamb that is led to the slaughter,
>   and like a sheep that before its shearers is silent,
>   so he did not open his mouth. . . .
> He was cut off from the land of the living,
>   stricken for the transgression of my people. . . .
> Out of his anguish he shall see light;
>   he shall find satisfaction through his knowledge.

Yet in the very shadow of his shame and suffering Jesus spoke of his sense of union with God and his hope of bringing his followers along into this union. Thus, he said, "I am in the Father and the Father is in me" (John 14:10), and "The Father and I are one" (John 10:30).

Indeed, "out of his anguish" he "saw light," and he tried to show it to us. In the high priestly prayer of John 17:22-26 Jesus raises his eyes to heaven and prays that

> As you, Father, are in me and I am in you, may [my followers] also be in us. . . . The glory that you have given me I have given them, so that they may be one, as we are one, I in them and you in me, so that they may be completely one.

And in Galatians 2:20, this theme of union, of dissolution of boundaries between the religious person and divinity, is asserted by Paul when he states, "I have been crucified with Christ; and it is no longer I who live, but it is Christ who lives in me."

Literature pertaining to religious material is full of references to the experience of union with God as the ultimate mystical achievement. William James states:

> The overcoming of all usual boundaries between the individual and the Absolute is the great mystic achievement. In mystic states we both become one with the Absolute and we become aware of our oneness. This is the everlasting and triumphant mystical tradition, hardly altered by differences in clime or creed.[60]

Later in his book, James makes the same point slightly differently. He notes that a person who has had the experience of "something wrong" may sense that "along with the wrong part there is a better part of him, even though it may be but a most helpless germ." Such a person may then become conscious

> that this higher part is coterminous and continuous with a MORE of the same quality, which is operative in the universe outside of him, and which he can keep in working touch with, and in a fashion get on board of and save himself when all his lower being has gone to pieces in the wreck.[61]

While "allow[ing] for the divided self and the struggle," this union involves a "change of personal centre" and expresses "the appearance of exteriority of the helping power and yet account for our sense of union with it; and . . . fully justify our feelings of security and joy."[62]

In mystical experience, *"the conscious person is continuous with a wider self through which saving experiences come."*[63] Finally, one of the conclusions of James' great tome is his assertion that among the three most basic characteristics of the religious life is the belief that "union or harmonious relation with the higher universe is our true end."[64]

One of the numerous testimonials of religious experiences for which James' book is well known expresses the experience as follows:

> I remember the night, and almost the very spot on the hilltop, where my soul opened out, as it were, into the Infinite, and there was a rushing together of the two worlds, the inner and the outer. It was deep calling unto deep. . . . I did not seek him, but felt the perfect unison of my spirit with His. The ordinary sense of things around me faded.[65]

Erich Fromm holds that deep religious experience involves "an attitude of oneness not only in oneself, not only with one's fellow men but with all of life and beyond that with the universe."[66] Paradoxically, this does not ultimately lead to a weakening of the experience of the self and one's uniqueness:

> That this is not so constitutes the paradoxical nature of this attitude. It comprises both the sharp and even painful awareness of one's self as a separate and unique entity and the longing to break through the confines of this individual organization and be one with the All. The religious attitude in this sense is the fullest possible experience of individuality and at the same time of its opposite; it is not so much a blending of the two as a polarity from whose tension religious experience springs.[67]

As James notes, many of the great Christian mystics have given voice to the experience of mystical unity. Saint Teresa of Avila, for example, writes in the spiritual classic *The Interior Castle:*

> [D]uring the time that the union lasts the soul is left as though without its senses, for it has no power to think even if it wants to. . . . In sum, it is like one who in every respect has died to the world so as to live more completely in God. . . . Though there is

not so much room for poisonous things to enter, some tiny lizards do enter; since these lizards have slender heads, they can
poke their heads in anywhere. And even though they can do no
harm, especially if one pays no attention to them, . . . they are often a bother since they are little thoughts proceeding from the
imagination.[68]

And what are the "tiny lizard" thoughts to which Teresa refers, in-
truding on the union of the God? I think it likely that they are intima-
tions of shame, or self-doubt, of the Jamesian "something wrongness" interfering with a sense of union that is otherwise experienced
as perfect. Teresa's autobiography contains ample evidence of the
shame she felt before God during the many years between her initial
entry into a convent and her eventual entry into the innermost dwelling places of "the interior castle" that ultimately bring the soul into
union with God. Here is one description:

> Into so many and such grave occasions of sin did I fall, and so
> far was my soul led astray by all these vanities, that *I was
> ashamed* to return to God and to approach Him in the intimate
> friendship that comes from prayer. *This shame* was increased by
> the fact that as my sins grew in number, I began to lose the plea-
> sure and joy which I had been deriving from virtuous things. I saw
> very clearly, My Lord, that this was failing me because I was
> failing Thee. The devil, beneath the guise of humility, now led
> me into the greatest of all possible errors. Seeing that I was so
> utterly lost, I began to be afraid to pray. (emphasis added)[69]

We thus see that the spiritual union that Teresa ultimately achieved
with God was not preceded by glorious years of contentment and a
sense of progress; rather, it was marked at times by a sense of *dis*-
union so severe that she could not even bring herself to pray. Further,
we see that Teresa was afflicted and assailed from her youth by shame
and self-doubt. The spiritual grace that she ultimately achieved—a
grace that shines through her writing and particularly in *The Interior
Castle*—came from ruthless self-examination and relentless prayer.
Thus, she said:

> I do not remember that He has ever granted me any of the out-
> standing favors of which I shall speak later save when *I have*

been consumed by shame by realizing my own wickedness; and his Majesty has even managed to help me to know myself by revealing to me things which I myself could not have imagined. I believe that, when a soul does anything to further its own progress in this Prayer of Union, it may seem to be deriving some immediate benefit but will very quickly fall again, because it has not laid the proper foundations. (emphasis added)[70]

It seems fair to suppose that Teresa would agree with this sentiment recorded by one of James' testimonials:

The first underlying cause of all sickness, weakness or depression is *the human sense of separateness* from that Divine Energy which we call God. The soul which can feel and affirm in serene but jubilant confidence, as did the Nazarene, "I and the Father are one," has no further need of a healer, or of healing. This is the whole truth in a nutshell, and other foundations for wholeness can no man lay than this fact of impregnable divine union.[71]

SOME OF DEPTH PSYCHOLOGY'S ACCOUNTS OF EXPERIENCES OF UNION

Depth psychologists from the time of Freud himself have struggled with questions relating to the experience of, or desire for, union with a larger whole. Occasionally, as in the case of Freud, this struggle has been undertaken in explicit or implicit conversation with religious persons.

This book has moved from a general description of the phenomenon of shame through psychological accounts for it, to theological and spiritual meanings and implications. Not the least of the spiritual implications of shame that have been discussed is its tendency to isolate the individual, removing her or him from the fullness of relationship with culture, with friends and lovers, and with God.

I have discussed in general terms the tension that exists between longing for union with others, with society, with God, and the longing for individuation and the living out of one's own "true" and creative self. I have maintained that pervasive shame stands on the boundary between union and individuation: that shame must be honestly dealt with and negotiated before there can be any satisfactory resolution of this tension. I have also suggested that the Christ event is an archetypal constellation around an individual who did just this and that Jesus' confrontation with shame contains the seeds of the psychic power of the Christ event.

Shame is an important way that God reaches out to us and touches us. We are frustrated, even overcome at times, by our physical, finite nature and by failings and inadequacies specific to us as individuals. It is in just these experiences that we meet God. It is just there—the godless vortex—that God is most often revealed to us, and that we feel most *known* and *seen* by God. It is in this place that we begin to get the sense of having a place in the heart of God. The experience of shame is transformative if and to the extent that we can avoid resorting to the various defenses which seek to deny our experience of shame. If we can stay in the godless vortex, we give grace the opportunity to enter.

Pastoral care can be helpful at this point. Pastors can convey a sense that it is all right to be in the godless vortex—a sense that this place may be a portal to deeper relationship with God and a fuller and more authentic sense of self. The task of the pastoral caregiver is thus to stand firm, to exhort courage, and to avoid the ever-present temptation to try to jolly people along with a simplistic "Things-are-not-so-bad-smile-Jesus-loves-you" approach. This approach is not helpful because it puts an end to honest relationship between the pastoral caregiver and the parishioner. Sometimes, pastoral caregivers will do this because they do not know what else to do. More often, however, pastoral caregivers resort to this because they do not really want to enter into the other's suffering. It is a cop-out.

And yet, having said all of this, pastors do need to be sensitive to different people's limitations in order to decide how hard to push people to try to stay in the godless vortex. This may be one of the greatest challenges of pastoral care. The godless vortex is a liminal place— a dangerous place. It would be a lie to suggest that every person can tolerate being there at any given time. It is possible for one to sink into mental illness from this place. It can be a place of grace, but it can also become a place of demons. Sometimes people need to think about medication or about pursuing activities—almost any activities—that will take them out of the shame vortex.

No human being can avoid resorting to the shame defenses all of the time: the suffering would be too great and often too incapacitating. Even the best of us will necessarily sometimes fall back on one or more of the shame defenses if only to get on with some of the everyday business and necessities of life. The best of us will succeed to a greater extent than will others in transforming shame, thus achieving both a sense of most creative individuality and unity with God. This is the achievement of the great religious geniuses such as Jesus, Buddha, and perhaps some few others. This was Jesus' struggle when, after his baptism, he was driven into the wilderness to do battle with Satan for forty days. He was tempted to seize power, to do that which would have enabled him to become a worldly ruler. He resisted the power defense. This was the parallel struggle of Siddhartha Gotama when, as Buddhist legend tells us, immediately before he attained enlightenment he did spiritual battle with Mara who urged him to pursue worldly power.[72]

Now, having discussed however briefly the existence of a human capacity for the experience of union with God, an experience that has been acknowledged and referred to by mystics (Christian and otherwise) throughout the ages, we are at a juncture where it is desirable to summarize some of the perspectives that depth psychologists have had regarding the sense of union.

Thus, in accordance with the methodology that has been articulated in Chapter 6, I will now set forth some of the parallel work that has been undertaken by depth psychologists in understanding feelings of and desire for union—with God and/or with creation and/or with others. This becomes highly relevant in moving toward an understanding of shame and both its spiritual and psychological dimensions and consequences.

THE "OCEANIC FEELING"

In 1927 Sigmund Freud published "The Future of an Illusion,"[73] which is his central work outlining his views on the emergence and role of religious ideations. Religious belief, said Freud, is but an illusion. Illusions are always suspect because they are "derived from human wishes," meaning that there is a motivation to believe something.[74] Freud offered that religion satisfies three basic desires of human beings. First, it helps us to come to terms with painful and destructive external forces of nature. Second, it helps us deal with the demands of instinct by setting forth moral prescriptions and rules.

Third, it satisfies what Freud saw as humankind's universal and absolutely paramount longing and need for a protecting father.[75]

Romain Rolland, winner of the 1929 Nobel Prize in literature and student of Oriental mysticism, sent a letter to Freud dated December 5, 1927, containing a respectful caveat to Freud's assertion that all manner of religious experience was so reducible. The relevant portion of Rolland's letter to Freud follows:

> Your analysis of religion is a just one. But I would have liked to see you doing an analysis of *spontaneous religious sentiment* or, more exactly, of religious *feeling,* which is wholly different from *religions* in the strict sense of the word, and much more durable.
>
> What I mean is: totally independent of all dogma, all credo, all Church organization, all Sacred Books, all hope in a personal survival, etc., the simple direct fact of *the feeling of the "eternal"* (which can not very well be eternal, but simply without perceptible limits, and like oceanic, as it were).
>
> This sensation, admittedly, is of a subjective character. But it is common to thousands (millions) of men actually existing, with its (thousands) millions of individual nuances, it is possible to subject it to analysis, with an approximate exactitude.
>
> . . . I have often had occasion to observe its rich and beneficent power, be it among the religious souls of the West, Christian or non-Christians, or among those great minds of Asia who have become familiar to me and some of whom I count as friends.
>
> I myself am familiar with this sensation. All through my life, it has never failed me; and I have always found in it a source of vital renewal. In that sense, I can say that I am profoundly "religious"—without this constant state (like a sheet of water which I feel flushing under the bark) affecting in any way my critical faculties and my freedom to exercise them. . . .
>
> [T]he sentiment I experience is imposed on me as a fact. It is a *contact.* And as I have recognized it to be identical (with multiple nuances) in a large number of living souls, it has helped me to understand that that was the true subterranean source of *religious energy* which, subsequently, has been collected, canalized and *dried up by the Churches,* to the extent that one could say

that it is inside the Churches (whichever they may be) that true
"religious sentiment" is least available.[76]

This letter from Rolland—a man whom Freud clearly respected
and perhaps even idealized—could not be easily dismissed.[77] The
letter seems to have created consternation and a preoccupying mental
struggle for Freud that continued for some time. The outcome of this
is contained in his 1930 "Civilization and Its Discontents."[78] This
conversation between Rolland and Freud is of particular interest to
students in the interdisciplinary field of psychology and religion because it presents a stunning example of a very prominent and articulate thinker, a person with a mystical bent, in conversation with the
founding father of depth psychology—a zealous atheist—about the
meaning and etiology of particular religious experience. In this conversation, one can see the beginnings of a dialogue between religious
experience and psychological theory that continues to this day, with
this book being but one example.[79] Those of us working in this interdisciplinary field labor in the interstices of the two fields. Thus, instead of coming down on the side of either psychology or religion, we
attempt to "contextualize religious studies in relationship to the theory and practice of psychotherapy and pastoral counseling."[80]
  While denying that he had any personal experience with this "oceanic feeling," Freud did not deny the possibility of the existence of
such feelings in others. He is dismissive of these feelings, character-
izing them as "nothing but" remnants of the earliest human condition,
i.e., "an infant at the breast does not distinguish his ego from the external world as the source of sensations flowing in upon him . . ."
Only later, as the infant finds the need to scream for what he desires
(the breast) is there an object, "in the form of something which exists
outside and which is only forced to appear by a special action." Thus,
"the ego detaches itself from the external world," and the mature ego-
feeling is "therefore only a shrunken residue of a much more inclusive—indeed all-embracing—feeling which corresponded to a more
intimate bond between the ego and the world about it."[81]
  Thus, for Freud, the oceanic feeling is "nothing but" a residue of
the sense of limitlessness, of lack of boundaries of the newborn ego
and the universe. Significantly, Freud likens the oceanic feeling as
described by Rolland to the experience of being in love, when the
"boundary between ego and object threatens to melt away. Against all
the evidence to his senses, the man who is in love declares that 'I' and

'you' are one, and is prepared to behave as if it were a fact."[82] However, Freud disputes Romain Rolland's contention that the oceanic feeling is the source of religious feelings because, states Freud,

> a feeling can only be a source of energy if it is itself the expression of a strong need. The derivation of religious needs from the infant's helplessness and the longing for the father aroused by it seems to me incontrovertible, especially since the feeling is not simply prolonged from childhood days, but is permanently sustained by fear of the superior power of Fate. I cannot think of any need in childhood as strong as the need for a father's protection. *Thus the part played by the oceanic feeling, which might seek something like the restoration of limitlessness narcissism, is ousted from a place in the foreground. The origin of the religious attitude can be traced back in clear outlines as far as the feeling of infantile helplessness. . . . I can imagine the oceanic feeling became connected with religion later on.* (emphasis added)[83]

It is worth noting that in an earlier letter from Freud to Rolland, he had referred to Rolland as an "apostle of love for mankind."[84] In "Civilization and Its Discontents," Freud suggests that the "love command"—i.e., "Thou shalt love they neighbor as thyself"—"originates in the remote regions where the distinction between ego and objects themselves is neglected. In other words, to the same developmental stage which, when preserved alongside the more narrow adult ego, is subjectively apprehended as the oceanic feeling."[85] As Parsons notes,

> One can see how this makes sense, for the love-command simply puts into an ideal and reified form the ethical meaning inherent in an early developmental state in which the self is the other and the other the self. . . . Freud seems willing to reduce Rolland's love for humanity to a residue of an early phase of ego-feeling.[86]

Thus, we see that for Freud, at least three experiences—the oceanic feeling; the state of being in love; and the experience of loving one's fellow human beings "as oneself"—all arise out of archaic primary narcissism.

Freud's dismissal of an original sense of union with the mother as the origin of religious feeling in favor of the "longing for the father" and the "need for a father's protection" is facile. The relationship between the infant and the mother's body begins at the time of conception—long before any possible realization of the "need for a father's protection," even assuming that only a "father," i.e., a male figure, can or does protect the child from danger. It is thus difficult to see how a mind as brilliant as Freud's could so easily dismiss the oceanic feeling, which he himself saw as arising out of a time when the infant felt himself or herself as one with the mother and the cosmos, as being the origin of religious feeling.[87]

Rolland insisted that there was something beyond the pre-Oedipal, that the kind of awareness the mystics had achieved entailed the deepest layer of the unconscious, and at that deepest layer was Unity. "Unity was the most archaic dimension of the unconscious, the very foundation of one's Being and the source of the most Real."[88] Rolland had an experience of Unity in his youth in which he felt that "All that is mine. It is me."[89] He was filled with a sense that his essence could not be harmed. The *Isa Upanishad* says that

> Who sees all beings in his own self, and his own self in all beings, loses all fear. . . . When a sage sees this great unity and his self becomes all beings, what delusion and what sorrow can ever be near him?[90]

Parsons quotes this analogous experience of the character Pierre, who, awaiting execution in Tolstoy's *War and Peace,* suddenly burst out laughing:

> "They have captured and imprisoned me. . . . Me? My immortal soul?" . . .The full moon was at its zenith. The woods and the fields were outlined around him; and beyond those fields and woods flooded with night, the view stretched out far as eye could reach towards a boundless horizon. "All that is mine," he thought. "All that is in me; all that is me! And that is what they have captured; that is what they have shut up in prison!" He smiled, and went to lie down by his comrades.[91]

In any event, Freud's speculation that the oceanic feeling is a psychic return to a state prior to the differentiation of an "I" from the cosmos, and that the original bond is between a "not-yet-I and the mother world"[92] is very significant.

In his recent contribution to the scholarship of the Rolland-Freud relationship, Parsons demonstrates from Rolland's autobiography that his relationship with his mother was central to his spiritual development. Rolland associated her with love, the church, and boundless nature. His writings about his spirituality were full of references to communion with nature. Thus Parsons contends that from his youth to his death Rolland's spirituality was marked by an "unconscious bond with a maternal matrix." His spirituality, including his description of the oceanic feeling, "evokes an overwhelming maternal presence."[93] It has been frequently observed that Freud, on the other hand, had little interest and put correspondingly little importance in pre-Oedipal experience. Freud was notoriously patriarchal and allowed the pre-Oedipal mother slight influence in the child's future development.[94]

In fact, Rolland had been directly engaged in conversation on this subject with Ferdinand Morel, who, in his study titled "Essai sur L'Introversion Mystique," had held that "mystics, as a special case of introverts, were sexually maladjusted and weak willed and had difficulty adjusting to social reality."[95] Furthermore, "in playing out their repressed desires, mystics regressed to narcissistic and autoerotic stages of development. . . . Deep ecstatic experiences . . . were interpreted as a longing for the security and quietude of the intrauterine state."[96]

Rolland met Morel on his own terms, insisting that indeed, "Unity was the most archaic dimension of the unconscious, the very foundation of one's being and the source of the most Real."[97] Thus, rather than dismissing unitive experience as nothing but regression, Rolland saw the possible archaic origin of unitive experience as probative of its authenticity in the human psyche.

When we consider the development and maintenance of the human embryo and fetus, we find that the womb has within it a whole organization developed out of the individual ovum that has been fertilized and implanted in the lining of the uterus. The mother's endometrium is intermingled with the placenta.[98] We might see the infant as beginning literally as part of the mother, slowly emerging from the state of identity with the mother.

SOME CONTRIBUTIONS OF OTTO RANK

Freud's renegade disciple Otto Rank was the first to develop a psychology in which one's original union with the mother and the process of separation from her becomes a prototype for all of the physical and psychological events that make for a meaningful and creative life. Rank's work is psychological as well as philosophical. In *The Trauma of Birth* (1924),[99] which Rank evidently at the time of writing saw as a development in complete continuity with Freud's theories of instinctual biological determinism, he developed a creative and comprehensive understanding of the central trauma of human life: separation. Every tiny newborn human comes face to face with his or her first object, the mother, only to begin gradually to lose her. This primal catastrophe is a harbinger of all of the losses and separations that await, and indeed is at the root of all of life's suffering. Rank had developed this conceptual framework as a result of an observation from his clinical work: he had found the "rebirth-phantasy," often expressed by clients as "feeling reborn" in the course of his work with them, to be a consistent metaphor. Rank "noticed that people, theoretically and therapeutically entirely uninfluenced, showed from the beginning the same tendency to identify the analytic situation with the intrauterine state."[100] Indeed,

> the fixation on the mother, which seems to be at the bottom of the analytic fixation (transference), includes the earliest physiological relation to the mother's womb. This rendered the regularity of the rebirth-phantasy intelligible and its underlying reality analytically comprehensible. The patient's "rebirth-phantasy" is simply a repetition in the analysis of his own birth.[101]

As for the issue of whether preobject union with the mother was at the root of mystical experience, Rank was clearly on the side of Rolland (although I know of no reference to the Freud-Rolland exchange in Rank's writings). Thus, Rank speaks of "the blessedness of child and mother in union" as an echo of a lost identity with the cosmos, "the All, which once existed and is now lost." This cosmic identification

> has to be surrendered and reasserted throughout every phase of self-development. The longing to restore Oneness, a preobjectual union with a cosmos floating in mystic vapors in which past, present and future are dissolved, "the *unio mystica,* or being at one with the All," a spiritual union in which space is not a barrier and time and death have vanished, is the primary stimulus for love and art. Affirming difference but paradoxically also releasing from difference, the meeting of I and you, leads on each side, to a feeling of unity with the other, the cosmos, the All, and finally with one's own self.[102]

Rank also described the cosmic or existential dimension of identification in his *Art and Artist:*

> At the highest level of human personality we have a process which psychoanalysis calls . . . identification. This identification is the echo of an original identity, not merely of child and mother, but of everything living—witness the reverence of the primitive for animals. In man, identification aims at reestablishing a lost identity: not an identity which was lost once and for all, phylogenetically through the differentiation of the sexes, or ontologically in birth, but an identity with the cosmic process, which has to be continually surrendered and continually reestablished in the course of self-development.[103]

Robert Kramer, who edited and compiled Otto Rank's American lectures, summarized the human situation as follows:

> Even with the kindest mothers and the least violent births, the human being is born afraid, a shivering bundle of *Angst* cast adrift in an uncaring world, a small island of pain floating on a vast ocean of indifference. At the moment of birth, feeling neglected and misunderstood, the *infans* [Latin: "not speaking"] is expelled weeping from the paradisal womb, like Adam, leaving behind it an ineffable past. The dividing line between the I, *das Ich,* and the universe is *Angst,* which vanishes only when I and you have become one, as parts of a greater whole. With birth, the feeling of oneness with the whole, *das Ganze,* is lost.[104]

The unconscious never gives up this desire for unification, which the ego has set aside (with varying degrees of success) in favor of social adjustment. This shows up in thumb sucking, bed-wetting, and dirtying oneself. Prescient of the later and better known and acclaimed work of Donald Winnicott on transitional objects, Rank wrote the following in *The Trauma of Birth:*

> The substitution of a finger for the mother's own breast shows . . . the child's first attempt to replace the mother's body by its own . . . or a part of its own. This leads to . . . the final and sublimest substitution for the reunion with the mother, namely the sexual act.[105]

For the male, penetrating the vaginal opening signifies a partial return to the womb, with the penis identified as a child. Ultimately, most females give up their wish to reenter the mother and receive satisfaction from their own ability to be the vessel of new life and to give birth.

For Rank, the conflict and tension between a desire to return to the whole, *das Ganze,* and the healthy human impulse to separate himself or herself from the collective by living creatively in art, music, invention, etc., is lifelong. We experience trauma at every liminal point along life's journey: birth, weaning, toilet training, our first steps, our first day of school, leaving home, marriage, loss of loved ones through illness and death, forced separation or rejection, and, ultimately, our own deaths and the illnesses and physical limitations that presage it.

According to Rank, the neurotic person refuses to embrace life because he or she is afraid of separation. He or she turns into a pillar of salt—like Lot's wife—frozen in time, looking back, afraid to move forward. The individual thinks he or she can cheat death by refusing life. Thus, Rank understood life as a loan with death the repayment. The neurotic cannot willingly accept the loan with its limits. "He refuses the loan (life) in order thus to escape the payment of debt (death)."[106] "At repayment time, the neurotic hopes—pathetically—to flout the limit. 'I haven't begun yet. I should not have to die—I have not really lived.'"[107]

Rank implicitly recognizes the fundamental existential dilemma of human existence that is so central to the ontological shame phenomenon: the finiteness of human life, the creaturely dimension of human life, the fact that we are out of nature yet conscious of our finiteness and long for the experience of unity with the whole even as we dread it. This latter experience too is part of our human birthright. We are reminded again of two of Kohut's "transformations of narcissism"—cosmic narcissism and wisdom. Both require a decathexis of self; wisdom in particular requires acceptance of one's limitations as a physical being, and particularly the inevitability of death.[108]

The fundamental tension in human life according to Rank is the fear of life, which is actually the fear of having to live as an isolated individual and the fear of loss or nondevelopment of individuality (death fear). Thus, there is a fear of separation from the whole and paradoxically a fear of the loss of whatever dearly bought individuality one has achieved, which is dissolution again into the whole. "Between these two fear possibilities . . . the individual is thrown back and forth all his life, which accounts for the fact that we have not been able to trace fear back to a single root, or to overcome it therapeutically."[109]

Even as one fears life, one is impelled toward life by the phenomenon that Rank calls "will." Will is a "positive guiding organization and integration of self which utilizes creatively, as well as inhibits and controls the instinctual drives."[110] It is the "vehicle for individual differentiation, the separation of the self from 'the other' or from the mass."[111]

The exercise of will, which is a good and healthy thing, necessarily involves guilt as well as fear. Guilt, notes Kramer,

> occupies a special position among the emotions, as a boundary phenomenon between the pronounced painful affects which separate and the more pleasurable feelings which unite. . . . [In lovers,] guilt feeling disturbs the harmony, and separates the lovers. Yet . . . we also see its uniting, binding power. It compels one to devote oneself to the object, to surrender. For many, especially neurotics, guilt feeling is the only way of expressing feelings at all.[112]

Rank's work provides important jumping-off points for thinking about how shame—as distinguished from guilt—mediates, facilitates, and interferes with the development of personality and the concomitant longing for union. I believe that shame, rather than guilt, is the significant "boundary phenomenon," and I cannot help but wonder whether Rank might not have agreed that the idea of shame is

nuanced way of talking about the boundary phenomenon that
...rwise articulates so convincingly. Shame is earlier than guilt.
It is ontological, an innate affect. It is based in the body, as well as being self-referential and existential. Guilt is a later development and is
much more easily expiated.

Shame provides a "way in" for God. It provides the boundaries that
reveal and shape the identity, even as it creates an opening for God to
enter through. It makes us painfully aware of our limitations, even as
it causes us to long for union with the source of being. It gives rise to a
liminal space, a godless space, the vacuum that is at the core of religious experience.

CONTRIBUTIONS OF LATER THEORISTS ON THE SUBJECT OF SEPARATION-INDIVIDUATION

The theme of separation from the maternal matrix and individuation is one that has been developed by many other depth psychologists, with or without reference to Rank's work. It has often struck me
as a common thread that meanders into and out of much depth psychology.
Michael Balint wrote that

> [t]he ultimate aim of libidinal striving is . . . the preservation or
> restoration of the original harmony. . . . This *unio mystica,* the
> reestablishment of the harmonious interpenetrating mix-up, be-
> tween the individual and the most important parts of the envi-
> ronment, his love objects, is the desire of all humanity.[113]

Researcher on infancy and theorist of separation-individuation
Margaret Mahler puts it this way:

> For the more or less normal adult, the experience of being
> both fully "in" and at the same time basically separate from the
> "world out there" is among the givens of life that are taken for
> granted. Consciousness of self and absorption without aware-
> ness of self are the two polarities between which we move, with
> varying ease and with varying degrees of alternation or simulta-
> neity. . . . *As is the case with any intrapsychic process, this one
> reverberates throughout the life cycle.* . . . Here, in the rap-

prochement subphase, we feel is the mainspring of man's eternal struggle against both fusion and isolation.

One could regard the entire life cycle as constituting a more or less successful process of distancing from and introjection of the lost symbiotic mother, an eternal longing for the actual or fantasied "ideal state of self," with the latter standing for a symbiotic fusion with the "all good" symbiotic mother, who was at one time part of the self in a blissful state of well-being.[114]

Likewise, in an early paper Hans Loewald wrote that "The deepest root of the ambivalence that appears to pervade all relationships, external as well as internal, seems to be the polarity inherent in individual existence of individuation and 'primary narcissistic' union."[115]

Donald Winnicott, whose work has already been alluded to, understood a whole person as one who has achieved "unit status," i.e., one who is able to distinguish between "Me" and "Not Me," inside and outside. The development begins with motility—the exercise of simple infantile movement inside and outside the womb, the kicking and twistings about that occasionally make pregnant women flinch. In these movements, the infant comes up against something that is not himself or herself.[116] Ultimately, however, achievement of unit status depends primarily on the infant's preconcern ruthlessness "relating to" the primal object—i.e., the breast. The newborn infant must be allowed the illusion that the breast is part of its own omnipotent self, present whenever desire for the breast is felt. Eventually, the infant begins to feel "concern" about its ruthless "destruction" of the object.

The "boundary phenomenon" of guilt that Rank describes as pertaining to an individual's assertion of his or her own individuality is conceptually similar to the "concern" that the infant begins to feel about the destruction of the object he or she once experienced as part of his or her own self. For reasons already stated, I would substitute the word *shame* for Rank's *guilt*. Shame is a more basic and ontological human affect than guilt. Guilt is subsumed under the rubric of shame and is less visceral and less self-referential than is shame. A good argument can likewise be made that the Winnicottian concept of "concern" might also be subsumed under the rubric of shame, since concern per se is likewise not an innate affect. At the risk of being presumptuous, I suspect that Winnicott in using the word *concern* as Rank uses the word *guilt,* is in fact getting at the burgeoning phenomenon of shame, broadly understood. The point is that this feeling of concern/guilt/shame is very much a part of the process by which the infant begins to distinguish between "Me" and "Not-Me"—i.e., between himself or herself and the breast and, for that matter, the cosmos. This feeling of concern has its roots in the infant's being permitted a time when it can exercise a ruthless *lack* of concern—one might call it untrammeled exercise of "will." Furthermore, notes Winnicott, in order to live abundantly and creatively one must live one's True Self, which requires creative living and separation from the collective. This goal is functionally identical with Rank's goal of self-realization and individuation through the emergence of or acting on will. The achievement of this goal allows us to have a sense of who we are, what we are, and who and what we are not.

Melanie Klein held that the infant's "mental and physical closeness to the gratifying breast in some measure restores, if things go well, the lost prenatal unity with the mother and the feeling of security that goes with it."[117]

Many, in addition of course to Rank himself, have understood this desire to restore the "lost prenatal unity" as the basis for erotic love and longing. Recall Freud's likening of the oceanic feeling to the feeling of being in love, when the "boundary between ego and object threatens to melt away."[118] Likewise, in his piece "Inhibitions, Symptoms and Anxiety" Freud wrote that love "desires contact because it strives to make the I and the love object one, to abolish all spatial barriers between them."[119]

One could say that the mother-infant bond, and later the bond between lovers, is an embodied, incarnational substitute for the *unio mystica.* The embodied experience may be seen as an entrance to—a concretization of—the *unio mystica.*

Karen Horney likewise wrote that, for a person with a "self-effacing" approach to life, longing for deep erotic love means

> to lose, to submerge himself in more or less ecstatic flings, to merge with another human being, to become one heart and one flesh, and in this merger to find a unity which he cannot find in himself. His longing for love thus is fed by deep and powerful sources: the longing for surrender and the longing for unity. And we cannot understand the depth of his emotional involvement without considering these sources. *The search for unity is one of the strongest motivating forces in human beings and is even more important to the neurotic, with his inner division. The*

longing to surrender to something bigger than we are seems to be the essential element of most forms of religion. And although the self-effacing surrender is a caricature of the healthy yearning, it nevertheless has the same power. . . . It is one factor in his propensity to lose himself in all kinds of feelings: in a "sea of tears"; in ecstatic feelings about nature; in wallowing in guilt-feelings; in his yearning for oblivion in orgasm or in fading out in sleep; and often in his longing for death as the ultimate extinction of self. (emphasis added)[120]

Heinz Kohut's discussion of what he called "cosmic narcissism" is another related phenomenon. In fact, Parsons contends that Romain Rolland's mature mysticism is akin to the transformative aspects of Kohut's metapsychology. Like Freud, Kohut seems to have interpreted the oceanic feeling as a transient return to the stage of primary narcissism. Still, Kohut spoke of " 'cosmic narcissism' as the religio-ethical goal of his psychology. Cosmic narcissism is seen as a developmentally mature attainment indicative of ethical and existential achievement."[121] Although Kohut "agreed that the mother-child relation genetically predetermined cosmic narcissism," he nevertheless

insisted that the latter was much more than the preservation of the pre-Oedipal feeling of unity. It signified that denouement of an existential process that consisted in a gradual decathexis of the individual self to participation in "supraindividual ideals and the world with which one identifies."[122]

In this state, one lives "without elation or anxiety, bathed in a continual communion with a contentless and supraordinate self." Moreover (and despite Freudian suggestions to the contrary),

[t]his process of self cannot be branded as defensive. On the contrary it demands not only engagement with and the transformation of archaic narcissistic structures into empathy, humor, wisdom, and creativity but also the acknowledgment and successful navigation of life's inevitable vicissitudes and disappointments—particularly the seemingly insurmountable fact of transiency.[123]

Thus, human beings live in the constant tension of the fear of/desire for differentiation through separation and individuation and the fear of/desire to merge through union. The individual fears and desires both the becoming of the self and the dissolution of that same self in union with the whole. Recall that for Kohut the experience of shame is one pronounced consequence of pathological narcissistic rage. "Cosmic narcissism" and "wisdom" thus represent the opposite of pathological narcissism, the latter being identified by the shame-bound personality.

Ernest Becker says that "nature has arranged that it is impossible for man to feel 'right' in any straightforward way" because of "twin ontological motives" that are always in tension: there is the desire to merge with the rest of nature and the cosmic process, existing along-side the desire to stand out and be unique which Becker refers to as the narcissistic quest for cosmic "heroism":

> The problem of heroics is the central one of human life, . . . [I]t goes deeper into human nature than anything else because it is based on organismic narcissism and on the child's need for self-esteem as *the* condition for human life.[124]

The failure to find a way to live with this tension, to live creatively yet be able to join with others in erotic and/or agapic love, to feel oneself part of a large whole, is the heart of neurosis.

When the central tension of human life is seen as that between in-dividuality and relatedness, the dynamic of Freud's much vaunted Oedipal crisis emerges in a new light. Freud was onto something very important: the Oedipus complex is real, but at its core is not the child's desire to have sex with the mother or the father. It is about the emerg-ing independent self versus compliance with and dependence upon one's parents. In John McDargh's words, the real issue is as follows:

> First, what does it mean that compared with the entirety of other animate life we humans are born . . . without the guidance of those instincts which enable lower forms of life to separate from their mothers in a matter of hours or days? Secondly, what does it mean for human development that this long dependent child is born into the matrix of power relationships to which in his or her helplessness and need he or she must begin to adapt? This I take to be the enduring meaning of the "oedipus complex" in its

broadest sense, that the growing child is possessed of yearning and desires and a sheer energy for activity which confronts the invincible authority and physical supremacy of those more powerful persons, on whom the child is dependent not only for the physical necessities of life but more importantly, for the love and the recognition that is life itself for the human child.[125]

Taking his cue from Rank, Ernest Becker saw the "Oedipus project" in a similar way. It is a "flight from passivity, from obliteration, from contingency: the child wants to conquer death by becoming the *father of himself,* the creator and sustainer of his own life."[126] Erich Fromm sees the Oedipal conflict not most essentially as the sexual craving for the mother or the father:

> This craving is only one expression of the much more profound and fundamental desire to remain a child attached to those protecting figures of whom the mother is the earliest and most influential. The foetus lives with and from the mother, and the act of birth is only one step in the direction of freedom and independence. The infant after birth is still in many ways part and parcel of the mother, and its birth as an independent person is a process which takes many years—which, in fact, takes a whole life. To cut through the naval string, not only in the physical but in the psychological sense, is the great challenge to human development and also its most difficult task.[127]

Jung plays a related chord. The mother and the maternal uterus represent the unconscious. Individuation is the process by which the consciousness of a person becomes differentiated from others. Jung wrote, "I use the term 'individuation' to denote the process by which a person becomes a psychological 'in-dividual,' that is, a separate, indivisible unit or 'whole.'"[128] This is a painful process that involves expanding consciousness:

> The development of the personality is at once a blessing and a curse. We must pay dearly for it and the price is isolation and loneliness. "Its first fruit is the conscious and unavoidable segregation of the single individual from the unconscious herd." But to stand alone is not enough, above all one must be faithful to one's own law: "Only the man who can consciously assent to

the power of the inner voice becomes a personality." And only a personality can find a proper place in the collectivity; only personalities have the power to create a community, that is, to become integral parts of a human group and not merely a number in a mass. For the mass is only a sum of individuals and can never, like a community, become a living organism that receives and bestows life. Thus self-realization, both in the individual and in the extrapersonal, collective sense, becomes a moral decision which lends force to the process of self-fulfillment that Jung calls "individuation."[129]

One of the great symbols of Jungian transformation is the hero archetype. Archetypes are symbolic motifs that at the deepest unconscious level are common to all persons; they are charged with powerful psychic energy. For Jung, the universal essence of the hero archetype is the journey to the unconscious and confrontation with one's demons. The unconscious is often symbolized by the mother or a symbol for the maternal. The journey to the unconscious results in the heroic adventure in individuation. Often this involves literal death and rebirth, which results in transformation.

Jung derived a deeper meaning from the incest taboo than did Freud. While Freud contended that sexual drive was the simple root of the boy's longing for his mother, Jung saw incestuous desire as a longing for "reversion to the original passive state where the libido is invested in the objects of childhood."[130] Reviewing a series of myths worldwide, Jung argues that there is an archetypal longing to "attain rebirth through a return to the womb, and to become immortal."[131] He wrote that "the basis of 'incestuous' desire is . . . the idea of becoming a child again, and returning to the parental shelter, and entering into the mother in order to be reborn through her."[132] Yet as Jung points out,

> As long as the child is in that state of unconscious identity with the mother he is still one with the animal psyche and is as unconscious as it. The development of consciousness inevitably leads not only to separation from the mother, but to separation from the parents and the whole family circle and thus to a relative detachment from the unconscious and the whole world of instinct. Yet the longing for this lost world continues and, when

difficult adaptations are demanded, is forever tempting one to make evasions and retreats, to regress . . .[133]

Here too, then, we have echoes of the shame vortex, i.e., the tension between the desire to regress and the pull to move forward, to individuate. Jung's description of the experience of withdrawal of libido from the mother may be seen as a description of the experience of the shame vortex—the place of tension between our creatureliness and finiteness and our consciousness and spirit:

> The relation to the mother must cease, *must die,* and this is the same as dying oneself. That is to say, the violence of the separation is proportionate to the strength of the bond, . . . and the stronger this broken bond was in the first place, the more dangerously does the "mother" approach him in the guise of the unconscious. This is indeed the . . . "savage mother of desire," who in another form now threatens to devour the erstwhile fugitive.[134]

Here we begin to come as close as depth psychology will take us to theology and spirituality. Christ himself is a paradigmatic example of the hero—a symbol around whom transformation can take place. In one of his discussions of the hero archetype, Jung has this to say about the heroic Christ figure:

> The struggle of Christ's soul in Gethsemane, where he wrestles with himself in order to complete his work; then the "transitus," the carrying of the cross, when he takes on his shoulders the symbol of the deadly mother and in so doing carries himself to the grave, from which he will rise again after three days—all these images express the same fundamental thought: that Christ is a divinity who is eaten in the Lord's supper. His death transforms him into bread and wine, which we relish as mystical food.[135]

The mother is the first embodiment of the possibility of union. Incarnational union is later achieved in sexual love. Both, however, are representations of—one might say earthly substitutes for—the union we are hardwired to seek with God, who is the source and ground of our being.

SHAME AND BIBLICAL WITNESS

How important a concept is shame in scripture? This question is important because, as Wayne Rollins points out, the Bible may be seen "as a part and product, not only of a historical, literary and socio-anthropological process, but also of a psychological process."[136] This means that

> conscious and unconscious processes are at work in the biblical authors and their communities, in the texts they have produced, in readers and interpreters of these texts and in their communities, and in the individual, communal and cultural effects of those interpretations.[137]

Psychological biblical criticism examines texts and their interpretation "as expressions of the nature, structure, processes, and habits of the human psyche/soul, both in individual and collective manifestations, past and present."[138] With these premises in mind, let us then look at the biblical use of the word *shame.*

The word *shame* and its direct derivatives (i.e., *ashamed, shameful, shamed,* and *shameless*) appears some 218 times in the New Revised Standard Version of the Old and New Testaments. In the Old Testament, uses of the word *shame* seem to be roughly grouped into the following categories: shame experienced in connection with exposure of bodily nakedness (see, e.g., Isaiah 47:3); shame experienced in connection with failure of various sorts (e.g., Jeremiah 20:11); shame experienced in connection with defeat in war (e.g., Jeremiah 50:2); shame as the consequence of sin (e.g., Daniel 9:8); shame as an emotion attendant upon outcast status (e.g., Zephaniah 3:19).

We thus see that the scriptural uses of "shame" are in close accord with the phenomenology of shame already discussed at length in this book.[139] In sum and substance, shame is about *exposure*—e.g., of the body, which is proof positive of our creatureliness. It is also about failure and defeat. Finally, it is about being isolated and outcast, and it is often fused with guilt for perceived wrongdoing.

The word *guilt* as used in scripture is almost exclusively associated with wrongdoing, such as breaking the law and the Commandments. It appears approximately 135 times in the Old Testament, and not at all in the New Testament. The word *guilty* appears forty times in scripture but only four times in the New Testament. The emphasis shifts in the New Testament from guilt (in consequence of transgressions in keeping the law) to shame, an essential sense of unworthiness that is acknowledged, held, transformed, and expiated by God embodied in the man Jesus who suffered ultimate shame in his conception, life, and death.

The Old Testament contains 150 psalms—Hebrew poetry that articulates every conceivable affect. Within the 150 psalms, fifty—a full one-third—are psalms of lament. In a typical Christian church service, a psalm is read or chanted by the congregation. Many of those psalms pull no punches in the anguish of shame they express. It sometimes strikes me as ironic to sit in a congregation of well-educated, well-dressed, well-fed, and, although perhaps only on the surface, self-satisfied worshipers repeating such words as the following together: "All day long my disgrace is before me, and shame has covered my face . . ." (Psalm 44:15), and "You know the insults I receive, and my shame and dishonor; my foes are all known to you" (Psalm 69:19).

In the 150 psalms, the word *shame* or *ashamed* appears forty-four times, and I believe that the disproportionate number of appearances of the word is reflective of its centrality in religious feelings. Nine psalms plead for God never to let the psalmist "be put to shame." Eighteen psalms exhort God to put the psalmist's *enemies* to shame. The picture emerges from reading the psalms that shame is the worst experience of anguish and suffering one can have. Psalmists plead with God not to experience it, and they wish it on their worst enemies. The tone of this pleading does tend to corroborate Sandra Edelman's contention that deep shame experience is numinous in the horror and dread it evokes: "There they shall be in great terror, in terror such as has not been. For God will scatter the bones of the ungodly; *they will be put to shame, for God has rejected them*" (emphasis added; Psalm 53:5).

The psalms of lament often express our hurt and anger over our foolishness and ridiculousness, and/or anger over the ridicule and abuse we suffer at the hands of others. They help us to give voice to our feelings about our unlovability and sense of shame, abandonment, rejection, and isolation. "The wisdom of the psalms of lament is that deep feelings of frustration and agony cannot remain unexpressed without doing serious damage to the one who has them."[140]

THE NEW TESTAMENT'S USE OF SHAME

When we reach the New Testament, it seems to me that we can discern a subtle shift in the meaning, the significance, and the consequences of shame experiences. I have already outlined some of the shameful aspects of the life and death of Jesus of Nazareth: his irregular conception, his birth in a manger, his irregular itinerant lifestyle, his unmarried status, his shameful execution.

As for Jesus' earthly ministry, it is, of course, the stuff of timeless Sunday school lessons that Jesus was kind and compassionate to outcasts and sinners, and that we should strive to be like him.

It behooves us here, however, to look closely at the people to whom Jesus ministered. When we do, we see that most of them were individuals under clouds of shame[141]—shame that isolated them from and made them unacceptable in their communities. Here are some of the people whom Jesus healed, ministered to, and associated with:

- Zacchaeus, a tax collector despised by his people for his collaboration with the occupying Romans in exacting taxes from the Jews (Luke 19:1-9), and other "tax collectors and sinners" with whom Jesus ate and otherwise associated (Matthew 9:10-13);
- the woman with the menstrual hemorrhage who was ritually impure under Jewish law (Mark 5:25; Luke 8:43-48);
- the sinner woman—presumably a prostitute—who barged into the Pharisee Simon's dinner party and washed Jesus' feet with her tears and hair (Luke 7:36-50);
- various and sundry lepers, who were ritually impure and outcasts from the community[142] (e.g., Mark 1:40-44; Luke 17:11-19);
- women, such as the Samaritan woman at the well with whom Jesus engaged in conversation about matters of shame to her, and the Syrophoenician woman who pleaded with him on behalf of her daughter (Matthew 15: 21-28; John 4:7-30; Mark 7:24-30);
- the raving Gerasene demoniac (Mark 5:1-20);
- various other persons who were "possessed by demons" (Matthew 8:28-34; Matthew 17:14-20; Luke: 8:1-2; Luke 9:37-43; Luke 11:14; Mark 1:23-27; Mark 3:22);
- an adulteress who was about to be stoned to death (John 8:4);

- a blind man who was presumed to have sinned, or had parents who sinned, about whom Jesus announced that the blindness was not due to anyone's sins (John 9:1-3).

Jesus' teachings were, in general, antithetical to the rigid honor/shame system by which people of his time were judged and measured. Jesus told parables about love and acceptance of shamed and defiled individuals, such as the prodigal son whose behavior in demanding and then dissipating his inheritance in dissolute living before his father's death, sleeping with pigs, etc., would have been heard by his listeners as completely beyond the pale (Luke 15:11-32). Jesus told those who are insulted by being slapped on the right cheek to turn the other as well (Matthew 5:39). In a culture in which an assault to the face or head was viewed as a great humiliation, this was a radical directive. We also understand that Jesus was shamed during his trial when his face was struck (Mark 14:65; Luke 22:65; John 18:22) and his head was mockingly crowned with thorns.[143]

Jesus repeatedly exhorted people that "the greatest among you must become like the youngest, and the leader like one who serves" (e.g., Matthew 18:2-5; Luke 9:46-47; Luke 22:26-27), thereby exalting the humble at the expense of the prideful and the powerful. Even as he was believed to be, at the very least, a great teacher, he humbled himself by washing the feet of lesser men at the Last Supper and exhorting them to do likewise (John 13:1-8).

Jesus taught that the shamed and outcast tax collector who prostrated himself at the temple was exalted by God, but the prideful Pharisees who "trusted in themselves" and their righteousness and "regarded others with contempt" would be "humbled" (Luke 18:9-14).

As he himself hung on the cross half naked after being spat upon, whipped, ridiculed, and crowned with thorns, Jesus conversed lovingly with self-confessed criminals (Luke 23:39-44).

Jesus returned to his disciples after his crucifixion and death not in a glorified body but rather still bearing the wounds of his humiliating death. Indeed, it was these wounds in his hands and side that he displayed to Thomas in order to clearly identify himself as the Christ (John 20:24-28). As Pilch and Malina put it, "honor and shame as they touch Jesus are best evidenced in the passion account, and this in a culture where crucifixion was the most humiliating of all possible forms of death."[144] However, "God's raising Jesus from the dead demonstrates God's vindication of Jesus and the ascription of paramount honor to him. It equally underscores God's approval of Jesus' standards for what is honorable and what is shameful."[145]

Jesus turned shame on its head. We see it everywhere in the gospels. In an honor/shame culture in which a male's honor was *the* most fundamental core value,[146] Jesus did not shrink from being shamed. Jesus did not shame people—*except* perhaps for those who shamed others. He seemed particularly attracted to shamed outcasts and perhaps was not far from being one himself,[147] by reason of the irregular circumstances of his conception and birth, his life and ministry, and his crucifixion and death. John Dominic Crossan has in fact contended that the "healing miracles" of Jesus recounted in scripture were not intended to be read as literal interventions in the physical world but as healing of a sense of rejection and isolation. Jesus "refused to accept the disease's ritual uncleanness and social ostracization."[148]

It is a very great mistake, however, to limit our understanding of the meaning of the gospels to an exthortation that we modern day Christians, like Jesus, should be kind to and inclusive of outcasts. Yes, of course we should be kind to and inclusive of outcasts, but there is a much deeper meaning to be gleaned from the gospels. The gospels are truly chronicles of shame. They are about the outcast, the unlovable, the impure, the abandoned—the shamed—*in* all of us, not just *outside* of us. We do well to take in this message, and not just the message that we should be kind and compassionate to others. New Testament scholar Robin Scroggs has written that "The psychological realities coming to expression in the biblical texts may be either descriptions of the imprisonment of the self needing release, or those of the liberated, transformed person."[149] The main point is that "God's acts of salvation, insofar as they lead to transformation happen not outside us or to us, but primarily *within* us. Salvation means *changes.* Changes in how we think, in how we feel, in how we act."[150] Jesus' transformation of shame—i.e., his resurrection—is a description of a "liberated, transformed person." He is, indeed, the "bearer of archetypal truths about the human condition that are alive and at work in the conscious and unconscious haunts of the human psyche or mind."[151]

We—all of us—carry sexual shame; fear of abandonment; loss of love; fear of exposure; dread of public shaming and ridicule; fear of disease, of physical, spiritual, and emotional infirmity (call them

"demons" if you will); horror regarding our physicality, our lust, and
greed. We are not just exhorted to be kind to outcasts. We—all of us to
a greater or lesser extent—experience ourselves as outcasts.

To the extent that the gospels are about being kind, generous, compassionate, and inclusive to *others* who are outcasts, I believe that they are most fundamentally about the shame defense of *projection*— projection of our own shame onto others. If and to the extent that we were honestly and courageously to confront our own shame, our own isolation, and our own outcast status, we would not be tempted to treat others as outcasts and seek to isolate and stigmatize them. Jesus commanded us to "Love your neighbor as yourself." This Commandment has no meaning if and to the extent that shame causes us to despise ourselves.

Here is an example of how depth psychology is helpful in religious life: Jung taught us that the protagonists in dreams are none other than different aspects of the dreamer. He relates two dreams—one of a theologian dreaming of a drunken tramp, the other of a high society lady dreaming of a dissolute prostitute. Jung says that

> Both of them were outraged and horrified, and absolutely re-
> fused to admit, that they had dreamed of themselves. . . . The
> "other" person we dream of is not our friend or neighbor, but the
> other in us, of whom we prefer to say: "I thank thee Lord, that I
> am not this publican or sinner."[152]

Depth psychology helps us to look for and own the publican, the sinner, the dissolute prostitute, the hypocrite—all of the shamed, exiled pieces—of ourselves. Why do this? Nobody wants to see these things, but we are impelled toward psychic and spiritual growth, just as a child is impelled to walk and talk and otherwise achieve independence. Psychic and spiritual growth can be attained only in this process of owning the fragments of ourselves, and this is what God asks of us. This is the pursuit of wholeness, and there is a cost to it because seeking wholeness does not mean finding only the good parts of ourselves but all of ourselves. This is what is involved in transformation of shame and the integration of shame experience. Unless we are willing to enter into this process of naming and owning the shameful, shamed, and isolated parts of ourselves, we will be unable to achieve any sense of unity with God. This is so because we cannot have this experience if we are willing to bring to God only what we see as "the good" in ourselves. This may be the ultimate meaning of Jesus' exhortation to his disciples, after feeding 5,000 people with two fishes and five loaves of bread, to "Gather up the fragments . . . so that nothing may be lost" (John 6:4-15).[153]

In choosing to become human and in allowing himself to be shamed in so many profound ways and then in the phenomenon of the resurrection and glorification of Jesus to the Godhead, God presented humankind with a paradigm of the transformation of shame. Jesus seemed to see an inevitability to his final shaming, telling his followers, "The Son Man must undergo great suffering, and be rejected by the elders, chief priests and scribes, and be killed, and on the third day be raised" (Luke 9:22). This final shaming must take place in order to demonstrate the ultimate transformation of ultimate shame: God incarnate standing in the shame vortex, ultimately raised to the Godhead in the resurrected Christ. In suffering the shame vortex without any resort to shame defenses, Jesus achieved ultimate union with God. We all can, to some lesser extent, experience the transformation of shame through grace—if not the sense of mystical union (call it "cosmic narcissism," if you will) with God that the best among us achieve.

Hebrews (12:1-2) is quite explicit about Jesus' achievement:

> Therefore, since we are surrounded by a great cloud of witnesses, let us also lay aside every weight and the sin that clings so closely, and let us run with perseverance the race that is set before us, *looking to Jesus the pioneer and perfecter of our faith, who for the sake of the joy that was set before him endured the cross, disregarding its shame, and has taken his seat at the right hand of the throne of God.* (emphasis added)

God's resurrection of Jesus demonstrates God's "vindication of Jesus and the ascription of paramount honor to him."[154]

In First Corinthians, Paul spells out what he sees as a central meaning of the Christ event:

> Consider your own call, brothers and sisters: not many of you were wise by human standards, not many were powerful, not many were of noble birth. *But God chose what is foolish in this world to shame the wise; God chose what is weak in this world to shame the strong; God chose what is low and despised in the world, things that are not, to reduce to nothing things that are,*

so that no one might boast in the presence of God. He is the source of your life in Christ Jesus, who became for us wisdom from God, and righteousness and sanctification and redemption, in order that, as it is written, "Let the one who boasts, boast in the Lord." (emphasis added; 1 Corinthians 1:26-30)

This theme of transforming weakness—i.e., shame—to strength that is so present in the Christ event is also seen in 2 Corinthians 12:6-10, where Paul explains how he appealed three times to God to remove from him an unspecified "thorn in the flesh." God did not grant the request but instead replied

"My grace is sufficient for you, for power is made perfect in weakness." So I will boast all the more gladly of my weaknesses, so that the power of Christ may dwell in me. Therefore I am content with weaknesses, insults, hardships, persecutions, and calamities for the sake of Christ; for whenever I am weak, I am strong.

How did Jesus transform shame into resurrection and exaltation to the Godhead? First, he was faithful to his own calling, regardless of the cost. He courageously accepted the terrible anguish and defeats that went along with the triumphs. The Gospels of Matthew, Mark, Luke, and John proclaim the commencement of Jesus' earthly ministry at his triumphant baptism, at which time the heavens open up and God's spirit descends upon him (Matthew 3:13-17; Mark 1:9-11; Luke 3:21-22; John 1:29-34) with the pronouncement, "This is my Son, the Beloved, with whom I am well pleased." Immediately thereafter, however, according to the Gospels of Matthew (4:1-11), Mark (1:12-13), and Luke (4:1-13), Jesus is driven "by the Spirit" (Luke 4:1) into the wilderness with wild beasts and is tempted there by the devil for forty days. Here we see a subtext that continues throughout the gospels of triumph followed by anguish. The story of Jesus' anguish and temptations in the wilderness is typically seen and preached in the light of his ultimate triumph over those temptations, but it could not have been experienced at the time this isolated and famished individual was going through it as other than agonizing and most probably frightful. I would think too that the experience of being driven into the wilderness by the Spirit and being tempted by the devil in a frighteningly vulnerable, famished state would have been experienced as shaming. These are instances in which, in the words of Jung, Jesus confronts his shadow, which must necessarily include his own shame issues.

Next, Jesus stayed in intentional, prayerful relationship with God. There are many other instances in the gospel in which Jesus intentionally retreats from his encounters with crowds into prayerful communication with God (e.g., Luke 9:28-36; Matthew 14:13-14; Matthew 14:22-27; John 6:15). These are times in which Jesus may well have experienced the kind of oceanic unity with God that has been discussed—times that might well have fueled and fed his deeply held conviction that "I and the Father are one." Yet, even so, when in his journeys he came to minister in his hometown of Nazareth, he was reminded that he was just a carpenter, the "son of Mary" (Mark 6:3)—and this last identification would have been shaming in a time, place, and culture in which one who was honorably conceived would be identified by his father's lineage.[155]

It is not surprising, given the paralysis and self-negation that attends shame, that Jesus found himself unable to accomplish "deeds of power" in his hometown, and said, "Prophets are not without honor, except in their hometown, and among their own kin, and in their own house" (Mark 6:4). It is not much of a stretch to conclude that Jesus' impotence in Nazareth resulted from the shaming reminders he received there of his humble—and in at least one respect, even shameful—origins. According to the Gospel of Luke, Jesus was actually driven out of town by the townspeople and led to the brow of the hill "so that they might hurl him off the cliff" (Luke 4:29-30).

Jesus' own family seems to have questioned his sanity: having heard (and evidently credited) news that he had lost his mind, his mother and siblings came at one point to collect him (Mark 3:21).

The final time when Jesus retreats to pray is in the garden immediately prior to his capture by Roman authorities which leads to his passion and death. Here we find the most painful struggle of all—a struggle which includes sweating blood and terrible fear, anguish and an obvious sense of profound isolation, loneliness, and betrayal—all elements of the shame experience. Jesus interrupts his prayer two or three times to beg his disciples to stay awake while he prays, but to no avail. They dissociate from the situation by sleeping.

Jurgen Moltmann stresses Jesus' rejection. He was rejected and abandoned by humanity, but this was not the worst of it: on the cross, he "was abandoned by his Father, whose immediate presence he proclaimed and experienced in his life."[156] According to Mark 15:37, he died with a loud, inarticulate cry, just after remonstrating, "My God, my God, why have you forsaken me?"(Mark 15:34). Hebrews (5:7) says that he died with "loud cries and tears." However,

> because, as the Christian tradition developed, this terrible cry of the dying Jesus was gradually weakened in the passion narratives and replaced by words of comfort and triumph, we can probably rely upon it as a kernel of historical truth. Jesus clearly died with every expression of the most profound horror.[157]

Moltmann suggests that Jesus' worst "torment was his abandonment by God." Furthermore, "what happened on the cross" must be understood as "something that took place between Jesus and his God . . ." Thus,

> the origin of Christology . . . lies not in Jesus' understanding of himself or in his messianic consciousness, nor in the evaluation of him by his disciples. . . . It lies in what took place between Jesus and his God . . . in what was given expression in his preaching and his actions and was literally "put to death" in his abandonment as he died.[158]

Jesus was, indeed, "folly to the wise, a scandal to the devout and a disturber of the peace in the eyes of the mighty. That is why he was crucified."[159]

This is the man, rejected and abandoned by his fellows and feeling himself rejected by God on the cross, that we call the Christ. The experience of rejection, isolation, and abandonment is, as we have seen, the very essence of shame. This sense of the ultimate abandonment of Christ is profoundly salvific for us all. It is what we reenact and reexperience during Lent and Holy Week, for *we* know what Jesus did *not* know as he suffered on the cross: that he had not been forsaken and abandoned. We know that this rejection did not have the last word, and that Jesus was enlivened and exalted to the Godhead. He achieved ultimate unity with God, even as he achieved his unique individual personal identity. If we could not understand Jesus as experiencing shame and suffering, the Christ event would be all but meaningless. Dietrich Bonhoeffer, writing from prison shortly before his own execution, stated it this way:

> God lets himself be pushed out of the world on to the cross. He is weak and powerless in the world, and that is precisely the way, the only way, in which he is with us and helps us. Matt. 8:17 makes it quite clear that Christ helps us, not by virtue of his omnipotence, but by virtue of his weakness and suffering. . . . *Only the suffering God can help. . . . That is a reversal of what the religious man expects from God. Man is summoned to share God's sufferings at the hands of a godless world.* (emphasis added)[160]

The Jesus of the gospel narratives accomplishes great deeds of healing and power; he teaches and ministers from a profoundly powerful place in his center which is filled with God consciousness. But the Jesus of the gospel narratives, when stripped of his Sunday-school gloss, also suffered isolation, loneliness, anguish, and shame. His own triumphant struggle with these feelings, accomplished through constant prayer and brutal honesty, allowed their transformation in himself, and gave him the ability to be a channel for transformation of shame in others. Christians are confronted with a reality of cosmic significance: a human being whose substance was God and who

> emptied himself,
>   taking the form of a slave,
>   being born of human likeness,
> and being found in human form
>   he humbled himself
>   and became obedient to the point of death—
>   even death on a cross.
> Therefore God also highly exalted him. (Philippians 2:7-9)

We contemporary people can take in Jesus' real lessons. We can struggle honestly and courageously with our own shame issues; we can "look to Jesus as the pioneer and perfecter of our faith" who "endured the cross, disregarding its shame" and thus took his "seat at the right hand of the throne of God" (Hebrews 12:2). What does this involve? I cannot put it better than Paul, who exhorted early Christians to "work out your own salvation with fear and trembling" (Philippians 2:12). For Paul, this meant coming to feel that "I have been crucified with Christ; and it is no longer I who live, but it is Christ who lives in me" (Galatians 2:20). It is possible for us to achieve the oneness with God that Jesus wanted for us, even as we grow into our own personal identities:

> As you, Father, are in me and I am in you, may they also be in us so that the world may believe that you have sent me. The glory that you have given me I have given them, so that they may be one, as we are one, I in them and you in me, that they may become completely one. (John 17:21-23)

We can only do this if and to the extent that we are willing and able to let go of shame defenses that avert our gazes from the fact and sources of our shame. Can we stop blaming others, transferring our shame to others, assuming postures of righteousness, acting out in rage, withdrawing, and just giving up? The efforts that we make to face our own shame is how we work out our salvation, with fear and trembling. The ability to see this is the lens that depth psychology provides. Because we are human creatures, our efforts can never be complete. Because we are of God, we are impelled to keep trying.

Chapter 9

Reflections on the Orientation of the Institutional Church and Its Ministers Toward the Meaning and Phenomenon of Shame

Oh God, by the passion of your blessed Son you made an instrument of shameful death to be for us the means of life: Grant us so to glory in the cross of Christ, that we may gladly suffer shame and loss for the sake of your Son our Savior Jesus Christ, . . .

Prayer for Tuesday of Holy Week,
Episcopal Book of Common Prayer, 1979

The measure of [human] life is not . . . freedom from inner struggle, but . . . discovery of how the whole of life, including its dark side, can be brought into the service of growth in love. In this sense salvation must transcend all particular therapies.

Daniel Day Williams, *The Minister and the Care of Souls*

One of the *sub silentio* debates in the extensive literature that has developed on the subject of shame over the past twenty-five years devolves from the question of whether shame can ever be a good thing—that is, whether it has any value in human life or whether it is just something we need to try to rid ourselves of in order to live creative, abundant lives.

John Bradshaw has contended that although toxic shame is debilitating and destructive and needs to be dealt with, still, shame is paradoxically what defines us as human and is the foundation of spirituality.[1] Others, such as Vicki Underland-Rosow, have taken issue with the notion that shame can ever be "either good or necessary," but rather is "integral to an addictive culture which promotes disconnection, dishonesty and judgmental attitudes."[2] She argues that "shame is antithetical to spirituality" and contends that institutional religion invidiously separates humans from themselves and from one another.

I have already discussed at some length the paradoxical nature of shame: how in its healthy forms it lends itself to individuation and creativity, allowing the individual the privacy to develop his or her inner life. At the same time, the human propensity for shame is what binds groups together by instituting rules for fitting in and adapting to one's culture.

The human propensity for shame may be seen as a kind of abyss into which good and evil can be thrown. It is, I think, much too simplistic to say as Underland-Rosow does that shame is per se a "bad thing." As James Fowler has said, "spiritually, shame is related to the deepest places of truth in our souls." He continues:

> Shame provides a primary foundation for conscience and for the instinctive sense of what is worthy or unworthy, right or wrong. Shame, as an emotion, relates to the sensitive feelings touched in love and deep communion with others. Shame protects the intimacy of our closest relations with friends, lovers, spouses, or children. It surrounds our relation with the Holy or the domain of what is sacred to us. Shame, in its positive influence, is the caretaker of our worthy selves and identities.[3]

Only in its distorted forms does shame destroy individuals and communities. In its distorted forms, shame takes over the entire personality and the result is paralysis, depression, addiction, contempt, violent acting out of rage, and last but not least "shamelessness." This is what Bradshaw calls "toxic shame." This is the shame that kills spirituality and abundant life rather than assisting it.

As we have seen, people's personalities are more or less bound in shame based upon many factors, including family of origin, social location, and some even say inborn temperament. It would stand to reason that the more intensely shame is experienced and the more one's personality is bound up in it, the more difficult it is to be positively transformed by it. Shame is always toxic when it has not been confronted honestly, i.e., when it distorts the personality by violence, contempt, depression, addiction, etc. There a here: The first is the degree to which shame penetrates e the personality; the second is the intensity with which it is on enced. Although all humans feel shame, undoubtedly there are those whose experience of it is a great deal less than that of most others. Some of these people are what William James called "healthy minded."[4] They may not feel much if any pressure toward conversion or transformation, and this makes them both blessed and cursed—blessed because they live on a more or less even keel; cursed because nothing impels them toward the ineffable experience of living on a different plane. On this plane the individual feels not simply "all right" but as if he or she is held, embraced, and contained by the source and ground of being. The shameful things do not magically disappear; rather the individual sees them, has acutely felt them, and then, as shame is gradually transformed, experiences a much greater perspective in which his or her own shameful aspects are seen but accepted and held, along with everything else about the self. The individual feels himself or herself of a piece and a part of a boundless fabric, and all feels well in spite of that which is not well. One does one's best, and that usually feels good enough. One feels oneself to be part of an infinite, eternal, benign, and intelligent whole. These individuals feel that they have their life's journey to live and that, at the end of their individual human lives and all that may be inherently shameful about it, they will return wholly to the source and ground of being which has been there all along. They are more transparent, more permeable, than those who have not confronted shame head-on because they have dropped some of the boundaries that isolate them without dropping the boundaries that provide them privacy and personal integrity. They may sometimes have experiences of oceanic unity which, although transient, result in an ongoing, expanded sense of self in relation to God and others. Yet there will be times of regression when shame smacks them in the face in spite of all the work they have done to transform it. These may be times of physical illness, terminal conditions, deaths of those they love, and other losses and failures. This is as close as I can come to explaining the experience of shame transformed.

Because of the innate nature of shame and, for that matter, its positive implications, the institutional Church cannot and should not have as one of its goals the "elimination" of all shame. Sandra Edelman put it best when she said,

> To shed ourselves of shame we would have to shed our histories, our parentage, our personalities as they now are, and start from the beginning again. Attractive as that prospect may seem at times, despite its patent impossibility, it is implicit with unwillingness to embrace our unique life and our special destiny. *To use a Christian metaphor, it is Jesus refusing to be crucified, or Jesus refusing to be Christ.* And even if it were possible, to lose a sense of shame is to risk being shameless, to fly to the other polarity where decency, justice, fairness, the capacity for awe, all the elements which make up an ethical life, are obliterated. There we would lose the capacity for humility, our groundedness in our status as human. (emphasis added)[5]

Some authors do, I believe, go too far in the suggestions they make to the institutional Church for elimination of toxic shame. Stephen Pattison, a priest of the Church of England, has written a bruising critique of the role of Christianity and the institutional Church in fostering and exploiting shame-based personalities. He relates the rise of the monarchical deity to a rise of human shame and he attacks the ideas of God as "wholly different from human beings," God as being without a body, God as "pure and holy," God as "perfect, good, and complete," God as omnipotent, and God as omnipresent. Pattison attacks the sacrament of baptism because of its purpose of "washing away sin." He even goes so far as to suggest that Christian symbols need to be reinvented and its God needs to be deidealized in order to help eliminate the human sense of smallness and shame.[6]

Pattison proves too much. Human beings do not create symbols or God images. Symbols, myths, and God images arise from the depths of the human psyche and address us. Human beings experience the *mysterium tremendum* as a place of awe, of power and immensity beyond imagining. It is preposterous to set out to remake our experience of God in such a way that we are cozy and comfortable with God, to bring God to our own level so that we do not feel reduced by God. As Paul Tillich stated, "A god whom we can easily bear is not God at all, and has no reality."[7]

The experience of smallness and creatureliness in the presence of the living God *is* a "fearful thing" or, at the very least, is likely to bring us to our knees in awe. The emotion and potentiality of shame in the face of the living God is innate, like sexuality, and also like sexuality it can be used for good or ill. "If experiences of shame can be fully faced, if we allow ourselves to realize their import, they can inform the self, and become a revelation of oneself, of one's society and of the human situation."[8] The experience of shame in the presence of the living God is what made Peter "fall down at Jesus knees," exclaiming: "Go away from me, Lord, for I am a sinful man!"(Luke 5:8). It is what caused Isaiah to say, "Woe is me! I am lost, for I am a man of unclean lips, and I live among a people of unclean lips; yet my eyes have seen the King, the Lord of hosts" (Isaiah 6:5). It is why, in so many of the epiphanies recounted in both the Old and New Testaments, God or God's messengers upon appearing to people first say, "Do not be afraid."

In addition, as Pattison himself points out, we need to recognize the contributions that shamed people have made to articulating relationship with God and to be less inclined to view them merely as "objects of compassion."[9] Volumes have been written about the shame and transformation of shame that has informed the religious experience of Christians such as Augustine, Teresa of Avila, Ignatius of Loyola, Peter Abelard, Margery Kempe, Richard Rolle, Martin Luther, Nietzsche, Søren Kierkegaard, Theresa of Lisieux, and Simone Weil, to name just a few. People who are able to transform profound shame experience make the most profound religious contributions of all. Contemporary examples that come to mind are, again, Anton Boisen, the founder of clinical pastoral education, and Bill W., the shamed alcoholic who, in his encounter with Christ, founded the Alcoholics Anonymous movement and the Twelve-Step concept that has been the salvation of millions of shamed-bound addicted people.

So I do proceed from the working proposition that to attempt to rid ourselves and our parishioners of shame would be like "Jesus refusing to be crucified," for Jesus' embrace of the ultimate shame experience and the transformation of that experience—his resurrection—may well be the most powerful psychic meaning of his birth, his life, his ministry, his death, his resurrection, and the greatest agent of healing.

To say that we have to work toward elimination of all shame would be like throwing the baby out with the bathwater. Yet, having said this, clearly the Christian Church through the centuries has, unwittingly or not, capitalized on the innate human shame potential and the symbolism of the cross in ways that have often been destructive and have promoted toxic shame and the development of the shame-bound personality. The Church has at times promoted the development of a kind of shame that has led to "a pervasive, chronic and radical over-shadowing of our innermost self."[10]

This is not to suggest that this tendency of the Church to capitalize on the human shame potential has always been deliberate or conscious. The Church is an enormous and unwieldy institution including at any given time millions of theologians, professional clergy, and others in religious orders. It has existed for many centuries. To suggest that there has been some kind of grand conspiracy to instill and promote shame, as Pattison sometimes comes close to saying, borders on paranoia. Yet there is an innate shame affect in human beings, and the Christ event has often been mercilessly used to shame and browbeat people instead of to reach out to them with the consolatory news of shame transformed in Christ. It may well be that the central Christian story of the passion of Christ has tended to draw into its most active participation and service individuals who have not adequately dealt with their own shame and who deploy shame defenses such as righteousness, power, and projection. I was struck by this recently in the middle of a Sunday liturgy I participated in. One of the hymns chosen for the morning appalled me in its message to the worshipers:

> Before thy throne, O God, we kneel: give us a conscience quick to feel, a ready mind to understand, the meaning of thy chastening hand; whatever the pain and shame may be, bring us, O Father, nearer thee.

> Search out our hearts and make us true; help us to give to all their due. From love of pleasure, lust of gold, from sins which make the heart grow cold, wean us and train us with thy rod; teach us to know our faults, O God.[11]

Words such as these do not, in my opinion, promote a healthy shame or embrace a shame that leads to life or to transformation and redemption of unhealthy shame. Words such as these tell people that they are, as they may already believe and fear, worthy only of being beaten and punished into submission by the chastising Father God, the ultimate judge who needs to take us to the woodshed and teach us a lesson we will not forget. These kinds of words only feed into the shame that all too many parishioners already feel as a result of being physically and psychically beaten or verbally shamed and abused by their earthly parents. This kind of experience of God is the opposite of grace, the opposite of everything that Jesus' birth, ministry, death, and resurrection were all about.

The Christian Church has sometimes seemed to regale in teaching the doctrines of "original sin" and human "fallenness"—the notion that "I was born guilty, a sinner when my mother conceived me" (Psalm 51:5). Many of our churches have taken this to the next step, teaching that the Christian Church (and, more specifically, *their particular flavor and denomination* of the Christian Church) is the only hope for redemption from this condition of original sin and human fallenness. It sometimes seems as though the Church intuitively grasps the human shame potential as the root of much religious feeling but, instead of working with it positively to encourage growth and transformation, the Church all too often uses the very shame defenses that impede both—righteousness being perhaps the most pronounced. That is, the Church and its hierarchy see themselves as "righteous," and they urge identification of the Church's faithful members with it.

At the root of it all is the shame vortex—the tension between our finite creatureliness and mind and spirit—our consciousness of God within. Illustrations of this are so abundant that it is difficult to choose among them. I will use as a prominent expression of this Augustine, one of the great fathers of the Church. Augustine saw original sin as being, at its most basic, about "concupiscence"—i.e., "the inordinate desire for temporal ends which has its seat in the senses."[12] By this thinking, we are all conceived in the sin of the sexual act, which puts us collectively in the shame vortex by reminding us of our creatureliness which is always in tension with our potential for godliness. Original sin—the doctrine that the transgression and curse of the primal couple (Genesis 3:1-24) implicated all of their human posterity—was understood by Augustine to mean that "rampant concupiscence had accompanied Adam's transgression, and thus his sin was transmitted by sexual procreation, through the medium of lust. . . . Augustine concluded that even infants were not exempt from guilt and thus required baptism."[13]

Thandeka has suggested that Augustine's *Confessions* is really not one biography but two, and must be read as such.

> One account by Augustine gives voice to the sentiments expressed by his body. The other account gives voice to the sentiments expressed by his rational mind. He called the mental moods produced by his body "carnal affection" *(carnalis affectus).* He called the other disposition of his mind "spiritual affection" *(caritas),* the sentiments produced within him when his thoughts focused solely on God. To keep the stories discrete, Augustine constructed a theology of the body and a theology of the mind. Each theology was based on a separate system of human sentiment and communication.[14]

Sandra Lee Dixon says that Augustine's work expanded upon the claim of the ancient philosopher Plotinus that "human souls have emanated from the One and lost touch with it by turning away from it and becoming involved in the world of the senses." Dixon illustrates this contention with this quote from the *Confessions:*

> Wherever the human soul turns itself, other than to you [God], it is fixed in sorrows, even if it is fixed upon beautiful things external to you and external to itself, which would nevertheless be nothing if they did not have their being from you.[15]

When we read Augustine's *Confessions,* we cannot help being struck by the revulsion he feels for all things related to the needs, comforts, consolations, delights, and desires of the human body—all things that remind us that we are not just of spirit but also out of nature. Even an infant who cries to be fed is evidence of human sinfulness.[16] The human longing for sexual intimacy is depraved to the point that Augustine even upbraids himself for his involuntary nocturnal emissions.[17]

Here we see the internal struggle that comes from understanding the body as a problem. It seems to me that in Augustine's work we find in exaggerated, highlighted form the universal dilemma: the body is the unavoidable, agonizing reminder that we are not just spirit but out of nature. However, as we have seen, the story of Adam and Eve's expulsion from paradise might better be seen not as being about sex or original sin but about original *shame:* it is the archetypal story of humankind's first understanding of its creatureliness which separated it from God, and its first experience of shame. Thus, Augustine writes:

> The enemy had a grip on my will and so made a chain for me to hold me a prisoner. The consequence of a distorted will is passion. . . . So my two wills, one old, the other new, one carnal, the other spiritual, were in conflict with one another, and their discord robbed my soul of all its concentration.[18]

This lamentation of Augustine echoes the words of Paul:

> For I know that nothing good dwells within me, that is, within my flesh. I can will what is right, but I cannot do it. For I do not do the good I want, but the evil I do not want is what I do. Now if I do what I do not want, it is no longer I that do it, but sin that dwells within me. So I find it to be a law that when I want to do what is good, evil lies close at hand. For I delight in the law of God in my inmost self, but I see in my members another law at war with the law of my mind, making me captive to the law of sin that dwells in my members. Wretched man that I am! Who will rescue me from this body of death? (Romans 7:15-25)

In his *Confessions,* Augustine acknowledged that some sensual pleasures still tempted him. Yet in his transformation of shame he seems to have been able to take the delights of his senses and convert them to a remarkable degree to love of God. Thus he says of a time before his conversion:

> How stupid man is to be unable to restrain feelings in suffering the human lot! That was my state at the time. So I boiled with anger, sighed, wept and was at my wit's end. I found no calmness, no capacity for deliberation. I carried my lacerated and bloody soul when it was unwilling to be carried by me. I found no place where I could put it down. There was no rest in pleasant groves, nor in games or songs, nor in sweet-scented places, nor in exquisite feasts, nor in the pleasures of the bedroom and bed, nor, finally, in books and poetry. Everything was an object of horror, even light itself; all that was not he made me feel sick and was repulsive—except for groaning and tears. In them alone was there some slight relief. [19]

Then, in his transformed state, Augustine is able to say this of God:

> But when I love you, what do I love? It is not physical beauty nor temporal glory nor the brightness of light dear to earthly eyes, nor the sweet melodies of all kinds of songs, nor the gentle odor of flowers and ointments and perfumes, nor manna or honey, nor limbs welcoming the embraces of the flesh; it is not these I love when I love my God. Yet there is a light I love, and a food, and a kind of embrace when I love my God—a light, voice, odor, food, embrace of my inner man, where my soul is floodlit by light which space cannot contain, where there is sound that time cannot seize, where there is a perfume which no breeze disperses, where there is a taste for food no amount of eating can lessen, *and where there is a bond of union that no satiety can part. That is what I love when I love my God.* (emphasis added)[20]

Contemporary Christians who have written about shame that the Church inflicted upon them by reason of the longing for sexual intimacy have included James Joyce, author of *Portrait of the Artist As a Young Man* (and many other great works), and Frank McCourt, author of the acclaimed *Angela's Ashes.*[21] A vivid depiction of the infliction of severe sexual shame by the Roman Catholic Church in Ireland appears in the movie *The Magdalene Sisters* (2002), which is the story of laundries where girls who appeared to be sexually active— either because they had been raped or because they might have had sexual encounters—were imprisoned, enslaved, and made to do commercial laundry. These laundries were run by the Church, in particular by nuns who continually shamed and abused the women. It cannot be denied that professionals working in the mental health field have all too often had to deal "with the pathologies created by a petty and self-righteous religiosity."[22]

We do not need to be told in our churches that we are shameful, because even the most healthy of us already feel and experience ourselves as shameful. This is the human condition. It is the condition of Job who, sitting alone, isolated, friendless, among the ashes, inflicted with loathsome sores, having lost all of his property and children, his good name, and then, finally, his own health, knows the fragility of human life and the illusoriness of security. Job's condition is, most basically, a condition of shame. To God he finally says, "See, I am of small account; what shall I answer you? I lay my hand upon my mouth" (Job 40:4).

Thus, the mistake that the Christian Church has made for the better part of 2,000 years is in telling people, in sum and substance, that they are miserable sinners and *should be ashamed* of themselves. This entirely misses the point. The fact of the matter is that people *are* ashamed of themselves. What we need to be saying to them is not that they *should* be ashamed but rather that God knows they *are* ashamed and that, in the words of Isaiah 30:18, God "waits to be gracious" to them.

Here something needs to be said about "feelings of guilt over willed misdeeds" as distinguished from shame, for it cannot be denied that human beings do sin—willfully act contrary to God's will— or that shame is and should be intertwined with guilt for actual wrongs committed. This is conscience. "Realistic and appropriate guilt cannot be analyzed away" by psychotherapists or by ministers, "nor should it be."[23] As Thomas Oden notes, for those grieving over real guilt for actual misdeeds the Church is in the pastoral position to make three things available that help: penitence, pardon, and reparation. "The pastoral intention must be to help keep the remorse or regret in due proportion to the values that have actually been negated."[24]

AMELIORATING THE CHURCH'S COMPLICITY IN FOSTERING TOXIC SHAME

Where can we start in ending the Church's complicity in the fostering of toxic shame?

In the first place, it seems to me that all pastors must labor to be conscious of the places of shame in themselves. There is far too much projection by members of the clergy, as well as among professionals in the mental health professions, of disease and pathology on those whom we serve, and far too little introspection and examination of our own motives, disease, and pathology. Adolph Guggenbuhl-Craig has pointed out that persons in the mental health professions (including clergy) often show an "enthrallment" with their charges' "negative potentialities" as reflected "in conversations between analysts, by the obvious relish with which one tells the other about the grave danger" facing a person he or she is supposed to be helping. "The nearly compulsive concentration on the patient's negative possibilities is linked to a destructive side in the analyst. . . ."[25] He continues, "Shadow in the analyst constellates shadow in the patient."[26] I believe that the same is true of clergy and their parishioners.

Pattison says it is small wonder that clergy are reluctant to admit and work for transformation of their own places of shame. Church order and discipline makes "exclusion and rejection" the tool of choice for dealing with behavior deemed "shameful." In the Episcopal Church in the United States of America, a priest who observes persons "living a notoriously evil life," or those "who have done wrong to their neighbors and are a scandal to the other members of the congregation," or when there is "hatred between members of the congregation" may exclude such persons from the Eucharist.[27]

Clergy fare no better when they engage in conduct deemed "immoral" or "unbecoming a member of the clergy."[28] Clergy are regularly cast out with little or no pastoral care or concern because of conduct deemed "immoral" or "unbecoming a member of the clergy"—often involving consensual sexual relationships with members of the parish served by the clergy person.

As Pattison notes, a good part of the problem lies with the fact that clergy are idealized and expected to be moral exemplars for their denominations. Thus, " 'higher' and more visible standards of behavior are expected" of clergy than of laypeople. The Church is much more concerned with the visible sexual relationships of ordained people than with those of nonordained people. If clergy are "discreet" about "irregular" sex lives (e.g., homosexual or otherwise extramarital behavior) so that they do not cause a scandal to the Church, they will usually go unscathed. If, however, their behavior becomes known and an embarrassment to the Church, they could well lose their orders or at least their jobs.[29] What does this lead to? It creates a situation in which

> if clergy perceive themselves to be in any way defective, they are likely to conceal this from themselves, their co-religionists and those in authority over them. This traps them in a web of shame and economy with the truth so they are unable to behave openly, morally, responsibly.[30]

For example, as I write this, an uproar has arisen in the Episcopal Church and, indeed, throughout the Anglican Communion by reason of the election to the episcopacy of an open, self-affirming gay man living in a committed relationship. However, it is an undisputed fact that there have always been homosexual clergy and bishops in the church. Thus, it seems clear the "value" that those opposed to Gene Robinson's consecration as bishop seek to uphold is not an exclusively heterosexual episcopacy but rather the unspoken "values" of shame, secrecy, self-hatred, and dishonesty.

Pattison reminds us that defenses against shame include "self-righteousness, contempt for others and the attempt to project shame on to others":

> Perhaps this helps to maintain the shaming attitudes that clergy and religious communities so often appear to enjoy placing on those who are perceived to be outsiders. It certainly does little to foster genuine forgiveness, openness to others, and the benevolent rather than the authoritarian use of pastoral power.[31]

Daniel Day Williams was right when he said that the ordination vows should include a promise to be engaged in "clarification of motive and search for integrity of self which we mean by self knowledge."[32] It occurs to me that those of us attracted to vocations in ordained ministry in the first place tend to be persons who have a particular need to establish their own piety, goodness, and purity before the world, before themselves, and before God. As previously noted, the Church has notoriously used the shame defense of "righteousness" to shame its members. Many clergy do, out of their own places of shame, seek to overidentify with the Church's smug and self-satisfied righteousness, its position of being purely good and having all of the answers.

Pattison acknowledges being a shame-bound individual himself and says that his religion has not freed him from his profound sense of personal shame. However, his extensive study of the shame phenomenon has led him to understand it better and this in turn helped him to come to some acceptance of it. It led him to feel that he "has a sense of shame and defilement rather than it having me."[33]

We must be honest in acknowledging that far from being part of the solution in helping people to deal with their shame, the Church has often been a big part of the problem. With few exceptions, pastoral theologians have generally proceeded from the assumption that Christianity helps rather than hurts people in dealing with shame. Unfortunately this is not always true. The Christian community needs to become more aware of its own exploitation of the innate shame affect that the Christ event would be helping us deal with if it were taught and preached more graciously and more truly. In addition, as Pattison points out, the Church—which perhaps too often and in too many respects identifies itself with God, effectively part of and fused with God—must "undertake some de-idealization of itself."[34]

One important way for the institutional Church to become more aware of its role in exploiting the shame affect is for its professional representatives—i.e., clergy—to receive more education and training in depth psychology and more encouragement to clarify their own motives in seeking ordination.[35] Few seminaries offer, much less require, courses in depth psychology. Too many seminaries and denominations implicitly encourage students to feel that their job is to "save" their flocks merely by exhorting them to adhere to ethical prescriptions and prohibitions. Too few seminaries or denominations do much to encourage their students and those who aspire to be ordained to examine their own places of shame, or to interrogate their deepest motives for seeking ordination.

It is ironic but perhaps not surprising that a faith which exalts as part of the Godhead itself a man who spent his life loving and accepting people out of shame, a person who took upon himself the ultimate shame—a man/God who "endured the cross, disregarding its shame, and has taken his seat at the right hand of the throne of God" (Hebrews 12:2)—has emerged as the "shamingest" institution of all.

PASTORAL RESPONSES TO TOXIC SHAME

> Anoint and cheer our soiled face
> With the abundance of thy grace.
> *Veni, creator spiritus*
>
> Hymn 503, *1982 Hymnal of the Episcopal Church*

Assuming pastors have confronted their own shame, how can they begin to help those who suffer from shame-bound personalities in their ministry?

It is commonly agreed that shame must be acknowledged and owned if it is in any sense to be mitigated. Healing toxic shame requires us to become aware of our shame, to notice our defenses against shame, and to accept a certain amount of shame as part of the human condition.[36]

Helen Block Lewis established this in a phenomenological study of shame published in 1971. Lewis refers to unacknowledged, unexplored shame as "undischarged" or "bypassed" shame. She reaches the following conclusions, based upon the examination of extensive clinical work of herself and others:

First, undischarged shame is fused with guilt, leading to obsessive or paranoid ideation. Second, undischarged shame, "with its florid imagery of the self and the 'other,' has an affinity for the development of hysterical 'scenes.'" Third, undischarged shame is sometimes experienced as simple depression. Fourth, the "simultaneous pull of undischarged shame toward depression, and toward 'turning of the tables' and humiliating the 'other,' can be experienced as excited or agitated depression." Fifth, since "the target of hostility with shame is the self, and the self is not an easily identifiable object, there is an affinity between undischarged shame affect and diffuse anxiety."[37]

Pastoral caregivers who, like psychotherapists, are occasionally witnesses to others' shame experiences may find themselves objects of "humiliated fury, which is likely to be either by-passed or unacknowledged. It is a repetition of past relationships with parental and other figures who witnessed humiliation."[38]

Lewis's study supported the conclusion that many patients who had had initial good results would return to analysis with exacerbated symptoms, "an even harsher superego than they had when treatment began, and the vocabulary of self-denigration . . . increased by their acquaintance with analysis."[39] Examining transcripts of case studies, Lewis was struck with "the way in which unanalyzed shame evoked in the patient vis-à-vis the therapist issued in an exacerbation of the . . . symptoms."[40] She concluded that "there are therapeutic advantages to a focus on undischarged shame and guilt in symptom formation. There are advantages in the phenomenological stance toward shame and guilt during treatment."[41]

Michael Lewis agrees that, from a therapeutic point of view, if a therapist focuses only upon the symptoms of depression and aggression he is "likely to miss the underlying stimulus . . . namely, the global, internal attribution of failure associated with being shamed."[42]

John Bradshaw says that the antidote to toxic shame is an "externalization process." However, "Embracing our shame involves pain. . . . The tendency to avoid emotional suffering . . . is the primary basis for all human mental illness."[43] Bradshaw's "externalization methods" include working a twelve-step program, honestly sharing our feelings with accepting, nonshaming others, and "learning through prayer and meditation to create an inner place of silence wherein we are centered and grounded in a personally valued Higher Power."[44] Bringing shame out of isolation and hiding by joining a nonshaming community, such as a twelve-step group or a therapy group, is key to healing the loneliness fostered by toxic shame.[45]

John Patton is realistic about the fallible, unpredictable nature of both the Church and pastoral care. The real pastoral work, he says, is not in teaching forgiveness, but in helping persons "with the pain of being themselves. . . . The pastor can think of his or her task as helping persons to accept and experience their shame so that they can be responsible enough to be guilty."[46]

Donald Capps suggests that pastors can provide some of the "good mirroring" that responds to the need to "affirm a brighter world than we had known." This affirmation or "reliable mirroring" comes from God but is refracted through pastoral relationships. It can help provide some sense that we are the "gleam in God's eye, that we are God's beloved, in whom God is well pleased."[47]

Clinicians' work clearly points to the conclusion that shame issues cannot become constructive agents for self-understanding and change until they are confronted directly. How can pastors best serve our people in view of this reality? How do we fail to serve our people? The following is an example of a time that I believe I failed to externalize a shame issue and place it in the context of faith for a parishioner.

One Saturday morning a single, middle-aged male parishioner, Ed, dropped by my office without an appointment and sat down. I had received the impression in the past that Ed was lonely. He was hard-working—a construction worker—and lived with and cared for his invalid mother and younger brother. Ed had generally struck me, if anything, as overly pious and sanctimoniously "sweet." In the past, I had felt that, although knowing nothing about me personally, he idealized me as a priest and as a woman. In fact, on several occasions I found it necessary to place boundaries on the relationship. On this particular morning, however, I was slightly more open with him than I had previously been. Then, quite out of the blue, Ed told me in great detail of an anonymous sexual encounter he had recently had with another man he met at a highway rest stop. Ed did not consider himself to be homosexual; he said he had done this "for the heck of it, just to have the experience." I did not experience this revelation to be in the spirit of confession. To the contrary, it was told to me in a rather defiant and frankly crude and vulgar manner that made me feel extremely uncomfortable. I felt anger and aggression coming from Ed, even contempt. I feel sure in retrospect that what I was hearing was a recounting of an experience that was deeply shaming to Ed, but I found myself unable to sit and hold his shame. I was not in the least bit uncomfortable about the revelation that he had engaged in this activity, but I was uncomfortable with the manner in which he was describing it to me. Before Ed demonstrated any inclination to stop talking, I stood up and told him I needed to leave. He reluctantly took the cue and departed from my office. Ed never came back to worship in my church again. Nor, I must confess, did I ever call him and entreat him to return.

This was, I now believe, a case in which I failed as a pastoral caregiver. I believe that Ed was, in a highly defensive way, crying out to me in shame. In retrospect, I think I could have better handled the situation. We might have explored why he was telling me about the incident. I might have asked him how he felt about himself concerning this situation. I might also have explored with him how he felt telling me about it, and I might have named the defiance I was experiencing from him in the telling. At the very least, I might have just stayed with him until he was finished saying whatever he felt he needed to say. Instead, I think I exacerbated his shame by, in essence, rejecting him and shutting him down.

I recount this incident to illustrate how difficult it can sometimes be to listen to shame, particularly when it masquerades as bravado, contempt, rage, and shamelessness. What a shamed person needs most is a sense of acceptance, and coming from me in that situation I think acceptance would have been helpful to Ed. However, I felt confused, shamed, even defiled, hearing the details of his sexual encounter. I felt somehow "smeared" by it. That is, I think, not an uncommon reaction to a disclosure of a shame scene. I let that get in the way of my call to accept what I was feeling as unacceptable, including possibly the exploration of his own negative feelings about the incident as conveyed in the hostility of the recounting of it. I am reminded of the woman at the well's confession to Jesus that she had no husband, and his response: "You are right in saying, 'I have no husband'; for you have had five husbands, and the one you have now is not your husband. What you say is true!" (John 4:17-18). Jesus did not hesitate to name the places of people's shame.

Perhaps we need to learn how to truly accept the unacceptable in ourselves and others, without suspending judgment altogether. As Paul Tillich has pointed out, "the human predicament . . . involves the fact of being guilty, the threat of that despair which is connected with the questions of guilt."[48] It is not helpful or honest, says Tillich, to suspend judgment. "The negative must be honestly faced as negative," and for pastoral counseling to be therapeutic, there must be "acceptance 'in spite of.'"[49] The counselor needs to "help the other accept himself in the situation of guilt. This *cannot* be done by suspending judgment, but it can by no means be done at all by continuing and strengthening moral demands."[50]

Only a spiritual sense of grace can heal—what Lewis Smedes calls "the experience of being accepted without regard to whether we are acceptable."[51] Grace works to remove the experience of rejection that lies at the heart of shame. Although grace can be experienced by individuals directly within themselves on their own, grace can also be experienced in embodied form in the accepting attitudes of other people such as friends and within religious communities. One way of externalizing shame is in the setting of sacramental confession. This is perhaps most appropriate in situations where shame is fused with guilt for actual wrongdoing. Sacramental confession can help persons feeling shame to experience in embodied form the "lightness of grace" which helps individuals to gradually accept themselves and to move toward being their own best, true selves.[52] Priests are invested by the institutional Church with the authority to pronounce absolution on its (the Church's) behalf. This is an absolution that God gives, with or without the expression of absolution by a priest. Still, it is sometimes helpful for people to actually experience this grace, acceptance, and forgiveness flowing through an authorized representative of their church.

Recalling Nietzsche's resentment of God's omniscient, omnipresent gaze, James Fowler wrote that if only Nietzsche had been able to accept the grace that was apparent in Jesus' life and work instead of finding it a threat, "who can know what so fertile a mind and so sensitive a soul might have offered."[53] Acceptance of grace is difficult because it means letting go of illusions of control that we so like to maintain. We hold on for dear life to whatever shreds of power and control we can. Sometimes, as it did for Nietzsche, this means lashing out against the very thing that can save us—love. Nietzsche ultimately concluded that there was no God, because if there were a God it would be himself. This is a paradigmatic example of deployment of the power defense. Deborah van Deusen Hunsinger situates therapy for shame within a broad context of God's acceptance, love, and grace, relying on Karl Barth for her contention that because God has "entered into the shamefulness of sin" in Jesus, human beings now share the objective honor and worthiness that God gave to Jesus.[54] This is, it seems to me, a slightly different way of saying that God's glorification of the shamed Jesus assures us of acceptance as well. However, van Deusen Hunsinger and I differ in that I believe the Christ event is about our redemption from shame rather than being about atonement for sin.

The antidote to the destructive potential of shame is "the healing response of acceptance of the self, despite its weakness, defects and failures."[55] Being healed in the sense of "cure, of being rid of the condition, is out of the question because the past cannot be brought into the present and made different from what it was, and shall always be." However, what we *can* do in our churches, and what I think we should always be working toward doing, is, again borrowing the words of Edelman, assisting people in *surrounding* the condition "with a strengthened ego position, enabling a broader perspective, more compassion for self, and freer access to creativity and life."[56] Ironically, this means a kind of validation of shame so that, at the very least, one is not ashamed of being ashamed. Validation of shame removes at least one layer of shame. It lets people know that we are all "in the soup" together.

Pastors need to be realistic about what they can do to help people to deal with toxic shame. Ideally, what the Church offers is a nonshaming community in which (among other things) human shame is understood and life is sustained by a hope that is grounded in God. Pastors need to know about and use, not just recite, the great symbols and concepts of faith. When we genuinely feel that the Church's language of grace, redemption, and hope can be used, we should use it without apology or embarrassment, and without pretending to be secular people. Pastors sometimes have to carry and in some sense incarnate the divine for their people. Sometimes that incarnational experience is all people have to hold tight to.[57]

It is, in general, a fallacy to see most pastoral care and counseling as occurring in well-defined sessions by regular and recurring appointment. "Most pastoral counseling comes by surprise and in disguise," James Dittes says.[58] Instead, typically, a parishioner will begin talking to the pastor in between times—when he is early for a meeting or at coffee hour or in the middle of a church cleanup day. One wise pastor said that most pastoral work is in the "interruptions"—with the person who sticks his or her head in the door, the person who phones about one thing and begins to talk about something entirely different, the person we run into when we are on our way to our cars and just want to go home.

Dittes also notes that "more needs for pastoral counseling emerge out of chronic, slowly evolving feelings of alienation and distress than out of sudden crises like death and illness."[59] When it comes to ministering to people's shame issues, we need to be realistic about our innate limitations as pastors and the complexity of the problem. Pattison is, I think, correct in stating that many theorists and theologians obscure the complexity and problematic nature of shame with overly simplistic responses that beg the question. He goes so far as to state that "the beginning of wisdom lies with the acknowledgment of ignorance and acceptance of practical impotence and inadequacy."[60] Pastoral theologians have said that we need to display "unconditional positive regard" and create a sense of "agapeic person-centredness."[61] However, Pattison asks, "Where are the agapeic pastoral counselors to be found? How can people be helped to develop agapeic skills? Many pastoral workers are poor at counseling and relationships, perhaps needing agapeic pastoral counseling themselves."[62]

Pattison makes a good point in questioning the training, experience, and skills of many people who happen to be ordained. In his unremittingly bleak assessment of the possibility of their being helpful, however, I think Pattison again goes too far. Perhaps we cannot "cure" people of their shame, but for reasons already stated I do not think that should be the goal. What we *can* do is to bring shame out of the closet. We need first of all to stop pretending that shame is a condition which applies only to others. We need to be more aware of the ways in which the shame dynamic can tend to attract persons to ordained ministry in the Church and how it can be exploited by needy, compulsive caregivers who seek to expiate their own shame by trying to rescue others.[63]

We can help to orient our people toward "surrounding the condition with a strengthened ego position, enabling a broader perspective, more compassion for the self, and freer access to creativity and life."[64] How can we do this? First, we need to stop promoting the illusion that authentic relationship with God means constant joy and peace. God in Christ never promised this: to the contrary, we were exhorted that we need to "take up the cross daily" (Luke 9:23) to follow Christ. It a mistake to imply that a faithful life means a "blissful absence of tensions." To be sure, "tensions which are seriously maladjusted"—e.g., between individuation and conformity—"and are therefore stretched to the breaking point do result in mental breakdown."[65] As Rollo May states, an important part of healing is "utilization of suffering," and I believe that an honest and caring pastor can, like a therapist, help hold people's suffering to enable transformation. May is correct when he states that "a human being will not change his or her personality patterns, when all is said and done, until forced to do so by suffering. . . . Suffering is one of the most potentially creative forces in nature."[66]

It has been said that shame in particular can be heroically transformed in creativity. Shame theorist Leon Wurmser contends that when one is grasped by creative power,

> the boundaries between self and parts of the outside world, between various objects, between different feelings, moods, images and memories melt away. A heightened sense of being alive, of attaining the best within, the ultimate meaning of oneself, even an increasing feeling of bodily vitality, is accompanied by a reaching out to others. The creative experience is a form of love with strong narcissistic aspects.[67]

However, Wurmser continued that this "bursting through of boundaries on so many levels, . . . stands against the dark foil of destruction":

> The old, stale forms must be broken; in the creative zeal there is a sense of ferocity, ruthlessness, contempt, even cruelty against what is confining and limiting. And this is not restricted to the artistic plane but extends to social life. The creative effort is clearly not merely a freeing up of love in its broadest sense, but an unbinding of aggression as well—at time in vicious forms.[68]

What can ministers do to make space for that which is authentic and real and potentially transformative? Are we up to the power of what we might unleash? Can we deal with the transformations and resurrections of personality that can ultimately follow from lives lived authentically and creatively? Or would we rather stick with the pious old formulas and language of guilt, sin, and repentance?

Pastoral caregivers need to communicate the felt sense that they, as well as the counselee, "stand in need of acceptance-*in-spite-of!* When this is realized, we have a relationship which in itself has the character of transformation."[69] We must be "grasped" (a favorite word of Tillich's) by the power of God which transcends the situation: "One can accept someone else ultimately only in the power of the ultimate."[70] In essence, one could see Tillich's theology of pastoral care as requiring the counselor to have confronted his or her own shame issues, enabling him or her to approach the counselee as fellow traveler rather than as object upon whom he or she will bestow superiority, expertise, spiritual groundedness, and insight.

Ministers invariably have an opportunity to make transformative space during their weekly sermons. I have tried to make it a habit *not* to tell people what they *should* do, say, think, or feel. It is all too easy to slide into righteous moralism which in itself is a kind of defense to shame. For 2,000 years preachers have been exhorting people in this manner, and the results speak for themselves: the Crusades, inquisitions, the Holocaust, religious wars, intolerance—in short, enormous manifestations of all of the defenses to shame discussed herein, including narcissistic rage, projections, righteousness, depression, defeatism, and killing perfectionism. However, Jesus was not primarily a reformer demanding repentance. John the Baptist preached "repent now or be damned," but Jesus' message was "God loves you in spite of yourself." I try to preach scripture in such a way that people will see that shame can be transformed in Christ, that God knows we are ashamed and "waits to be gracious to us" (Isaiah 30:18).

Let us take, by way of example, the story of the woman who appeared at Simon the Pharisee's home when Jesus was there for dinner and began to wash his feet with her tears and her hair. This, I think, is a touching story of shame transformed in Christ, and I use it as an example because the shame theme is particularly prominent. Here are some excerpts of a sermon I preached on this to the urban poor, working-class, ethnically diverse parish I was serving:

> In first-century Palestine, when this happened, there were very strict rules in Judaism about whom you ate with and whom you did not eat with, whom you touched and whom you did not touch. These were the religious laws, and it was shameful to disregard them. Women could not eat with men. Women did not let their hair down in public. Prostitutes were not permitted to touch holy men at respectable dinner parties. But this woman was not daunted by the setting. She does not ask to be admitted. The woman's emotions are extravagant and inappropriate. She is "over the top." Tears flow from the well of her heart and cascade to the feet of Jesus. She uses her tears and her hair to wash his feet, then pours costly oil on him.
>
> What is this woman feeling? I believe she is feeling the welling up of shame and the release of shame. This is a woman who has been cast out, rejected by her community. A woman who has been engaged in activity—we don't know exactly what but most likely it was sexual—that puts her "beyond the pale." In Jesus' acceptance of her approach and her intimate touch, she is feeling the grace of "all rightness" for all that is not all right in her, all that is broken.
>
> Many of us have a sense at some time or another that there is something wrong in us as we stand. In fact, this sense of something wrongness may be the first thing that is needed in order for grace to enter in. And what is grace? Grace is the felt sense of God's presence in the wake of sorrow and despair.
>
> I bet many of you can relate to this if you think about it.

At this point in the sermon I risked telling a story of personal shame and ensuing transformative grace from my own life. Specifically, I talked about how I related to the woman's feelings going back to a time in my life when I abused alcohol. I talked about the tears and the grace that enabled me to stop. I admit that I felt quite vulnerable in telling this story; I worried about how the congregation would feel having a minister who had had a drinking problem, albeit many years before. But I believe that in telling the story I showed them that I trusted them, and my trust did not turn out to be misplaced. In fact, I think it opened the door to some storytelling of their own on later occasions. In the sermon, I also talked about the beloved hymn "Amazing Grace," written by a slave trader turned Anglican priest. What I tried to do in that sermon was to create space for people to think about their own places of shame. Jesus welcomed the woman who was willing and able to experience her shame and come to him with it. He was less warmly disposed toward Simon the Pharisee, one who, in his punctilious obedience of the rules, covered himself in a mantle of righteous contempt for the woman. As a minister, I try very hard not to be like Simon the Pharisee, pretending that obedience to the rules and laws is the key to salvation, telling people what they *should* do, think, and feel, or, worst of all, suggesting that my own feelings or behavior are being held up as exemplary. I think that this kind of preaching encourages "hiding"—life on the "guilt axis" that Helen Lynd talks about, the False Self life that Winnicott talks about, and the "fear of life" that Rank talks about. Furthermore, I think that it completely distorts the gospel message. It is the kind of preaching that encourages people to come to church in their Sunday best, leaving (or trying to leave) the shamed and broken parts at home and more or less ignoring or forgetting about what they hear as soon as they leave the church. Furthermore, it renders church irrelevant. It is part of the reason for the dead and lifeless feeling that exists in so many churches, including the empty pews and the resulting panic of church professionals about declining church membership.

People need to understand that from the broken, wounded, and shamed parts of themselves, from suffering honestly experienced, can emerge strength, creativity, and the peace that can come only from a sense of life deeply experienced and authentically lived. This is a very freeing and hopeful thing to realize. Real mental health is not just a matter of "adjustment." Development of a strong, self-differentiated, and individuated personality requires radical inner struggle. The goal should not be to possess a personality with no edges. The goal is to find meaning and creative understanding through the process of our inner struggles. One finds integrity and hope through creative engagement in life, rather than despair.[71]

Ministers are in a unique position to foster that attitude by our words and by our examples. We need to be honest and real with people about what they might encounter on a spiritual journey, should they wish to embark on one. Where else will people hear this perspective? They will not hear it from most of the self-help books which are so popular and which purport to show people how they can live without conflict, shame, or suffering; not from television; not from political leaders or movie stars; not from exercise classes or pottery classes or most popular novels; not in most undergraduate or graduate classrooms; not from television or radio evangelists who preach a simplistic and false "happy-clappy" path to salvation. Ministers who are serious about fostering spiritual growth and transformation must

> offer a firm and big enough space that people trust enough to bring all of themselves into it—the bad, the troubled, the uncertain, the vengeful and resentful parts of themselves, and the eager, lively, glad, and ambitious parts. All are invited to the banquet.[72]

One of the difficulties with this is that we must have a big enough space in ourselves to deal with some of the suffering that is experienced by people when they open themselves up in this way. People are at different places in their journey, and it is unlikely that more than a handful at a time in any given congregation will be at the agonizing transitional phase analogous to the phase of childbirth when the baby's head enters the birth canal:

> In the birth process, the dark, seemingly chaotic period of transition is the time of greatest discomfort. . . . In our spiritual lives, too, it is a pivotal time. The old ways no longer serve. The comfortable rhythms of worship and solitary prayer feel empty and sterile.[73]

However, as Henri Nouwen once said, for many people, churches "decorated with words announcing salvation and new life are little more than parlors for those who feel quite comfortable in their old life."[74] Clergy need to accept this too. We need to meet people where they are, understanding that there will come a time in most people's lives when they finally face the Gorgon and need the depth that a seasoned, honest, and courageous minister can provide—one who has faced the Gorgon herself or himself. Edelman asks a question that clergy might well ask:

> Do we collaborate with the Gorgon by agreeing with her message of unworth and defilement, falling unconsciously into the victim position and refusing to claim the gold of the original self? Do we deny any relationship with her by trying to ignore, distract, override her? Or by projecting her? Do we feed her berserker aspect by acting out unconscious rage and aggression, inevitable products of the infantile wound—and by acting out, add yet another layer of shame when we finally reflect on that behavior? (How much of the Gorgon's monstrosity and potency for annihilation is our own primitive rage?) Or do we, like Athene, claim her and the wound from which she was birthed, thereby making possible her transformation?[75]

The shaman metaphor is also very useful here. The shaman is found in one form or another in most cultures. A shaman attains his or her true vocation as a healer, seer, and visionary through the experience of self-wounding, death, and rebirth. "Knowing intimately and personally the realm of sickness, decrepitude, dying and death readies the shaman for his or her actual mission."[76] Jesus of Nazareth acted as a shaman in suffering ultimate shame and emerging victorious. Many of us who are called to ordained ministry are people who happen to carry shame that can also be used and channeled in a transformative manner in effecting grace. Orthodox theories of atonement have it that Jesus bore the sins of humanity and suffered the punishment due to us. However, I believe that the enduring power of the cross comes rather from his having borne the felt shame of humanity and transforming it. "Sin" is, ironically, incidental and largely a by-product of the defenses of shame. Sebastian Moore argues that self-disesteem—i.e., shame—is "the root of all evil, the basis of what might be called original sin. . . ."[77] I think of this weekly as I celebrate the Eucharist. The communion wafer is broken and the priest proclaims "Alleluia! Christ our Passover is sacrificed for us." At this moment the broken wafer is held aloft, the pieces apart, until the congregation responds, "Therefore let us keep the feast. Alleluia!" The shamefully broken body of Christ is then, week after week, reconstituted in Christians everywhere. He—and we—are put back together again, resurrected as it were. Perhaps we cannot be whole without first being broken.

Chapter 10

Conclusion

O God of unchangeable power and eternal light; . . . by the effectual working of your providence, carry out in tranquility the plan of salvation; let the whole world see and know that things which were cast down are being raised up, and things which had grown old are being made new, and that all things are being brought to their perfection by him through whom all things were made, your son Jesus Christ our Lord.

Episcopal Book of Common Prayer, 1979

I have attempted to demonstrate the ubiquity in human life of the shame experience and its centrality in the tension between the human condition of creatureliness and our awareness of godliness and spirit. I have also attempted to show the place of shame as boundary phenomenon in the concomitant tension between the longing for union and the impulse toward striving to be one's own separate and unique person, creatively alive in the world. The negotiation of these tensions is the fundamental work we human beings are called to do in this life, and it is fraught with much anguish. The work of depth psychologists gives us a place to stand in understanding the roots of and the power of shame in human life. This understanding gives us hope and courage as we seek God's grace in transforming unhealthy shame.

I have tried to show a distinction between healthy shame as a boundary phenomenon between the emergence of the individual and his or her creativity and the need to conform and be part of a larger whole—family, culture, the human family, creation, God itself—and shame that hijacks and distorts the entire personality, like a terrorist.

The Christ event—the incarnation—constellates the shame archetype for us. Jesus' birth, his ministry, his death, and his resurrection give us a paradigmatic model of shame transformed and resurrected. It is a model that ordained representatives of the Church are in a unique position of holding out—through the sacraments, preaching, and pastoral care.

Notes

Chapter 1

1. Rollo May, *The Art of Counseling,* Revised Edition (Lake Worth, FL: Gardner Press, 1989), p. 123.

2. John Hick and Michael Goulder, *Why Believe in God?* (London: SCM Press, Ltd., 1983), p. 80.

Chapter 2

1. Donald Capps, *Jesus: A Psychological Biography* (St. Louis, MO: Chalice Press, 2000), p. 149, citing Andries Van Aarde, "Social Identity, Status Envy and Jesus' Abba," *Pastoral Psychology* 45 (1997): 451-472.

2. Ibid.

3. Ibid.

4. Capps, *Jesus: A Psychological Biography,* p. 150, quoting Van Aarde, "Social Identity," p. 464.

5. Ibid., p. 149.

6. Ibid.

7. Jane Schaberg, *The Illegitimacy of Jesus: A Feminist Theological Interpretation of the Infancy Narratives* (San Francisco: Harper & Row, 1987).

8. Capps, *Jesus: A Psychological Biography,* p. 148.

9. See Elaine Pagels, *The Origins of Satan* (New York: Random House, 1995), in which she comments that Matthew was preoccupied with the refutation of "damaging rumors about Jesus—for example, that his birth was illegitimate, which would disgrace and disqualify him as a suitable candidate for Israel's Messiah," p. 77.

10. K.C. Hanson and Douglas Oakman, *Palestine in the Time of Jesus: Social Structures and Social Conflicts* (Minneapolis: Fortress Press, 1998), p. 57.

11. In Jerome Neyrey (Ed.), *The Social World of Luke Acts* (Peabody, MA: Hendrickson Publishers, Inc., 1991), p. 25.

12. Ibid., pp. 25-26.

13. John Pilch and Bruce Malina (Eds.), *Handbook of Biblical Social Values* (Peabody, MA: Hendrickson Publishers, Inc., 1998), pp. 106-107.

14. Bruce J. Malina, *The New Testament World: Insights from Cultural Anthropology,* Revised Edition (Louisville, KY: Westminster/John Knox Press,1993), pp. 96-97.

15. Ibid., p. 34.

16. Ibid., p. 50.

17. Capps, *Jesus: A Psychological Biography,* p. 161.

18. Ibid., p. 103, quoting John Dominic Crossan, *The Historical Jesus: The Life of a Mediterranean Jewish Peasant* (San Francisco: HarperSanFrancisco, 1991), p. 14.

19. See Ann Belford Ulanov, *The Female Ancestors of Christ* (Boston: Shambhala, 1993).

20. See discussion in Hanson and Oakman, *Palestine in the Time of Jesus,* pp. 53-57.

21. Jerome H. Neyrey, *Honor and Shame in the Gospel of Matthew* (Louisville, KY: John Knox Press, 1998), p. 98.

22. Ibid., quoting E.D. Freed, "The Women in Matthew's Genealogy," in *Journal for the Study of the New Testament,* 29 (1987): 15.

23. Jack Miles, "Before Jesus Could Talk," *New York Times Magazine,* Sunday, December 24, 1995.

24. Crossan, *The Historical Jesus,* p. 10.

25. Pierre Bourdieu, "The Sentiment of Honour in Kabyle Society," in John G. Peristiany (Ed.), *Honor and Shame: The Values of Mediterranean Society* (Chicago: University of Chicago Press, 1966), pp. 211-212.

26. Ibid., p. 54.

27. Capps, *Jesus: A Psychological Biography,* pp. 14, 131.

28. Ibid., p. 149.

29. Ibid., pp. 66-74.

30. Pilch and Malina, *Handbook of Biblical Social Values,* p. 113.

31. "When someone is convicted of a crime punishable by death and is executed, and you hang him on a tree, his corpse must not remain all night upon the tree; you shall bury him that same day, *for anyone hung on a tree is under God's curse*" (emphasis added).

32. Martin Hengel, *Crucifixion in the Ancient World and the Folly of the Message of the Cross* (Philadelphia: Fortress Press, 1977), p. 87.

33. John Dominic Crossan, *Jesus, A Revolutionary Biography* (HarperSanFrancisco, 1994), pp. 123 *ff.*

34. James D. Whitehead and Evelyn Eaton Whitehead, *Shadows of the Heart* (New York: Crossroad, 1994), pp. 155-156. Edward P. Wimberly has very profitably considered the shame experience of Jesus as set forth, implicitly and explicitly, in the gospels and its potential value as story narrative in pastoral care and preaching. See his book *Moving from Shame to Self-Worth* (Nashville: Abingdon Press, 1999).

35. Carl Jung, "The Psychology of Christian Alchemical Symbolism," in *Collected Works,* Volume 9ii (Princeton: Princeton University Press, 1959), p. 179.

36. Albert Schweitzer, *The Quest of the Historical Jesus* (New York: MacMillan Publishing Company, 1968), pp. 370-371.

37. Malina, *The New Testament World,* p. 66.

38. Carl Jung, "Answer to Job," in *Collected Works,* Volume 11 (Princeton: Princeton University Press, 1958), p. 441.

39. Carl Jung, "Psychological Approach to the Trinity," in *Collected Works,* Volume 11 (Princeton: Princeton University Press, 1958), p. 154.

40. Carl Jung, "Answer to Job," p. 409.

41. Carl Jung, "The Psychology of Christian Alchemical Symbolism," p. 181.

42. Carl Jung, "The Development of Personality," in *Collected Works,* Volume 17 (Princeton: Princeton University Press, 1954), p. 181.

43. Carl Jung, "The Relations Between the Ego and the Unconscious," in *Collected Works,* Volume 7, trans. R.F.C. Hull (Princeton: Princeton University Press, 1953), p. 144.

44. Martha Nussbaum, *Upheavals of Thought* (Cambridge: Cambridge University Press, 2001), p. 198.

Chapter 3

1. *Jacobellis v. Ohio,* 378 U.S. 184, 197 (1964).

2. Martha Nussbaum, *Upheavals of Thought* (Cambridge: Cambridge University Press, 2001), p. 196.

3. Ibid.

4. *Book of Common Prayer* (New York: Church Hymnal Corporation, 1979), p. 360.

5. Ibid., p. 337.

6. *Book of Common Prayer* (New York: Oxford University Press, 1928), p. 6.

7. Vicki Underland-Rosow, *Shame: Spiritual Suicide* (Shorewood, MN: Waterford Publications, 1995), p. 46.

8. Helen Lynd, *On Shame and the Search For Identity* (London: Routledge, 1999 [1958]), p. 23.

9. Merle Fossum and Marilyn Mason, *Facing Shame: Families in Recovery* (New York: WW Norton & Company, 1986), pp. 5-6.

10. See Edwin H. Friedman, *From Generation to Generation* (New York: Guilford Press, 1985).

11. Sylvan Tompkins, *Affect, Imagery, and Consciousness.* Volume 2, *The Negative Affects* (New York: Springer, 1963), p. 118.

12. Helen Block Lewis, *Shame and Guilt in Neurosis* (New York: International Universities Press, Inc., 1971), p. 34.

13. Ibid., p. 36.

14. Ibid.

15. Lynd, *On Shame,* p. 208.

16. The two positive affects Tompkins posits are interest/excitement and enjoyment/joy. There is one "neutral" affect: surprise/startle. See discussion in Donald Nathanson (Ed.), *Shame and Pride: Affect, Sex and the Birth of Self* (New York: W. W. Norton & Company, 1992), p. 136.

17. Ibid., p. 149.

18. Ibid., p. 136.

19. Ibid., pp. 137-138.

20. Ibid.

21. Michael Lewis, *Shame: The Exposed Self* (New York: The Free Press, 1995), p. 2.

22. Carl Jung, "Synchronicity: An Acausal Connecting Principle," in *Collected Works,* Volume 8, 1960, pp. 436-437, para. 841.

23. Nathanson, *Shame and Pride,* p. 144.

24. See discussion in John Patton, *Is Human Forgiveness Possible?* (Nashville: Abingdon Press, 1985), p. 50, citing Gerhart Piers and Milton B. Singer, *Shame and*

Guilt: A Psychoanalytic and a Cultural Study (New York: W. W. Norton & Company, 1971), p. 50.

25. Lewis, *Shame and Guilt in Neurosis,* p. 33.

26. Ibid., p. 34.

27. Ibid.

28. Ibid., p. 37.

29. Ibid.

30. Lynd, *On Shame,* p. 207.

31. Donald Capps, *The Depleted Self: Sin in a Narcissistic Age* (Minneapolis: Fortress Press, 1993), p. 81.

32. Ibid., pp. 81-82.

33. Patton, *Is Human Forgiveness Possible?,* p. 52.

34. Lynd, *On Shame,* p. 68.

35. Gershen Kaufman, *Shame: The Power of Caring* (Rochester, VT: Schenkman Books, Inc., 1992), p. 32. See Erving Goffman's *Stigma: Notes on the Management of Spoiled Identity* (New York: Simon & Schuster, 1963).

36. See Donald Winnicott, *Holding and Interpretation* (New York: Grove Press, 1986), p. 52.

37. Andrew Morrison, *Shame: The Underside of Narcissism* (Hillsdale, NJ: Analytic Press, 1989), p. 13 *ff.*

38. Gershen Kaufman, *The Psychology of Shame* (New York: Springer, 1996), p. 21; Paul Gilbert, "What Is Shame, Some Issues and Controversies," in Paul Gilbert and Bernice Andrews (Eds.), *Shame: Interpersonal Behavior, Psychopathology and Culture* (New York: Oxford University Press, 1992), pp. 3-30.

39. See Stephen Pattison, *Shame: Theory, Therapy, Theology* (Cambridge, England: Cambridge University Press, 2000), p. 75.

40. Ibid., p. 93.

41. John Bradshaw, *Healing the Shame That Binds You* (Deerfield Beach, FL: Health Communications, Inc., 1988), p. viii, quoting Gershen Kaufman, *Shame: The Power of Caring.*

42. Bradshaw, *Healing the Shame,* p. 14.

43. Piers and Singer, *Shame and Guilt,* p. 16.

44. Franz Alexander, "Remarks About the Relation of Inferiority Feelings to Guilt Feelings," *International Journal of Psychoanalysis* 19 (1938), 41.

45. Capps, *The Depleted Self,* p. 83.

46. Carl D. Schneider, *Shame, Exposure and Privacy* (Boston: Beacon Press, 1977), p. 78.

47. Ibid.

48. Patton, *Is Human Forgiveness Possible?,* p. 50.

49. Lewis, *Shame and Guilt in Neurosis,* p. 204.

50. Underland-Rosow, *Shame,* p. 26.

51. Ibid., p. 19.

52. Lewis, *Shame: The Exposed Self,* p. 34.

53. Erik Erikson, *Childhood and Society* (New York: W. W. Norton & Company, 1963), pp. 252-253.

54. Ibid., p. 253.

55. Ibid., pp. 253-254.

56. Ibid., p. 254.

57. Nussbaum, *Upheavals of Thought,* p. 196.

58. Erkison, *Childhood and Society,* p. 256.

59. Ibid., p. 257.

60. Ibid.

61. Kaufman, *Shame: The Power of Caring,* p. 14.

62. Lynd, *On Shame,* p. 32.

63. Ibid., p. 34.

64. Ibid., pp. 43-44.

65. Lewis, *Shame and Guilt in Neurosis,* p. 16.

66. Lynd, *On Shame,* p. 37.

67. Goffman, *Stigma,* p. 128.

68. Ram Dass, *Still Here* (New York: Riverhead Books, 2000), p. 11.

69. Goffman, *Stigma,* p. 129.

70. Moshe Halevi Spero, "Shame: An Object Relations Formulation." In Albert J. Solnit, Ruth S. Eissler, and Peter B. Neubauer (Eds.), *The Psychoanalytic Study of the Child,* Volume 39 (New Haven: Yale University Press, 1984), pp. 259-282, 268 *ff.*

71. See Kaufman, *Shame: The Power of Caring,* p. 197.

72. Ibid., pp. 74-75.

73. Gilbert and Andrews, *Shame: Interpersonal Behavior,* p. 26.

74. Lynd, *On Shame,* p. 28.

75. Alan Roland, *Cultural Pluralism and Psychoanalysis* (New York: Routledge Press, 1996), p. 106. In her book *The Chrysanthemum and the Sword* (Rutland, VT: Charles Tuttle, 1954), anthropologist Ruth Benedict argued that Eastern cultures tend to be "shame cultures," and Western cultures tend to be "guilt cultures." She contended that in the latter, individuals focus on specific wrongdoing which is subject to punishment—often legal. Benedict's work has generated much interest and dialogue but has been subject to criticism and ultimately rejected by most people who have seriously studied the matter, partly because guilt and shame are often fused, with guilt being a subsidiary affect of the shame affect. See Pattison, *Shame,* p. 54.

76. Lewis, *Shame: The Exposed Self,* pp. 215-216.

77. Ibid.

78. Sandra Edelman, *Turning the Gorgon: A Meditation on Shame* (Woodstock, CT: Spring Publications, 1998), pp. 19-20.

Chapter 4

1. Helen Merrell Lynd, *On Shame and the Search for Identity* (London: Routledge Press, 1958).

2. Ibid., p. 207.

3. Ibid.

4. Ibid., pp. 208-209. Reproduced with permission.

5. Ibid., pp. 209-210.

6. Ibid., p. 230.

7. Ibid., p. 231.

8. Ibid., p. 232.

9. Donald Winnicott, *Home Is Where We Start From* (New York: W. W. Norton & Company, 1986), p. 143.

10. Ibid.

11. Ibid.

12. D.W. Winnicott, *Human Nature* (New York: Schocken Books, 1988), p. 80.

13. Mario Jacoby, *Shame and the Origins of Self-Esteem* (New York: Routledge, 1994), p. 59.

14. Donald Winnicott, "Ego Distortion in Terms of True and False Self." In *Maturational Processes* (Madison: International Universities Press, Inc., 1965), p. 150.

15. This example is taken from Lynd, *On Shame,* p. 36.

16. Shaye J.D. Cohen, *From Macabees to the Midrash* (Philadelphia: Westminster Press, 1987), p. 149.

17. See Neill Elliot, *Liberating Paul: The Justice of God and the Politics of the Apostle* (Marynoll, NY: Orbis Books, 1994), p. 67.

18. Erik Erikson, *Young Man Luther* (New York: W. W. Norton, 1958), p. 257.

19. Quoted in Martin Hengel, *Crucifixion in the Ancient Word and the Folly of the Message of the Cross* (Philadelphia: Fortress Press, 1977), pp. 4-5.

20. Ibid.

21. Ibid., p. 22.

22. *Apology I, 13.4,* quoted by Hengel, *Crucifixion,* p. 1.

23. Quoted by Hengel, *Crucxifixion,* p. 21.

24. Carl Schneider, *Shame, Exposure and Privacy* (Boston: Beacon Press, 1977), p. xv.

25. Gershen Kaufman, *Shame: The Power of Caring* (Rochester, VT: Schenkman Books, Inc., 1992), pp. xx-xxi.

26. Lynd, *On Shame,* p. 32.

27. Ibid., p. 20.

28. Schneider, *Shame, Exposure and Privacy,* p. 25.

Chapter 5

1. John Patton, *Is Human Forgiveness Possible?* (Nashville: Abingdon Press, 1985), p. 13.

2. Jane Middelton-Moz, *Shame and Guilt: Masters of Disguise* (Deerfield Beach, FL: Health Communications, Inc., 1990), p. 55.

3. Ibid.

4. Michael Lewis, *Shame: The Exposed Self* (New York: The Free Press, 1992), pp. 149-153.

5. Helen Block Lewis, *Shame and Guilt in Neurosis* (New York: International Universities Press, 1971), p. 58.

6. Ana M. Alaya, "Ex-Boyfriend Tells Jury He Blacked Out Before Slaying," *The Star Ledger,* October 17, 2001, p. 15 (Newark, NJ).

7. Heinz Kohut, "Thoughts on Narcissism and Narcissistic Rage," *The Psychoanalytic Study of the Child,* Volume 27 (New York: International Universities Press, 1972), pp. 360-399, 386.

8. James Gilligan, *Violence: Reflections on a National Epidemic* (New York: Random House, 1996), pp. 47-48; 66-67.

9. See Frederick Turner, *Beauty: The Value of Values* (Charlottesville, VA: University Press of Virginia, 1991), p. 17.

10. John Patton, *Is Human Forgiveness Possible?* (Nashville: Abingdon Press, 1985), p. 75.

11. Ibid.

12. Gershen Kaufman, *Shame: The Power of Caring* (Rochester, VT: Schenkman Books, Inc., 1992), p. 85, quoted by Patton, *Is Human Forgiveness Possible?*, p. 75.

13. Patton, *Is Human Forgiveness Possible?* p. 77, quoting Rollo May, *Power and Innocence* (New York: W. W. Norton & Company, 1972), pp. 95, 97.

14. Leon Wurmser, *The Mask of Shame* (Northvale, NJ: Jason Aronson, Inc., 1995), p. 260.

15. Eugene Kennedy, *The Unhealed Wound: The Church and Human Sexuality* (New York: St. Martin's Griffin, 2001).

16. Ibid., p. 165.

17. Patton, *Is Human Forgiveness Possible?*, p. 14.

18. Sandra Edelman, *Turning the Gorgon: A Meditation on Shame* (Woodstock, CT: Spring Publications, 1998), p. 32.

19. See Eugene Kennedy, *The Unhealed Wound.*

20. Edelman, *Turning the Gorgon,* p. 100.

21. Martha Nussbaum, *Upheavals of Thought* (Cambridge: Cambridge University Press, 2001), p. 197.

22. Kaufman, *Shame: The Power of Caring,* p. 87.

23. Edelman, *Turning the Gorgon,* p. 32.

24. Sigmund Freud, "Mourning and Melancholia," *The Standard Edition of the Complete Psychological Works of Sigmund Freud,* Volume 14, pp. 243-258. Original work published 1917.

25. Kaufman, *Shame: The Power of Caring,* p. 93.

26. Andrew Morrison, *Shame: The Underside of Narcissism* (Hillsdale, NJ: Analytic Press, 1989), pp. 107 *ff.*

27. Melanie Klein, "Envy and Gratitude," in *Envy and Gratitude and Other Works* (New York: Free Press, 1975), pp. 186-235.

28. Ann Belford Ulanov, *Cinderella and Her Sisters* (Philadelphia: Westminster Press, 1983), pp. 30-31.

29. Andrew Morrison, *Shame: The Underside of Narcissism,* pp. 108-109.

Chapter 6

1. Morton Kelsey, *The Other Side of Silence: Meditation for the Twenty-First Century* (New York: Paulist Press, 1997), pp. 13-14.

2. *Book of Common Prayer* (New York: Church Publishing Company, 1979), p. 531.

3. Ann Belford Ulanov, "Clinical Encounters with the Spirit," Union Theological Seminary, New York, 1998, unpublished.

4. Kathleen O'Connor, "What Is Our Present?" In Diane Jonte-Pace and William B. Parsons (Eds.), *Religion and Psychology: Mapping the Terrain* (New York: Routledge Press, 2000), p. 83.

5. April Greiman, *The Fusion of Technology and Graphic Design* (New York: Watson-Guptill Publishing, 1990), p. 41.

6. See Mary Ruberry, "Introduction," *3-D Bible Stories* (Newport Beach, CA: 3-D Revelations Publishing, 1994).

7. Gospel of Thomas 45:30-33, from Elaine Pagels, *The Gnostic Gospels* (New York: Random House, 1979), p. 126.

8. Gospel of Thomas 32:14-19, from Pagels, *The Gnostic Gospels,* p. 127.

9. Teresa of Avila, *The Life of Teresa of Jesus* (New York: Doubleday Books, 1991), p. 145.

10. Curtis Hart, "Anton Boisen: Madness, Mental Health and Ministry," in S. Severino and R. Liew (Eds.), *Pastoral Care and the Mentally Disabled* (Binghamton, NY: The Haworth Press, Inc., 1994), pp. 49-65.

11. Anton Boisen, *Out of the Depths* (New York: Harper & Brothers, 1960), pp. 196-197.

12. Ibid.

13. In fact, in his autobiography Boisen relates that his parents were so alarmed with his early signs of "sex organ excitement" that he was circumcised at the age of four. This did not help, however, because (again according to Boisen) "the trouble lay in a more than average interest in matters eliminative and sexual" (Ibid., p. 24).

14. Anton Boisen, *Exploration of the Inner World* (New York: Harper & Brothers, 1936), p. 1.

15. Ibid., p. 60.

16. Ibid.

17. Daniel Day Williams, *The Minister and the Care of Souls* (New York: Harper & Brothers, 1961), p. 27.

18. Boisen, *Out of the Depths,* p. 9.

19. Boisen, *Exploration of the Inner World,* p. 222.

20. For a coherent summary of the history of religious, scientific, and pseudoscientific developments presaging the work of Sigmund Freud, see Henri F. Ellenberger, *The Discovery of the Unconscious* (New York: Basic Books, 1970), pp. 3-417.

21. Richard Tarnas, *The Passion of the Western Mind* (New York: Ballantine Books, 1991), p. 328.

22. Daniel Day Williams, *The Minister and the Care of Souls,* p. 13.

23. Ibid., p. 21.

24. Ibid., p. 118.

25. Ana Maria Rizzuto, *The Birth of the Living God* (Chicago: University of Chicago Press, 1979), p. 7.

26. O'Connor, "What Is Our Present," p. 75.

27. Ibid., p. 83.

28. Ibid., pp. 83-84.

29. Sigmund Freud, "New Introductory Lectures on Psychoanalysis," in *The Standard Edition of the Complete Psychological Works of Sigmund Freud,* Volume 22 (1933), p. 95.

30. See Ann Belford Ulanov, "Mending the Mind and Minding the Soul: Explorations Towards the Cure of the Whole Person," *Journal of Religion in Disability and Rehabilitation* 1(2) (1994), 85-101.

31. Ellenberger, *The Discovery of the Unconscious,* pp. 3-48; Otto Rank, *Psychology and the Soul,* trans. Gregory Richter and E. James Lieberman (Baltimore: The Johns Hopkins University Press, 1998 [1930]), p. 1. Daniel Day Williams preferred "care of souls." So do I.

32. Gordon Allport, *The Individual and His Religion* (New York: MacMillan Publishing Co., Inc., 1950), p. 88.

33. Stanislov Grof, *Beyond the Brain* (Albany: State University of New York Press, 1985), p. 331.

34. Allport, *The Individual and His Religion,* pp. 1-2.

35. See discussions in Ann Belford Ulanov's works, *Religion and the Spiritual in Carl G. Jung* (Mahwah, NJ: Paulist Press, 1999); and *The Feminine in Jungian Psychology and in Christian Theology* (Evanston, IL: Northwestern University Press, 1971), pp. 85 *ff.*

36. Carl Jung, "Introduction to the Religious and Psychological Problems of Alchemy," in R.F.C. Hull (Ed. and Trans.) *Collected Works of C.G. Jung,* Volume 12 (Princeton, NJ: Princeton University Press, 1953), p. 13, para. 14. (Original work published in 1944.)

37. Ibid., p. 10, para. 11.

38. See, e.g., Meister Eckhart, who believed that the soul was "the tabernacle" or "castle" of "the spark" of God, the "Grund" or core of it. This spark is, according to the proposition of Eckhart's which was condemned by the medieval church in 1329, something in the soul that is uncreatable as well as uncreated: "To find union with God, one has merely to incarcerate himself in this fortress of the soul," R. Petry, *Late Medieval Mysticism* (London: SCM Press, Ltd., 1957), p. 173. See generally D. Carmody and J. Tully, *Mysticism: Holiness East and West* (New York: Oxford University Press, 1996).

39. Other translations say, "The Kingdom of God is *among* you." See *Harper Collins Study Bible, New Revised Standard Version* (New York: HarperCollins, 1989), p. 1989, which uses "among" but states in a footnote that "within" is an alternate translation.

40. See Carmody and Tully, *Mysticism,* p. 10.

41. See generally Ann Belford Ulanov, *The Functioning Transcendent* (Wilmette, IL: Chiron Publications, 1996).

42. Williams, *The Minister,* p. 27.

43. Wayne Rollins, lecture, November 19, 2001, American Academy of Religion, Denver, Colorado.

44. D. Andrew Kille, *Psychological Biblical Criticism* (Minneapolis: Fortress Press, 2001).

45. Paul Tillich, "The Theological Significance of Existentialism and Psychoanalysis." In J. Heaney, ed., *Psyche and Spirit* (Ramsey, NJ: Paulist Press, 1973), p. 264. Paul Ricoeur (1970) saw it as necessary to avoid a false dialectic between spirit and psyche: "The only way to avoid this caricature of dialectic is to show in each discipline of thought, considered in and for itself, the presence of the other. These two contrary disciplines are not external opposites but are intrinsically inter-

related." (*Freud and Philosophy,* trans. David Savage, New Haven, CT: Yale University Press), pp. 468-469.

46. Ernest Becker, *Denial of Death* (New York: Free Press Paperbacks, 1973), p. 275.

47. Ann Ulanov and Barry Ulanov, *Religion and the Unconscious* (Philadelphia: Westminster Press, 1975), p. 13.

48. Ibid.

49. Ibid.

50. Ibid.

51. Ann Ulanov, "Clinical Encounters with the Spirit."

52. Augustine, *Confessions,* trans. Harry Chadwick (Oxford: Oxford University Press, 1991), p. 3.

53. Ricoeur, *Freud and Philosophy,* p. 525.

54. Julian of Norwich, *Showings* (Mahwah, NJ: Paulist Press, 1978), p. 296.

55. Erich Fromm, *Psychoanalysis and Religion* (New Haven, CT: Yale University Press, 1950), p. 25.

56. John McDargh, *Psychoanalytic Object Relations Theory and the Study of Religion* (New York: University Press of America, 1983), p. xv.

57. Ibid.

58. Moshe Halevi Spero, *Religious Objects As Psychological Structures* (Chicago: University of Chicago Press, 1992), p. 30.

59. Allport, *The Individual and His Religion,* p. 10.

60. Paul Pruyser, "Religion in a Psychiatric Hospital: A Reassessment." In H. Maloney and B. Spilka (Eds.), *Religion in Psychodynamic Perspective* (New York: Oxford University Press, 1991), p. 97.

61. Deborah van Deusen Hunsinger, *Theology and Pastoral Counseling: A New Interdisciplinary Approach* (Grand Rapids, MI: William B. Eerdmans Publishing Company, 1995), p. 14.

62. Paul Pruyser, *The Minister As Diagnostician* (Philadelphia, PA: The Westminster Press, 1976), p. 85.

63. Margaret Kornfeld, *Cultivating Wholeness* (New York: Continuum, 1998), p. 103.

64. Allport, *The Individual and His Religion,* pp. 91-92.

65. Ibid.

66. Edward Wimberly, *Moving from Shame to Self-Worth* (Nashville: Abingdon, 1999), p. 18.

67. Williams, *The Minister,* pp. 100-101.

Chapter 7

1. Sigmund Freud, "Draft K, The Neuroses of Defense," in *The Standard Edition of the Complete Psychological Works of Sigmund Freud,* Volume 1 (London: Hogarth Press), pp. 224-225. Original work published 1894; "The Neuro-Psychoses of Defense," in *The Standard Edition of the Complete Psychological Works of Sigmund Freud,* Volume 3 (London: Hogarth Press), p. 171 ("*self-reproach* [for having carried out the sexual act in childhood] can easily turn into *shame* [in case someone else should find out about it]"). Original work published 1894.

2. Sigmund Freud, "Extracts from the Fleiss Papers," in *The Standard Edition of the Complete Psychological Works of Sigmund Freud,* Volume 1 (London: Hogarth Press), p. 258. Original work published 1896; "Interpretation of Dreams," in *The Standard Edition of the Complete Psychological Works of Sigmund Freud,* Volume 4 (London: Hogarth Press), pp. 238, 242. Original work published 1900.

3. Freud, "Neuro-Psychoses of Defense," p. 178.

4. Sigmund Freud, "Leonardo Da Vinci," in *The Standard Edition of the Complete Psychological Works of Sigmund Freud,* Volume 11 (London: Hogarth Press), p. 96. Original work published 1910.

5. *Cassell's German Dictionary* (New York: McMillan Publishing Company, 1978), p. 519.

6. Sigmund Freud, "Civilization and Its Discontents," in *The Standard Edition of the Complete Psychological Works of Sigmund Freud,* Volume 21 (London: Hogarth Press), p. 99. Original work published 1930.

7. Sigmund Freud, "The Psychopathology of Everyday Life," in *The Standard Edition of the Complete Psychological Works of Sigmund Freud,* Volume 6 (London: Hogarth Press), p. 83. Original work published 1901.

8. Freud, "Extracts from the Fleiss Papers," p. 268, original work published 1950; Freud, "Psychotherapy of Hysteria," in *The Standard Edition of the Complete Psychological Works of Sigmund Freud,* Volume 2 (London: Hogarth Press), p. 269. Original work published 1895; Freud, "Three Essays on Sexuality," in *The Standard Edition of the Complete Psychological Works of Sigmund Freud,* Volume 7 (London: Hogarth Press), pp. 161, 164, 219, 231. Original work published 1950; Freud, "Jokes and the Unconscious," in *The Standard Edition of the Complete Psychological Works of Sigmund Freud,* Volume 8 (London: Hogarth Press), pp. 97, 101, 133. Original work published 1905; Freud, "An Autobiographical Study," in *The Standard Edition of the Complete Psychological Works of Sigmund Freud,* Volume 20 (London: Hogarth Press), pp. 37, 211. Original work published 1925.

9. Freud, "Extracts from the Fleiss Papers," p. 270; Freud, "Three Essays on Sexuality," pp. 219, 231. See discussion in Andrew Morrison, "Shame, Ideal Self and Narcissism," in *Essential Papers on Narcissism* (New York: New York University Press, 1986), pp. 348, 349.

10. Freud, "New Introductory Lectures on Psychoanalysis," in *The Standard Edition of the Complete Psychological Works of Sigmund Freud,* Volume 22 (London: Hogarth Press), p. 132.

11. Freud, "Totem and Taboo," in *The Standard Edition of the Complete Psychological Works of Sigmund Freud,* Volume 13 (London: Hogarth Press). Original work published 1913.

12. Freud, "Civilization and Its Discontents," in *The Standard Edition of the Complete Psychological Works of Sigmund Freud,* Volume 21 (London: Hogarth Press), p. 132. Original work published 1930.

13. Michael Lewis, *Shame: The Exposed Self* (New York: The Free Press, 1992), p. 60.

14. Helen Block Lewis, *Shame and Guilt in Neurosis* (New York: International Universities Press, 1971), p. 100.

15. Morrison, "Shame, Ideal Self and Narcissism," p. 349.

16. See Heinz L. Ansbacher and Rowena R. Ansbacher, *The Individual Psychology of Alfred Adler* (New York: Harper & Row, 1956), pp. 23, 258. See discussion of

Adler's use of the word *shame* in Peer Hultberg's "Shame: A Hidden Emotion," *Journal of Analytical Psychology* 33 (1988): 112.

17. Sigmund Freud, "Mourning and Melancholia," *The Standard Edition of the Complete Psychological Works of Sigmund Freud,* Volume 14 (London: Hogarth Press, 1917), p. 244.

18. Ibid., p. 245.

19. Ibid., p. 246.

20. Ibid., p. 257.

21. Ibid., p. 249.

22. Ibid., pp. 249-250.

23. Ibid., p. 251.

24. Andrew Morrison, *Shame: The Underside of Narcissim* (Hillsdale, NJ: Analytic Press, 1989), p. 113.

25. Sigmund Freud, "Outline of Psychoanalysis," *The Standard Edition of the Complete Psychological Works of Sigmund Freud,* Volume 23 (London: Hogarth Press), p. 150. Original work published 1938.

26. See Lewis, *Shame and Guilt in Neurosis,* pp. 394, 431.

27. Morrison, "Shame, Ideal Self and Narcissism," p. 352.

28. Sigmund Freud, "On Narcissism," *The Standard Edition of the Complete Psychological Works of Sigmund Freud,* Volume 14 (London: Hogarth Press), p. 95. Original work published 1914.

29. Morrison, "Shame, Ideal Self and Narcissism," p. 352.

30. Lewis, *Shame and Guilt in Neurosis,* p. 37.

31. Karen Horney, *Neurosis and Human Growth* (New York: W. W. Norton & Company, 1950), p. 111.

32. Ibid., p. 38.

33. Ibid., pp. 41 *ff.*

34. Ibid., p. 194.

35. Ibid., p. 196.

36. Ibid., p. 198.

37. Ibid., p. 215.

38. Ibid., p. 231.

39. Ibid., p. 286.

40. Ibid., p. 286.

41. William James, *Varieties of Religious Experience,* ed. with Introduction by Martin Marty (New York: Penguin Books, 1982), p. 508.

42. Alice Miller, *For Your Own Good: Hidden Cruelty in Child-Rearing and the Roots of Violence* (New York: Farrar, Straus, Giroux, 1990), pp. 3 *ff.*

43. Ibid., p. 59.

44. Alice Miller, *The Drama of the Gifted Child* (New York: Basic Books, 1997), p. 2.

45. Ibid., p. 73.

46. Lewis, *Shame: The Exposed Self,* p. 72.

47. Miller, *The Drama of the Gifted Child,* p. 14.

48. Quoted in Stephen Pattison, *Shame: Theory, Therapy, Theology* (Cambridge: Cambridge University Press, 2000), p. 48.

49. Heinz Kohut and Ernest S. Wolf, "The Disorders of the Self and Their Treatment: An Outline," in *Essential Papers on Narcissism,* ed. Andrew P. Morrison (New York: New York University Press, 1986), p. 178.

50. Donald Capps, *The Depleted Self* (Minneapolis: Fortress Press, 1993), p. 31.

51. Ibid., p. 31.

52. Ibid., p. 33.

53. Capps, *The Depleted Self;* Heinz Kohut, *Restoration of the Self* (New York: International Universities Press, 1977), pp. 206-207, 224-225.

54. Capps, *The Depleted Self,* p. 33.

55. Heinz Kohut, *The Analysis of the Self* (New York: International Universities Press, 1971), p. 20.

56. Heinz Kohut, "Forms and Transformations of Narcissism," *The Search for the Self,* Volume 1, ed. Paul Ornstein (New York: International Universities Press, 1978), p. 427.

57. Kohut, "Forms and Transformations of Narcissism," p. 432.

58. Ibid., p. 433.

59. Allen M. Siegel, *Heinz Kohut and the Psychology of the Self* (London: Routledge, 1996), p. 71.

60. See, e.g., Lisa Cataldo, "Jesus As Transforming Selfobject: Kohution Theory and the Life of St. Francis of Assissi," presented at the American Academy of Religion, Person Culture and Religion Section, Denver, Colorado, November 20, 2001. In this paper, Cataldo argues that St. Francis effectively used Jesus as a perfect idealized object to undergo a transmuting internalization which transformed him from a callow youth to a spiritual giant.

61. Kohut, *The Analysis of the Self,* p. 9.

62. Siegel, *Heinz Kohut,* p. 61.

63. Kohut, "Forms and Transformations of Narcissism," p. 439.

64. Kohut, *The Search for the Self,* Volume 2, p. 655.

65. Thandeka, "White Racial Induction and Christian Shame Theology." In *Gender and Psychoanalysis* 4(Fall 1999): 461.

66. Siegel, *Heinz Kohut,* p. 61.

67. Ibid., pp. 61-62, quoting "Forms and Transformations of Narcissism."

68. Andrew D. Morrison, *The Culture of Shame* (Northvale, NJ: Jason Aronson, Inc., 1998), p. 206, n. 3.

69. Kohut, *The Analysis of the Self,* p. 116.

70. Siegel, *Heinz Kohut,* pp. 91-92.

71. Ibid., p. 92.

72. Paul Ornstein (Ed.), *The Search for the Self, Selected Writings of Heinz Kohut,* Volume 1 (New York: International Universities Press, 1978), p. 69.

73. Ibid.

74. Siegel, *Heinz Kohut,* p. 61.

75. Kohut, "Forms and Transformations of Narcissism," p. 440.

76. Ibid., p. 441.

77. Mara Sidoli, "Shame and the Shadow," *Journal of Analytical Psychology* 33 (1988): 128.

78. Ornstein (Ed.), *The Search for Self,* p. 69.

79. See Gershen Kaufman, *Shame: The Power of Caring* (Rochester, VT: Schenkman Books, Inc., 1992), p. 69.

80. Pattison, *Shame,* p. 86.

81. Kohut, *The Analysis of the Self,* p. 185.

82. Siegal, *Heinz Kohut,* p. 94.

83. Ibid., p. 4.

84. Ibid., p. 165.

85. Ibid.

86. Ibid.

87. Ibid.

88. Ibid., p. 64.

89. Sandra Edelman, *Turning the Gorgon: A Meditation on Shame* (Woodstock, CT: Spring Publications, 1998), p. 31.

90. Morrison, *Shame: The Underside of Narcissism,* p. 57.

91. Kaufman, *Shame: The Power of Caring,* p. 77.

92. Morrison, *Shame: The Underside of Narcissism,* p. 78.

93. Ibid.

94. Ibid., p. 79.

95. Ibid.

96. See Siegel, *Heinz Kohut,* p. 8.

97. Kohut, "Forms and Transformations of Narcissism," pp. 446-447.

98. Ibid., p. 447.

99. Ibid., p. 449.

100. Ibid., pp. 449-450.

101. Ibid., p. 448.

102. Ibid., p. 450.

103. Ibid., p. 451.

104. Ibid., p. 453.

105. Ibid., p. 455.

106. Ibid., pp. 455-456.

107. Ibid. See William B. Parsons, *The Enigma of the Oceanic Feeling* (New York: Oxford University Press, 1999), which contains a brilliant discussion of Kohut's conception of cosmic narcissism, characterized by Parsons as "the religious-ethical goal of his psychology," p. 163.

108. Kohut, "Forms and Transformations of Narcissism," p. 458.

109. Ibid.

110. Ibid.

111. Ibid., p. 459.

112. Carl Jung, *Collected Works,* Volume 20, trans. R. F. C. Hull (Princeton: Princeton University Press, 1966), p. 614.

113. Peer Hultberg, "Shame: A Hidden Emotion," *Journal of Analytical Psychology* 33 (1988): 109-110.

114. Ibid., p. 117.

115. Ibid., p. 115.

116. Sidoli, "Shame and the Shadow," p. 131.

117. Edelman, *Turning the Gorgon,* pp. 21-22, quoting Jung, "Aion," in *Collected Works,* 1959, Volume 9ii, pp. 8-9.

118. See discussion in Mario Jacoby's *Shame and the Origins of Self-Esteem* (New York: Routledge, 1991), pp. 16-20.

119. Edelman, *Turning the Gorgon,* p. 68.

120. Ibid.

121. Ibid.

122. Ibid., p. 35.

123. Ibid., quoting Gershen Kaufman, *The Psychology of Shame: Theory and Treatment of Shame-Based Syndromes,* Revised Edition (New York: Springer, 1996), p. 5, and Hultberg, "Shame: A Hidden Emotion," p. 116.

124. Ibid., quoting Leon Wurmser, *The Mask of Shame* (Northvale, NJ: Jason Aronson, Inc., 1997), p. 83.

125. Lewis, *Shame and Guilt in Neurosis,* p. 41.

126. Edelman, *Turning the Gorgon,* pp. 35-36, quoting Rudolph Otto, *The Idea of the Holy,* trans John W. Harvey (London: Oxford University Press, 1923), p. 13.

127. Ibid., p. 76, quoting Paul Pruyser, *A Dynamic Psychology of Religion* (New York: Harper & Row, 1968), p. 336.

128. Ibid.

129. Paul Ricoeur, *The Symbolism of Evil,* trans. Emerson Buchanan (Boston: Beacon Press, 1967), p. 43.

130. Edelman, *Turning the Gorgon,* p. 98, quoting Otto, *The Idea of the Holy,* p. 124.

131. Edelman, *Turning the Gorgon,* p. 98.

132. Ibid., p. 39.

133. Ibid.

134. Ibid., p. 40.

135. Ibid, p. 38.

136. Ibid., p. 47.

137. Ibid., p. 58.

138. Ibid.

139. Ibid., p. 61.

140. Ibid., p. 63.

141. Ibid., p. 87, quoting Kohut, *The Restoration of the Self,* p. 189.

142. Edelman, *Turning the Gorgon,* p. 87.

143. Robin Briggs, *Witches and Neighbors* (New York: Penguin Books, 1996), p. 384.

144. Edelman, *Turning the Gorgon,* p. 99, quoting D. W. Winnicott, *From Pediatrics to Psychoanalysis* (New York: Basic Books, 1975), pp. 303-304.

145. See D.W. Winnicott, "The Concept of Trauma," in Clare Winnicott, Ray Shepherd, and Madelaine Davis (Eds.), *Psychoanalytic Explorations* (Cambridge, MA: Harvard University Press, 1989), p. 139; "Fear of Breakdown," in Clare Winnicott, Ray Shepherd, and Madelaine Davis (Eds.), *Psychoanalytic Explorations* (Cambridge, MA: Harvard University Press, 1989), p. 90.

146. Heinz Kohut, *How Does Analysis Cure?* (Chicago: University of Chicago Press, 1984), p. 16.

147. Ibid.

Chapter 8

1. Dietrich Bonhoeffer, *Ethics* (New York: MacMillan Company, 1955), p. 23.

2. Jean-Paul Sartre, *Being and Nothingness* (New York: Washington Square Press, 1984), p. 302.

3. Ibid., p. 350.

4. Ibid., p. 301.

5. Ibid., p. 302.

6. *Book of Common Prayer* (New York: Church Hymnal Corporation, 1979), p. 355.

7. Carl Schneider, *Shame, Exposure and Privacy* (Boston: Beacon Press, 1977), p. 130.

8. Ibid., p. 131.

9. Ibid., p. 131, quoting Sartre's *Being and Nothingness,* p. 222.

10. Ibid., quoting *Being and Nothingness,* p. 410.

11. Ibid., p. 132, quoting *Being and Nothingness,* p. 290.

12. Helen Block Lewis, *Shame and Guilt in Neurosis* (New York: International Universities Press, 1971), pp. 24-25.

13. Ibid., p. 25.

14. Erik Erikson, *Young Man Luther* (New York: W. W. Norton & Company, 1958), p. 256.

15. Ibid., quoting Luther, p. 256.

16. Schneider, *Shame, Exposure and Privacy,* p. 133.

17. Ibid., quoting C.S. Lewis, *They Asked for a Paper* (London: Geoffrey Bles, 1962), p. 134.

18. Ibid., p. 135.

19. Paul Tillich, *Shaking the Foundations* (New York: Charles Scribner's Sons, 1948), p. 40.

20. Ibid., p. 42.

21. William James, *The Varieties of Religious Experience,* ed. with Introduction by Martin Marty (New York: Penguin Books, 1985), p. 508.

22. Ibid., p. 87.

23. Ibid., p. 127.

24. Ibid., pp. 139-140.

25. Julius Rubin, *Religious Melancholy and Protestant Experience in America* (New York: Oxford University Press, 1994), p. 199.

26. James, *The Varieties of Religious Experience,* p. 91.

27. Ibid., p. 163.

28. Rubin, *Religious Melancholy,* p. 198.

29. James, *The Varieties of Religious Experience,* pp. 170-171.

30. See generally Mario Jacoby, *Shame and the Origins of Self-Esteem: A Jungian Approach* (New York: Routledge Press, 1994), and Sandra Edelman, *Turning the Gorgon: A Meditation on Shame* (Woodstock, CT: Spring Publications, 1998), both written from a Jungian perspective and both containing lengthy expositions regarding the archetypal nature of shame.

31. Eric Heller, "Man Ashamed," *Encounter* 42:2 (February 1974): 23-30, quoted in Schneider, *Shame, Exposure and Privacy,* p. xiii.

32. Paul Tillich, *Systematic Theology,* Volume II (Chicago: University of Chicago Press, 1957), p. 35.

33. Ernest Becker, *The Denial of Death* (New York: Free Press Paperbacks, 1973), p. 26.

34. Rudolph Otto, *The Idea of the Holy,* trans. John W. Harvey (London: Oxford University Press, 1928), p. 51.

35. Gershen Kaufman, *Shame: The Power of Caring* (Rochester, VT: Schenkman Books, Inc., 1992), p. 196.

36. Jacoby, *Shame,* p. 19.

37. Bonhoeffer, *Ethics,* p. 20.

38. Ibid., p. 21.

39. Ibid., p. 20.

40. Ibid.

41. Dacher Keltner and Lee Anne Harker, "The Forms and Functions of the Nonverbal Signal of Shame," in Paul Gilbert and Bernice Andrews (Eds.), *Shame: Interpersonal Behavior, Psychopatholgy and Culture* (New York: Oxford University Press, 1998), p. 78.

42. Peer Hultberg, "Shame: A Hidden Emotion," *Journal of Analytical Psychology* 33 (1988): 117; Jacoby, *Shame,* p. 22.

43. Hultberg, "Shame," p. 112, quoting Alfred Adler, *Understanding Human Nature* (New York: Greenberg, 1971), p. 225.

44. Kaufman, *Shame: The Power of Caring,* pp. 56, 60.

45. Ibid., p. 61.

46. Lewis, *Shame and Guilt in Neurosis,* pp. 31-32.

47. Schneider, *Shame, Exposure and Privacy.*

48. Ibid., p. 22.

49. Ibid.

50. Jacoby, *Shame,* p. 21.

51. Ibid., p. 22.

52. Vicki Underland-Rosow, *Shame: Spiritual Suicide* (Shorewood, MN: Waterford Publications, 1995), p. 52.

53. Leon Wurmser, *The Mask of Shame* (Northvale, NJ: Jason Aronson, Inc., 1997), p. 65.

54. Ibid., pp. 65-66.

55. Bonhoeffer, *Ethics,* pp. 22-23.

56. Erich Fromm, *Escape from Freedom* (New York: Avon Books, 1941), p. 39.

57. Ibid., p. 40.

58. Donald Capps, *The Depleted Self: Sin in a Narcissistic Age* (Minneapolis: Fortress Press, 1993), p. 35.

59. Stephen Pattison, *Shame: Theory, Therapy, Theology* (Cambridge, England: Cambridge University Press, 2000), p. 204. The "Aaronic blessing" refers to Numbers 6:24.

60. James, *The Varieties of Religious Experience,* p. 419.

61. Ibid., p. 508.

62. Ibid., p. 509.

63. Ibid., p. 515.

64. Ibid., p. 485.

65. Ibid., p. 66.

66. Erich Fromm, *Psychoanalysis and Religion* (New Haven: Yale University Press, 1950), p. 95.

67. Ibid.

68. Teresa of Avila, *The Interior Castle.* Classics of Western Spirituality Series (Mahwah, NJ: Paulist Press, 1979), pp. 86-87.

69. Teresa of Avila, *The Life of Teresa of Jesus,* trans. E. Allison Peers (New York: Doubleday, 1991), p. 96. Originally written 1565.

70. Ibid., p. 215.

71. James, *The Varieties of Religious Experience,* p. 102.

72. See Karen Armstrong, *Buddha* (New York: Penguin, 2001), pp. 90-92.

73. Sigmund Freud, "The Future of Illusion," *The Standard Edition of the Complete Psychological Works of Sigmund Freud,* Volume 21 (London: Hogarth Press), pp. 5-56.

74. Michael Palmer, *Freud and Jung on Religion* (New York: Routledge, 1997), p. 34.

75. Ibid., p. 35.

76. This letter (as well as all of the other extant Freud-Rolland correspondence) is contained in full in William B. Parsons, *The Enigma of the Oceanic Feeling* (New York: Oxford University Press, 1999), pp. 173-174.

77. It was Freud who had initiated the acquaintance with Rolland. Parsons (1999) asserts that there was a bond of "mutual respect, admiration and love" between the two men, although they met only once (p. 20). For Freud, Rolland was an "ethical exemplar whose internationalist and pacifistic stands influenced" him, and Rolland also touched Freud "on a deeply personal level: through Freud's racial and cultural status as a Jew" (p. 23).

78. Sigmund Freud, "Civilization and Its Discontents," *Standard Edition of the Complete Psychological Works of Sigmund Freud,* Volume 21 (London: Hogarth Press), pp. 64-145.

79. Another religious person that Freud respected and with whom he maintained a long-standing correspondence was Oscar Pfister, a Lutheran pastor who endeavored to apply principles of Freudian psychoanalysis in his ministry. For an informative discussion of that relationship and quotations from some of the correspondence, see W. W. Meissner's *Psychoanalysis and Religious Experience* (New Haven, CT: Yale University Press, 1984), pp. 73-103. Freud once wrote to Pfister that psychoanalysis should be "a profession of *lay* curers of souls who need not be doctors and should not be priests," p. 100.

80. *Person, Culture and Religion Group of the American Academy of Religion* "Mission Statement," as quoted from *PCR News, Annual Meeting 2000.*

81. Freud, "Civilization," p. 68.

82. Ibid., p. 66.

83. Ibid., p. 72.

84. Parsons, *Enigma,* p. 172, Freud's letter to Rolland of January 29, 1926.

85. Ibid., p. 42.

86. Ibid.

87. There is, indeed, good reason to believe that Freud himself knew better. Parsons points out that elsewhere in "Civilization and Its Discontents," Freud states, "In my *Future of an Illusion* I was concerned much less with the deepest sources of the religious feeling than with what the common-man understands by his religion— with the system of doctrine and promises which on the one hand explains to him the riddles of the world with enviable completeness, and, on the other, reassures him that a careful providence will watch over his life and will compensate him in a future existence for any frustrations he suffers here." Parsons, *Enigma,* pp. 42-43, quoting from "Civilization and Its Discontents." Furthermore, Freud's "last known reference" to religion was contained in the following note written a month before his death: "Mysticism is the obscure self-perception of the realm outside the ego, of the id." Ana Maria Rizzuto, *Why Did Freud Reject God?* (New Haven: Yale University

Press, 1998), p. 155, quoting "Findings, Ideas, Problems," in *The Standard Edition of the Complete Psychological Works of Sigmund Freud,* Volume 23 (London: Hogarth Press), p. 300.

88. Parsons, *Enigma,* p. 70.

89. Ibid., p. 92.

90. Taken from Philip Novak's, *The World's Wisdom* (San Francisco: Harper-SanFrancisco, 1994), pp. 9-10.

91. Parsons, *Enigma,* p. 92.

92. Jonathan Lear, *Love and Its Place in Nature* (New York: Farrar Straus & Giroux, 1990), pp. 136-137.

93. Parsons, *Enigma,* p. 57.

94. In a 1926 lecture given by Otto Rank, he "criticized Freud for being unable to 'see' beyond the Oedipus situation to the 'primal object relationship.'" Robert Kramer, *A Psychology of Difference* (Princeton, NJ: Princeton University Press, 1996), p. 37.

95. Parsons, *Enigma,* p. 68.

96. Ibid.

97. Ibid., p. 70.

98. D.W. Winnicott, *Human Nature* (Levittown, PA: Brunner/Mazel, 1988), p. 157.

99. Otto Rank, *The Trauma of Birth* (New York: Dover Publications, Inc., 1993).

100. Ibid., p. 6.

101. Ibid., p. 4. Sandor Ferenczi, a close colleague of Rank's who was also a part of Freud's original inner circle, also broke with Freud at a later date in emphasizing the trauma of birth in human development and arguing that the longing to reunite with the mother remains with the individual throughout life. He compared the developmental process to phylogenesis: breaking out of the mother's body corresponds to being cast out of the primal sea. See Gyorgy Vikar, "The Budapest School of Psychoanalysis," in Peter L. Rudnytsky, Antal Bokay, and Patrizia Giampieri-Deutsch (Eds.), *Ferenczi's Turn in Psychoanalysis* (New York: New York University Press, 1996), p. 168.

102. Robert Kramer, *A Psychology of Difference* (Princeton: Princeton University Press, 1996), p. 4, quoting from one of Rank's American lectures.

103. Kramer, *A Psychology of Difference,* citing Otto Rank's *Art and Artist: Creative Urge and Personality Development,* trans. Charles Francis Atkinson (New York: W. W. Norton & Company, 1989), p. 175.

104. Kramer, *A Psychology of Difference,* p. 3.

105. Rank, *Trauma of Birth,* pp. 18-19.

106. Otto Rank, *Will Therapy* (New York: Alfred A. Knopf, 1929).

107. E. James Lieberman, *Acts of Will: The Life and Work of Otto Rank* (Amherst, MA: University of Massachusetts Press, 1985), p. 302.

108. Heinz Kohut, "Forms and Transformations of Narcissism," in Paul Ornstein (Ed.), *The Search for the Self,* Volume 1 (New York: International Universities Press, 1978) p. 459.

109. Rank, *Will Therapy,* p. 124.

110. Ibid., pp. 111-112.

111. Esther Menaker, *Otto Rank: A Rediscovered Legacy* (New York: Columbia University Press, 1982), p. 44.

112. Kramer, *A Psychology of Difference,* p. 158.

113. Michael Balint, *The Basic Fault: Therapeutic Aspects of Regression* (Evanston, IL: Northwestern University Press, 1994), p. 74.

114. Margaret Mahler, "On the First Three Subphases of the Separation-Individuation Process." In Peter Buckley (Ed.), *Essential Papers on Object Relations* (New York: New York University Press, 1986), pp. 223, 231-232.

115. Hans Loewald, "Internalization, Separation, Mourning and the Superego," in *Papers on Psychoanalysis* (New Haven: Yale University Press, 1980), pp. 257-276. It is recognized that Daniel Stern's work, *The Interpersonal World of the Infant* (New York: Basic Books, 1965), demonstrated to the satisfaction of many that the image of the infant who does not differentiate between himself or herself and other is incorrect. However, I think that the work of Rank and others discussed in this book as they pertain to the development of a distinct sense of self and ego boundaries as central to developmental, emotional, and spiritual issues throughout the life cycle remains of inestimable value. I would thus agree with Nancy Chodorow who on this subject wrote, "In this context, whether or not this life course preoccupation reflects an actual early infantile state is not really at issue." *Feminism and Psychoanalytic Theory* (New Haven: Yale University Press, 1989), p. 220, n. 15.

116. D. W. Winnicott, "Aggression and Its Roots," in C. Winnicott, R. Shepherd, and M. Davis (Eds.), *Depravation and Delinquency* (New York: Routledge Press, 1984), pp. 84-99, 93, 97.

117. Melanie Klein, *Envy and Gratitude and Other Works* (New York: The Free Press, 1975), pp. 178-179.

118. Sigmund Freud, "Civilization and Its Discontents," in *The Standard Edition of the Complete Psychological Works of Sigmund Freud,* Volume 21 (London: Hogarth Press), p. 66.

119. Freud, "Inhibitions, Symptoms and Anxiety," in *The Standard Edition of the Complete Psychological Works of Sigmund Freud,* Volume 20 (London: Hogarth Press, 1926) p. 122.

120. Karen Horney, *Neurosis and Human Growth* (New York: W. W. Norton & Company, 1950), pp. 240-241, 152.

121. Parsons, *Enigma,* p. 163.

122. Ibid., pp. 163-164, quoting Kohut, "Forms and Transformations of Narcissism," p. 458.

123. Parsons, *Enigma,* p. 164.

124. Becker, *Denial of Death,* pp. 7, 151.

125. John McDargh, *Psychoanalytic Object Relations Theory and the Study of Religion* (New York: University Press of America, 1983), p. 72.

126. Becker, *Denial of Death,* p. 36.

127. Fromm, *Psychoanalysis and Religion,* pp. 79-80.

128. C. G. Jung, "Conscious, Unconscious and Individuation," in *Collected Works,* Volume 9i (Princeton: Princeton University Press), p. 275.

129. Jolande Jacobi, *The Psychology of C. G. Jung* (New Haven, CT: Yale University Press, 1973), p. 106.

130. Carl Jung, "Origin of the Hero," in *Collected Works,* Volume 5 (Princeton: Princeton University Press), p. 174.

131. Carl Jung, "Symbols of the Mother and Rebirth," in *Collected Works,* Volume 5 (Princeton: Princeton University Press), p. 212.

132. Ibid., p. 223.

133. Ibid., p. 235.

134. Carl Jung, "The Dual Mother," in *Collected Works,* Volume 5 (Princeton: Princeton University Press), p. 312.

135. Ibid., p. 339.

136. Wayne Rollins, *Soul and Psyche: The Bible in Psychological Perspective* (Minneapolis: Fortress Press, 1999), p. 92.

137. Ibid.

138. Ibid., p. 93.

139. See extensive discussion of shame as "defeat" in John J. Pilch and Bruce J. Malina (Eds.), *Handbook of Biblical Social Values* (Peabody, MA: Hendrickson Publishers, 1998), pp. 45-48.

140. Edward Wimberly, *Moving from Shame to Self-Worth* (Nashville: Abingdon Press, 1999), p. 54.

141. See Karen A. McClintock, *Sexual Shame: An Urgent Call for Healing* (Minneapolis: Fortress Press, 2001), pp. 142-144.

142. For a general discussion of what it meant to be a "leper" in Jesus' time, see Pilch and Malina, *Handbook of Biblical Social Values,* pp. 104-106.

143. J. Neyrey, *Honor and Shame in the Gospel of Matthew* (Louisville, KY: John Knox Press, 1998), pp. 204-205.

144. Pilch and Malina, *Handbook of Biblical Social Values,* p. 113.

145. Ibid., p. 114.

146. Ibid., pp. 106-114.

147. Ibid., pp. 45-48.

148. John Dominic Crossan, *Jesus: A Revolutionary Biography* (San Francisco: HarperSanFrancisco, 1994), 82; see also Pilch and Malina, *Handbook of Biblical Social Values,* pp. 102-106.

149. Robin Scroggs, "Emerging Trends in Biblical Thought," *The Christian Century* (March 1982): 336.

150. Ibid.

151. Rollins, unpublished lecture at the American Academy of Religion, November 19, 2001.

152. Carl Jung, "The Meaning of Psychology for Modern Man," in *Collected Works,* Volume 10 (Princeton: Princeton University Press), pp. 151-152, para. 321.

153. Such was the message of a sermon delivered by C. Denise Yarbrough, "Fragments of Our Lives," in Roger Alling and David Schlafer (Eds.), *Preaching Through the Year of Mark: Sermons That Work VII* (New York: Morehouse Publishing, 1999), p. 28.

154. Pilch and Malina, *Handbook of Biblical Social Values,* p. 114.

155. *The New Interpreter's Bible Commentary,* Volume VIII (Nashville, TN: Abingdon Press, 1995), "Mark," Pheme Perkins, p. 592.

156. Jurgen Moltmann, *Crucified God* (Minneapolis: Fortress Press, 1993), p. 63.

157. Ibid., p. 146.

158. Ibid., p. 149.

159. Ibid., p. 24.

160. Dietrich Bonhoeffer, *Letters and Papers from Prison* (London: SCM Press, 1971), pp. 360-361.

Chapter 9

1. John Bradshaw, *Healing the Shame That Binds You* (Deerfield, FL: Heath Communications, Inc., 1988), p. 9.

2. Vicki Underland-Rosow, *Shame: Spiritual Suicide* (Shorewood, MN: Waterford Publications, 1995), p. 19.

3. James Fowler, *Faithful Change* (Nashville, TN: Abingdon Press, 1996), p. 92.

4. William James, *The Varieties of Religious Experience,* ed. with Introduction by Martin Marty (New York: Penguin Books, 1985), pp. 78 *ff.*

5. Sandra Edelman, *Turning the Gorgon: A Meditation on Shame* (Woodstock, CT: Spring Publications, 1998), p. 17.

6. Stephen Pattison, *Shame: Theory, Therapy, Theology* (Cambridge, England: Cambridge University Press, 2000), pp. 229-289.

7. Paul Tillich, *Shaking the Foundations* (New York: Charles Scribner's Sons, 1948), p. 42.

8. Helen Merrell Lynd, *On Shame and the Search for Identity* (London: Routledge, 1999 [1958]), p. 71.

9. Pattison, *Shame,* p. 223.

10. Edelman, *Turning the Gorgon,* p. 17.

11. *The Hymnal 1982, according to the use of the Episcopal Church* (New York: Church Hymnal Corporation, 1982), p. 574.

12. *Oxford Dictionary of the Christian Church*, Second Edition, ed. F.L. Cross (1983), p. 328.

13. *Encyclopedia of Early Christianity,* Second Edition (New York: Garland Publishing, Inc., 1997), p. 840, citing Augustine, *Nupt. et concup.,* 1.6.7, 1.24.27.

14. Thandeka, "The Split Self: A Self Psychology Analysis of Augustine's Doctrine of Human Nature," p. 1, unpublished paper presented on November 20, 2001, American Academy of Religion, Denver, Colorado.

15. Sandra Lee Dixon, *Augustine: The Scattered and Gathered Self* (St. Louis, MO: Chalice Press, 1999), p. 35.

16. Augustine, *Confessions* (Oxford: Oxford University Press, 1992), p. 9.

17. Ibid., pp. 203-204.

18. Ibid., p. 140.

19. Ibid., p. 59.

20. Ibid., p. 183.

21. See Karen A. McClintock, *Sexual Shame: An Urgent Call for Healing* (Minneapolis, MN: Fortress Press, 2001).

22. Pattison, *Shame: Theory, Therapy, Theology,* pp. 273 *ff.*

23. Nina Coltart, *Slouching Towards Bethlehem* (New York: Other Press, 2000), p. 47.

24. Thomas Oden, *Care of Souls in the Classical Tradition* (Philadelphia: Fortress Press, 1984), p. 105.

25. Aldolph Guggenbuhl-Craig, *Power in the Helping Professions* (Woodstock, CT: Spring Publications, 1971), pp. 51-52.

26. Ibid., p. 79.

27. *The Book of Common Prayer According to the Use of the Episcopal Church* (New York: Church Hymnal Corporation) p. 409.

28. *Constitutions and Canons of the Episcopal Church,* Title IV, Canon 1, Section 1 (b), (j) (1997).

29. Pattison, *Shame,* p. 269.

30. Ibid.

31. Ibid., p. 269.

32. Daniel Day Williams, *The Minister and the Care of Souls* (New York: Harper & Row, 1961), pp. 100-101.

33. Pattison, *Shame,* p. 8.

34. Ibid., p. 276.

35. According to a recent study reported and discussed by C. Wayne in the *Journal of Pastoral Care* 57(1)(Spring 2003), clergy candidates come to the ordained ministry with a higher need for approval and affirmation than 90 percent of people in the general population. The study further reported that clergy do not often find the affirmation and approval that they seek from their parishioners and colleagues. As a result, clergy are more likely to become physically ill from stress-related disorders than 90 percent of the people in the general population.

36. Ronald and Patricia Potter-Efron, *Letting Go of Shame* (Center City, MN: Hazelden, 1989), pp. 2-3.

37. Helen Block Lewis, *Shame and Guilt in Neurosis* (New York: International Universities Press, 1971), p. 46.

38. Ibid., p. 58.

39. Ibid., pp. 492-493.

40. Ibid., p. 494.

41. Ibid., p. 511.

42. Michael Lewis, *Shame: The Exposed Self* (New York: The Free Press, 1992), p. 142.

43. Bradshaw, *Healing the Shame,* pp. 115-116.

44. Ibid.

45. Ibid., p. 119.

46. John Patton, *Is Human Forgiveness Possible?* (Nashville: Abingdon Press, 1985), p. 186.

47. Donald Capps, *The Depleted Self: Sin in a Narcissistic Age* (Minneapolis: Fortress Press, 1993), pp. 68-69.

48. Paul Tillich, "Theology and Counseling." In *The Meaning of Health, Essays in Existentialism, Psychoanalysis and Religion* (Chicago: Exploration Press, 1984), p. 120.

49. Ibid., p. 121.

50. Ibid.

51. Lewis Smedes, *Shame and Grace* (London: SPCK, 1993), pp. 107-108.

52. Ibid., pp. 153 *ff.*

53. Fowler, *Faithful Change,* p. 144.

54. Deborah van Deusen Hunsinger, *Theology and Pastoral Counseling* (Grand Rapids: William B. Eerdmans Publishing, 1995), pp. 198 *ff.*

55. Andrew Morrison, *Shame: The Underside of Narcissism* (Hillsdale, NJ: Analytic Press, 1989), p. 82.

56. Edelman, *Turning the Gorgon,* p. 17.

57. Williams, *The Minister,* p. 105.

58. James Dittes, *Pastoral Counseling: The Basics* (Louisville, KY: Westminster John Knox Press, 1999), p. 5.

59. Ibid., p. 7.

60. Pattison, *Shame,* p. 189.

61. See discussion in Pattison, *Shame,* pp. 216-218.

62. Ibid., p. 217.

63. Ibid., p. 223.

64. Edelman, *Turning the Gorgon,* p. 78.

65. Rollo May, *The Art of Counseling,* Revised Edition (Lake Worth, FL: Gardner Press, 1989), p. 49.

66. Ibid., p. 123.

67. Leon Wurmser, *The Mask of Shame* (Northvale, NJ: Jason Aronson, Inc., 1997), p. 293.

68. Ibid.

69. Paul Tillich, "Theology of Pastoral Care," in *The Meaning of Health,* p. 128.

70. Ibid.

71. Williams, *The Minister,* p. 101.

72. Ann Belford Ulanov, *The Wisdom of the Psyche* (Cambridge, MA: Cowley Publications, 1988), p. 127.

73. Margaret Guenther, *Holy Listening: The Art of Spiritual Direction* (Cambridge, MA: Cowley Publications, 1992), p. 100.

74. Henri Nouwen, *The Wounded Healer* (New York: Doubleday, 1979), p. 86.

75. Edelman, *Turning the Gorgon,* p. 109.

76. Joan Halifax, *Shaman* (London: Thames and Hudson, 1982), p. 92.

77. See Pattison, *Shame,* p. 255, discussion of Sebastian Moore's *The Fire and the Rose Are One* (London: Dartmon, Longman & Todd, 1980).

Bibliography

Adler, Alfred. *Understanding Human Nature.* New York: Greenberg, 1971.

Albers, Robert H. *Shame, A Faith Perspective.* Binghamton, NY: The Haworth Pastoral Press, Inc., 1995.

Alexander, Franz. Remarks About the Relation of Inferiority Feelings to Guilt Feelings. *International Journal of Psychoanalysis* 19(1938): 41-49.

Allport, Gordon. *The Individual and His Religion.* New York: MacMillan Publishing Co., Inc., 1950.

Ansbacher, Heinz and Ansbacher, Rowena. *The Individual Psychology of Alfred Adler.* New York: Harper & Row, 1956.

Armstrong, Karen. *Buddha.* New York: Penguin, 2001.

Assagioli, Roberto. Transcendental Experiences and Meditation. In John J. Heaney (Ed.), *Psyche and Spirit.* Ramsey, NJ: Paulist Press, 1973, pp. 125-137.

Augustine. *Confessions.* Trans. Harry Chadwick. Oxford: Oxford University Press, 1992.

Balint, Michael. *The Basic Fault.* Evanston, IL: Northwestern University Press, 1994.

Becker, Ernest. *Denial of Death.* New York: Free Press Paperbacks, 1973.

Benedict, Ruth. *The Chrysanthemum and the Sword.* Rutland, VT: Charles Tuttle, 1954.

Berecz, John. *Beyond Shame and Pain.* Lima, OH: CSS Publishing, 1998.

Berecz, John and Helm, Herbert. Shame: The Underside of Christianity. *Journal of Psychology and Christianity* 17(1998): 5-14.

Boisen, Anton. *Exploration of the Inner World.* New York: Harper & Brothers, 1936.

——— . *Out of the Depths.* New York: Harper & Brothers, 1960.

Bonhoeffer, Dietrich. *Ethics.* New York: MacMillan, 1955.

——— . *Letters and Papers from Prison.* London: SCM Press, 1971.

Book of Common Prayer According to the Use of the Episcopalian Church. New York: Church Hymnal Corporation, 1979.

Bourdieu, Pierre. The Sentiment of Honor in Kabyle Society. In John G. Perstiany (Ed.), *Honor and Shame: The Values of Mediterranean Society.* Chicago: University of Chicago Press, 1966, pp. 191-241.

Bowlby, John. *Attachment and Loss.* New York: Basic Books, 1969.

Bradshaw, John. *Healing the Shame That Binds You.* Deerfield, FL: Health Communications, Inc., 1988.

Briggs, Robin. *Witches and Neighbors.* New York: Penguin Books, 1996.

Brown, Byron. *Soul Without Shame*. Boston: Shambhala, 1999.

Buckley, Peter (Ed.). *Essential Papers on Object Relations*. New York: New York University Press, 1986.

Capps, Donald. *The Depleted Self: Sin in a Narcissistic Age*. Minneapolis: Fortress Press, 1993.

———. *Jesus: A Psychological Biography*. St. Louis, MO: Chalice Press, 2000.

Carmody, Denise Lardner and John Tully. *Mysticism: Holiness East and West*. New York: Oxford University Press, 1996.

Cataldo, Lisa. Jesus As Transforming Selfobject: Kohutian Theory and the Life of St. Francis of Assisi. A paper presented to the Person, Culture, and Religion Group of the American Academy of Religion, November 20, 2001, Denver, Colorado.

Chodorow, Nancy. *Feminism and Psychoanalytic Theory*. New Haven: Yale University Press, 1989.

Cohen, Shaye. *From Macabees to the Midrash*. Philadelphia: Westminster Press, 1987.

Coltart, Nina. *Slouching Towards Bethlehem*. New York: Other Press, 2000.

Constitution and Canons of the Episcopal Church, 1997.

Coyne, James C. (Ed.). *Essential Papers on Depression*. New York: New York University Press, 1985.

Crossan, John Dominic. *The Historical Jesus: The Life of a Mediterranean Jewish Peasant*. San Francisco: HarperSanFrancisco, 1991.

———. *Jesus: A Revolutionary Biography*. San Francisco: HarperSanFrancisco, 1994.

Dass, Ram. *Still Here*. New York: Riverhead Books, 2000.

Dittes, James. *Pastoral Counseling*. Louisville, KY: Westminster John Knox Press, 1999.

Dixon, Sandra Lee. *Augustine: The Scattered and Gathered Self*. St. Louis, MO: Chalice Press, 1999.

Edelman, Sandra. *Turning the Gorgon: A Meditation on Shame*. Woodstock, CT: Spring Publications, 1998.

Ellenberger, Henri. *The Discovery of the Unconscious, The History and Evolution of the Dynamic Unconscious*. New York: Basic Books, 1970.

Elliot, Neill. *Liberating Paul: The Justice of God and the Politics of the Apostle*. Marynoll, NY: Orbis Books, 1994.

Encyclopedia of Early Christianity, Second Edition. New York: Garland Publishing, Inc., 1997.

Erikson, Erik. *Childhood and Society*. New York: W. W. Norton & Company, 1963.

———. *Young Man Luther*. New York: W. W. Norton & Company, 1958.

Forman, Robert. *Mysticism, Mind, Consciousness*. Albany: State University of New York Press, 1999.

Fossum, Merle and Mason, Marilyn. *Facing Shame: Families in Recovery*. New York: WW Norton & Company, 1986.

Fowler, James. *Faithful Change*. Nashville: Abingdon Press, 1996.

Frank, Jerome and Frank, Julia. *Persuasion and Healing.* Baltimore: The Johns Hopkins University Press, 1991.

Freed, E. D. "The Women in Matthew's Genealogy." *Journal for the Study of the New Testament* 29(1987): 3-19.

Freud, Sigmund. "An Autobiographical Study" (1925). In *The Standard Edition of the Complete Psychological Works of Sigmund Freud,* Volume 20, trans. James Strachey. London: Hogarth Press, 1966, pp. 7-70.

————. "Civilization and Its Discontents" (1930). In *The Standard Edition of the Complete Psychological Works of Sigmund Freud,* Volume 21, trans. James Strachey. London: Hogarth Press, pp. 64-145.

————. "Draft K, The Neuroses of Defense" (1896). In *The Standard Edition of the Complete Psychological Works of Sigmund Freud,* Volume 1, trans. James Strachey. London: Hogarth Press, pp. 220-229.

————. "Extracts from the Fleiss Papers" (1896). In *The Standard Edition of the Complete Psychological Works of Sigmund Freud,* Volume 1, trans. James Strachey. London: Hogarth Press, pp. 220-280.

————. "Findings, Ideas, Problems" (1938). In *The Standard Edition of the Complete Psychological Works of Sigmund Freud,* Volume 23, trans. James Strachey. London: Hogarth Press, pp. 299-300.

————. "The Future of an Illusion" (1927). In *The Standard Edition of the Complete Psychological Works of Sigmund Freud,* Volume 21, trans. James Strachey. London: Hogarth Press, pp. 5-56.

————. "Inhibitions, Symptoms and Anxiety" (1926). In *The Standard Edition of the Complete Psychological Works of Sigmund Freud,* Volume 20, trans. James Strachey. London: Hogarth Press, pp. 77-174.

————. "Interpretation of Dreams" (1900). In *The Standard Edition of the Complete Psychological Works of Sigmund Freud,* Volume 4, trans. James Strachey. London: Hogarth Press.

————. "Introductory Lectures on Psychoanalysis" (1916). In *The Standard Edition of the Complete Psychological Works of Sigmund Freud,* Volumes 15 and 16, trans. James Strachey. London: Hogarth Press.

————. "Jokes and the Unconscious" (1905). In *The Standard Edition of the Complete Psychological Works of Sigmund Freud,* Volume 8, trans. James Strachey. London: Hogarth Press.

————. "Leonardo Da Vinci" (1910). In *The Standard Edition of the Complete Psychological Works of Sigmund Freud,* Volume 11, trans. James Strachey. London: Hogarth Press, pp. 59-137.

————. "Mourning and Melancholia" (1917). In *The Standard Edition of the Complete Psychological Works of Sigmund Freud,* Volume 14, trans. James Strachey. London: Hogarth Press, pp. 243-258.

————. "The Neuro-Psychoses of Defense" (1894). In *The Standard Edition of the Complete Psychological Works of Sigmund Freud,* Volume 3, trans. James Strachey. London: Hogarth Press, pp. 159-185.

————. "New Introductory Lectures on Psychoanalysis" (1933). In *The Standard Edition of the Complete Psychological Works of Sigmund Freud,* Volume 22, trans. James Strachey. London: Hogarth Press, pp. 3-182.

————. "On Narcissism" (1914). In *The Standard Edition of the Complete Psychological Works of Sigmund Freud,* Volume 14, trans. James Strachey. London: Hogarth Press, pp. 67-102.

————. "Outline of Psychoanalysis" (1938). In *The Standard Edition of the Complete Psychological Works of Sigmund Freud,* Volume 23, trans. James Strachey. London: Hogarth Press, pp. 141-207.

————. "The Psychopathology of Everyday Life" (1901). In *The Standard Edition of the Complete Psychological Works of Sigmund Freud,* Volume 6, trans. James Strachey. London: Hogarth Press.

————. "Psychotherapy of Hysteria" (1895). In *The Standard Edition of the Complete Psychological Works of Sigmund Freud,* Volume 2, trans. James Strachey. London: Hogarth Press, pp. 253-305.

————. "Three Essays on Sexuality" (1950). In *The Standard Edition of the Complete Psychological Works of Sigmund Freud,* Volume 7, trans. James Strachey. London: Hogarth Press, pp. 123-243.

————. "Totem and Taboo" (1913). In *The Standard Edition of the Complete Psychological Works of Sigmund Freud,* Volume 31, trans. James Strachey. London: Hogarth Press, pp. 1-161.

Friedman, Edwin. *From Generation to Generation: Family Process in Church and Synagogue.* New York: The Guilford Press, 1985.

Fromm, Erich. *Escape from Freedom.* New York: Avon Books, 1941.

————. *Psychoanalysis and Religion.* New Haven: Yale University Press, 1950.

Gilbert, Paul and Andrews, Bernice (Eds.), *Shame: Interpersonal Behavior, Psychopathology and Culture.* New York: Oxford University Press, 1998.

Gilligan, James. *Violence: Reflections on a National Epidemic.* New York: Random House, 1996.

Goffman, Erving. *The Presentation of Self in Everyday Life.* New York: Doubleday, 1959.

————. *Stigma: Notes on the Management of Spoiled Identity.* New York: Simon & Schuster, 1963.

Goodenough, Erwin Ramsell. *The Psychology of Religious Experience.* New York: Basic Books, 1965.

Grainger, Roger. *Watching for Wings, Theology and Mental Illness in a Pastoral Setting.* London: Darton, Longmman & Todd, 1979.

Greiman, April. *The Fusion of Technology and Graphic Design.* New York: Watson-Guptill Publishing, 1990.

Grof, Stanislov. *Beyond the Brain.* Albany: State University of New York, 1985.

Guenther, Margaret. *Holy Listening.* Cambridge, MA: Cowley Publications, 1992.

Guggenbuhl-Craig, Adolph. *Power in the Helping Professions.* Woodstock, CT: Spring Publications, 1971.

Halifax, Joan. *Shaman.* London: Thames and Hudson, 1982.

Hanson, K.C. and Oakman, Douglas. *Palestine in the Time of Jesus: Social Structures and Social Conflicts.* Minneapolis: Fortress Press, 1998.

Hart, Curtis. Anton Boisen: Madness, Mental Health and Ministry. In S. Severino and R. Liew (Eds.), *Pastoral Care and the Mentally Disabled.* Binghamton, NY: The Haworth Press, 1994, pp. 49-65.

Hengel, Martin. *Crucifixion in the Ancient World and the Folly of the Message of the Cross.* Philadelphia: Fortress Press, 1977.

Hick, John and Goulder, Michael. *Why Believe in God?* London: SCM Press, Ltd., 1983.

Horney, Karen. *Neurosis and Human Growth.* New York: W. W. Norton & Company, 1950.

Hultberg, Peer. Shame: A Hidden Emotion. *Journal of Analytical Psychology* 33(1988): 109-126.

Jacobi, Jolande. *The Psychology of C. G. Jung.* New Haven, CT: Yale University Press, 1973.

Jacoby, Mario. *Shame and the Origins of Self-Esteem: A Jungian Approach.* New York: Routledge Press, 1996.

James, William. *The Varieties of Religious Experience.* Ed. with Introduction by Martin Marty. New York: Penguin Books, 1982.

Jones, James. *Contemporary Psychoanalysis and Religion.* New Haven: Yale University Press, 1991.

————. *Psychology and Religion in Transition.* New Haven: Yale University Press, 1991.

Jonte-Pace, Diane and Parsons, William (Eds.). *Religion and Psychology: Mapping the Terrain.* New York: Routledge Press, 2001.

Julian of Norwich. *Showings.* Mahwah, NJ: Paulist Press, 1978.

Jung, Carl Gustav. "Aion." In *Collected Works,* Volume 9ii, trans. R. F. C. Hull. Princeton: Princeton University Press, 1959.

————. Analytical Psychology and Education. In *Collected Works,* Volume 17, trans. R. F. C. Hull. Princeton: Princeton University Press, 1954, pp. 63-132.

————. Answer to Job. In *Collected Works,* Volume 11, trans. R. F. C. Hull. Princeton: Princeton University Press, 1958, pp. 357-470.

————. The Battle for Deliverance from the Mother; The Dual Mother. In *Collected Works,* Volume 5, trans. R. F. C. Hull. Princeton: Princeton University Press, 1956, pp. 274-393.

————. Conscious, Unconscious and Individuation. In *Collected Works,* Volume 9i, trans. R. F. C. Hull. Princeton: Princeton University Press, 1959, pp. 275-289.

————. The Development of Personality. In *Collected Works,* Volume 17, trans. R. F. C. Hull. Princeton: Princeton University Press, 1954, pp. 165-201.

————. Introduction to the Religious and Psychological Problems of Alchemy. In *Collected Works,* Volume 12, trans. R. F. C. Hull. Princeton: Princeton University Press, 1953, pp. 3-37.

————— . The Meaning of Psychology for Modern Man. In *Collected Works,* Volume 10, trans. R. F. C. Hull. Princeton: Princeton University Press, 1964, pp. 134-156.

————— . Origin of the Hero. In *Collected Works,* Volume 5, trans. R. F. C. Hull. Princeton: Princeton University Press, 1956, pp. 171-205.

————— . Psychological Approaches to the Trinity. In *Collected Works,* Volume 11, trans. R. F. C. Hull. Princeton: Princeton University Press, 1958, pp. 109-200.

————— . The Psychology of Christian Alchemical Symbolism. In *Collected Works,* Volume 9ii, trans. R. F. C. Hull. Princeton: Princeton University Press, 1959, pp. 173-183.

————— . The Relations Between the Ego and the Unconscious. In *Collected Works,* Volume 7, trans. R. F. C. Hull. Princeton: Princeton University Press, 1953, pp. 121-139.

————— . Symbols of the Mother and Rebirth. In *Collected Works,* Volume 5, trans. R. F. C. Hull. Princeton: Princeton University Press, 1956, pp. 207-273.

————— . Synchronicity: An Acausal Connecting Principle. In *Collected Works,* Volume 8, trans. R. F. C. Hull. Princeton: Princeton University Press, 1960, pp. 421-519.

Kaufman, Gershen. *Shame: The Power of Caring.* Rochester, VT: Schenkman Books, Inc., 1992.

————— . *The Psychology of Shame: Theory and Treatment of Shame-Based Syndromes,* Revised Edition. New York: Springer, 1996.

Kaufman, Gershen and Raphael, Lev. *Dynamics of Power: Fighting Shame and Building Self-Esteem.* Rochester, VT: Schenkman Books, Inc., 1991.

Kelsey, Morton. Interview with Morton Kelsey. *Your Church* 23 (March/April 1997): 11-12.

————— . *The Other Side of Silence: Meditation for the Twenty-First Century.* New York: Paulist Press, 1997.

Kelsey, Morton and Sprunger, Robert. Does Healing Have a Place in Your Ministry? *Your Church* 22(2)(March/April 1976): 14-18.

Keltner, Dacher and Harker, Lee Anne. The Forms and Functions of the Nonverbal Signal of Shame. In Paul Gilbert and Bernice Andrews (Eds.), *Shame: Interpersonal Behavior, Psychopathology and Culture.* New York: Oxford University Press, 1998, pp. 78-98.

Kennedy, Eugene. *The Unhealed Wound: The Church and Human Sexuality.* New York: St. Martin's Press, 2001.

Kille, Andrew. *Psychological Biblical Criticism.* Minneapolis: Fortress Press, 2001.

Klein, Melanie. *Envy and Gratitude and Other Works 1946-1963. The Writings of Melanie Klein, Volume III.* New York: The Free Press, 1975.

Kohut, Heinz. *The Analysis of the Self.* New York: International Universities Press, Inc., 1971.

————— . Forms and Transformations of Narcissism. In Paul Ornstein (Ed.), *The Search for the Self, Selected Writing of Heinz Kohut: 1950-1978,* Volume 1. New York: International Universities Press, 1978, pp. 427-460.

————— . *How Does Analysis Cure?* Ed. Arnold Goldberg and Paul Stepansky. Chicago: University of Chicago Press, 1984.

————— . *Restoration of the Self.* New York: International Universities Press, 1977.

————— . *The Search for the Self, Selected Writings of Heinz Kohut,* Volumes 1 and 2, ed. with Introduction by Paul Ornstein. New York: International Universities Press, 1978.

————— . Thoughts on Narcissism and Narcissistic Rage. *The Psychoanalytic Study of the Child,* Volume 27. New York: International Universities Press, 1972, pp. 360-399.

Kohut, Heinz and Wolf, Ernest S. "The Disorders of the Self and Their Treatment: An Outline." In Andrew P. Morrison (Ed.), *Essential Papers on Narcissism.* New York: New York University Press, 1986, pp. 175-196.

Kornfeld, Margaret. *Cultivating Wholeness.* New York: Continuum, 1998.

Kramer, Robert. *A Psychology of Difference.* Princeton: Princeton University Press, 1996.

Kung, Hans. *Christianity and the World Religions.* Trans. Peter Heinegg. Maryknoll, NY: Orbis Books, 1993.

Lear, Jonathan. *Love and Its Place in Nature.* New York: Farrar, Straus & Giroux, 1990.

Lee, Robert G. and Wheeler, Gordon. *The Voice of Shame: Silence and Connection in Psychotherapy.* San Francisco: Jossey-Bass Publishers, 1996.

Leuba, James H. *The Psychology of Religious Mysticism.* New York: Harcourt Brace, 1925.

Lewis, C.S. *They Asked for a Paper.* London: Geoffrey Bles, 1962.

Lewis, Helen Block. *Shame and Guilt in Neurosis.* New York: International Universities Press, 1971.

Lewis, Michael. *Shame: The Exposed Self.* New York: The Free Press, 1995.

Lieberman, E. James. *Acts of Will: The Life and Work of Otto Rank.* Amherst, MA: University of Massachusetts Press, 1985.

Loewald, Hans. Internalization, Separation, Mourning and the Superego. In *Papers on Psychoanalysis.* New Haven: Yale University Press, 1980, pp. 257-276.

Lynd, Helen Merrell. *On Shame and the Search for Identity.* London: Routledge, 1999 [1958].

Mahler, Margaret. On the First Three Subphases of the Separation-Individuation Process. In Peter Buckley (Ed.), *Essential Papers on Object Relations.* New York: New York University Press, 1986, pp. 222-231.

Mahler, Margaret, Pine, Fred, and Bermann, Anni. *The Psychological Birth of the Human Infant.* New York: Basic Books, 1975.

Malina, Bruce J. *The New Testament World: Insights from Cultural Anthropology,* Revised Edition. Louisville, KY: Westminster John Knox Press, 1993.

Maslow, Abraham. *Religions, Values and Peak Experiences.* New York: Penguin Books, 1964.

May, Rollo. *The Art of Counseling,* Revised Edition. Lake Worth, FL: Gardner Press, 1989.

——— . *Power and Innocence.* New York: W. W. Norton & Company, 1972.

McClintock, Karen A. *Sexual Shame: An Urgent Call for Healing.* Minneapolis, MN: Fortress Press, 2001.

McDargh, John. *Psychoanalytic Object Relations Theory and the Study of Religion.* New York: University Press of America, 1983.

McNeill, John. *A History of the Cure of Souls.* New York: Harper & Brothers, 1951.

Meadow, Mary Jo. The Dark Side of Mysticism: Depression and the "Dark Night." *Pastoral Psychology* 33(1984): 105-125.

Meissner, W.W. *Psychoanalysis and Religious Experience.* New Haven: Yale University Press, 1984.

Menaker, Esther. *Otto Rank: A Rediscovered Legacy.* New York: Columbia University Press, 1982.

——— . *Separation, Will and Creativity.* Ed. Claude Barbre. Northvale, NJ: Jason Aronson, Inc., 1996.

Middelton-Moz, Jane. *Shame and Guilt: The Masters of Disguise.* Deerfield Beach, FL: Health Communications, Inc., 1990.

Miles, Jack. "Before Jesus Could Talk." *New York Times Magazine,* Sunday, December 24, 1995.

Miller, Alice. *For Your Own Good: Hidden Cruelty in Child-Rearing and the Roots of Violence.* New York: Farrar, Straus, Giroux, 1990.

——— . *The Drama of the Gifted Child.* New York: Basic Books, 1997.

Moltmann, Jurgen. *Crucified God.* Minneapolis: Fortress Press, 1993.

Moore, Sebastian. *The Fire and the Rose Are One.* London: Dartmon, Longman & Todd, 1980.

Morrison, Andrew. *The Culture of Shame.* Northvale, NJ: Jason Aronson Inc., 1998.

——— (Ed.). *Essential Papers on Narcissism.* New York: New York University Press, 1986.

——— . *Shame: The Underside of Narcissism.* Hillsdale, NJ: Analytic Press, 1989.

Nathanson, Donald (Ed.). *The Many Faces of Shame.* New York: The Guilford Press, 1987.

——— . *Shame and Pride: Affect, Sex and the Birth of Self.* New York: W. W. Norton & Company, 1992.

Neyrey, Jerome. *Honor and Shame in the Gospel of Matthew.* Louisville, KY: John Knox Press, 1998.

——— (Ed.). *The Social World of Luke—Acts.* Peabody, MA: Hendrickson Publishers, 1991.

Nietzsche, Friedrich. *Beyond Good and Evil: Prelude to a Philosophy of the Future.* Trans. Walter Kaufmann. New York: Random House, 1966.

——— . *The Gay Science.* Trans. Walter Kaufmann. New York: Random House, 1974.

————. *Thus Spoke Zarathustra*. Trans. Walter Kaufmann. In *The Portable Nietzsche*. New York: Random House, 1966.

————. *The Will to Power*. Trans. Walter Kaufmann and R.J. Hollingdale. Ed. Walter Kaufmann. New York: Random House, 1967.

Nouwen, Henri. *The Wounded Healer*. New York: Doubleday, 1979.

Novak, Philip. *The World's Wisdom*. San Francisco: HarperSanFrancisco, 1994.

Nussbaum, Martha. *Upheavals of Thought*. Cambridge: Cambridge University Press, 2001.

Oates, Wayne. *The Psychology of Religion*. Waco, TX: Word Books, 1973.

O'Connor, Kathleen. What Is Our Present. In Diane Jonte-Pace and William B. Parsons (Eds.), *Religion and Psychology: Mapping the Terrain*. New York: Routledge Press, 2000, pp. 75-93.

Oden, Thomas C. *Care of Souls in the Classical Tradition*. Philadelphia: Fortress Press, 1984.

Ornstein, Paul (Ed.). *The Search for Self: Selected Writings of Heinz Kohut: 1950-1978*, Volume 1. New York: International Universities Press, 1978.

Otto, Rudolph. *The Idea of the Holy*. Trans. John W. Harvey. London: Oxford University Press, 1923 [1917].

Pagels, Elaine. *The Gnostic Gospels*. New York: Random House, 1979.

————. *The Origins of Satan*. New York: Random House, 1995.

Palmer, Michael. *Freud and Jung on Religion*. New York: Routledge, 1997.

Parsons, William B. *The Enigma of the Oceanic Feeling*. New York: Oxford University Press, 1999.

————. The Oceanic Feeling Revisited. *Journal of Religion* 78(1998): 501-523.

Pattison, Stephen. *Shame: Theory, Therapy, Theology*. Cambridge, England: Cambridge University Press, 2000.

Patton, John. *Is Human Forgiveness Possible?* Nashville: Abington Press, 1985.

Perkins, Pheme. The Gospel of Mark. In *New Interpreters Bible Commentary*, Volume VIII. Nashville: Abingdon Press, 1995, p. 509.

Perry, C. Wayne. "First Look: What Brings Clergy Candidates into Ministry," *Journal of Pastoral Care and Counseling,* Volume 7, no. 1 (2003).

Petry, Ray. *Late Medieval Mysticism*. London: SCM Press, Ltd., 1957.

Piers, Gerhart and Singer, Milton. *Shame and Guilt: A Psychoanalytic and a Cultural Study*. New York: W.W. Norton, 1971.

Pilch, John and Malina, Bruce (Eds.). *Handbook of Biblical Social Values*. Peabody, MA: Hendrickson Publishers, Inc., 1998.

Potter-Efron, Ronald and Potter-Efron, Patricia. *Letting Go of Shame*. Center City, MN: Hazelden, 1989.

Proudfoot, Wayne. *Religious Experience*. Berkeley: University of California Press, 1985.

Pruyser, Paul. Anxiety, Guilt and Shame in the Atonement. In H. Newton Malony and Bernard Spilka (Eds.), *Religion in Psychodynamic Perspective: The Contri-*

butions of Paul W. Pruyser. New York: Oxford University Press, 1991, pp. 99-116.

————. *Between Belief and Unbelief.* New York: Harper & Row, 1963.

————. *A Dynamic Psychology of Religion.* New York: Harper & Row, 1968.

————. *The Minister As Diagnostician.* Philadelphia: Westminster Press, 1976.

————. Nathan and David: A Psychological Footnote. *Pastoral Psychology* 13 (1962): 14-18.

————. Religion in a Psychiatric Hospital: A Reassessment. In H. Newton Malony and Bernard Spilka (Eds.), *Religion in Psychodynamic Perspective: The Contributions of Paul W. Pruyser.* New York: Oxford University Press, 1991, pp. 85-98.

Rank, Otto. *Art and Artist: Creative Urge and Personality Development,* trans. Charles Francis Atkinson. New York: W.W. Norton & Company, 1989 [1932].

————. *Beyond Psychology.* New York: Dover Publications, Inc., 1941.

————. *A Psychology of Difference: The American Lectures of Otto Rank,* ed. and Introduction, Robert Kramer. Princeton: Princeton University Press, 1996.

————. *Psychology and the Soul,* trans. Gregory C. Richter and E. James Lieberman. Baltimore: The Johns Hopkins University Press, 1998 [1930].

————. *The Trauma of Birth.* New York: Dover Publications, Inc., 1993 [1924].

————. *Will Therapy.* New York: Alfred A. Knopf, 1929.

Ricoeur, Paul. *Freud and Philosophy,* trans. Denis Savage. New Haven, CT: Yale University Press, 1970.

————. *The Symbolism of Evil,* trans. Emerson Buchanan. Boston: Beacon Press, 1967.

Rieff, Philip, *The Triumph of the Therapeutic.* New York: Harper & Row, 1966.

Rizzuto, Ana Maria. *The Birth of the Living God.* Chicago: University of Chicago Press, 1979.

————. *Why Did Freud Reject God?* New Haven: Yale University Press, 1998.

Roland, Alan. *Cultural Pluralism and Psychoanalysis.* New York: Routledge, 1996.

Rollins, Wayne. *Jung and the Bible.* Atlanta: John Knox Press, 1983.

————. *Soul and Psyche: The Bible in Psychological Perspective.* Minneapolis: Fortress Press, 1999.

Ruberry, Mary. Introduction. *3-D Bible Stories* (Newport Beach, CA: 3-D Revelations Publishing, 1994.

Rubin, Julius. *Religious Melancholy and Protestant Experience in America.* New York: Oxford University Press, 1994.

Sartre, Jean-Paul. *Being and Nothingness.* New York: Washington Square Press, 1984.

Schaberg, Jane. *The Illegitimacy of Jesus: A Feminist Interpretation of the Infancy Narratives.* San Francisco: Harper & Row, 1987.

Schneider, Carl D. *Shame, Exposure and Privacy.* Boston: Beacon Press, 1977.

Schweitzer, Albert. *The Quest of the Historical Jesus.* New York: MacMillan Publishing Company, 1968.

Scroggs, Robin. Emerging Trends in Biblical Thought. *The Christian Century* (March 1982): 335-338.

———. The Heuristic Value of a Psychological Model in the Interpretation of Pauline Theology. In Robin Scroggs (Ed.), *The Text and the Times, New Testament Essays for Today.* Minneapolis: Fortress Press, 1993, pp. 125-150.

Sidoli, Mara, Shame and the Shadow. *Journal of Analytical Psychology* 33(1988): 127-142.

Siegel, Allen. *Heinz Kohut and the Psychology of the Self.* London: Routledge Press, 1996.

Silber, John. Masks and Fig Leaves. In J. Roland Pennock and John Chapman (Eds.), *Privacy.* New York: Atherton Press, 1971.

Smedes, Lewis. *Shame and Grace.* London: SPCK, 1993.

Spero, Moshe. *Religious Objects As Psychological Structures.* Chicago: University of Chicago Press, 1992.

———. Shame: An Object Relations Formulation. In Albert J. Solnit, Ruth S. Eissler, and Peter B. Neubauer (Eds.), *The Psychoanalytic Study of the Child,* Volume 39. New Haven, CT: Yale University Press, 1984, pp. 259-282.

Steinke, Peter. *Healthy Congregations: A Systems Approach.* New York: The Alban Institute, Inc., 1996.

Stern, Daniel. *The Interpersonal World of the Infant.* New York: Basic Books, 1965.

Stone, Howard. Depression and Spiritual Desolation. *Journal of Pastoral Care* 52 (1998): 389-296.

Strozier, Charles. Heinz Kohut's Struggles with Religion, Ethnicity and God. In Janet Liebman Jacobs and Donald Capps (Eds.), *Religion, Society and Psychoanalysis.* Boulder, CO: Westview Press, 1997, pp. 165-180.

Tarnas, Richard. *The Passion of the Western Mind.* New York: Ballantine Books, 1991.

Taylor, Eugene. *Shadow Culture: Psychology and Spirituality in America.* Washington, DC: Counterpoint, 1999.

Teresa of Avila. *The Interior Castle.* Classics of Western Spirituality Series. Mahwah, NJ: Paulist Press, 1979.

———. *The Life of Teresa of Jesus: The Autobiography of Teresa of Avila,* trans. E. Allison Peers. New York: Doubleday Books, 1991.

Thandeka. White Radical Induction and Christian Shame Theology: A Primer. In *Gender and Psychoanalysis* 4(Fall 1999): 455-495.

———. The Split Self: A Self Psychology Analysis of Augustine's Doctrine of Human Nature. Unpublished paper presented on November 20, 2001, American Academy of Religion, Denver, Colorado.

Tillich, Paul. *The Meaning of Health: Essays in Existentialism, Psychoanalysis and Religion.* Ed. Perry Lefevre. Chicago: Exploration Press, 1984.

———. *Shaking the Foundations.* New York: Charles Scribner's Sons, 1948.

————— . *Systematic Theology,* Volume II. Chicago: University of Chicago Press, 1957.

————— . The Theological Significance of Existentialism and Psychoanalysis. In John J. Heaney (Ed.), *Psyche and Spirit.* Ramsey, NJ: Paulist Press, 1973, pp. 261-274.

————— . Theology of Pastoral Care. *Pastoral Psychology Journal* 10(October 1959): 21-26.

Tompkins, Sylvan. *Affect, Imagery, and Consciousness.* Volume 2, *The Negative Affects.* New York: Springer, 1963.

Turner, Frederick. *Beauty: The Value of Values.* Charlottesville, VA: University Press of Virginia, 1991.

Ulanov, Ann Belford. *Cinderella and Her Sisters.* Philadelphia: Westminster Press, 1983.

————— . "Clinical Encounters with the Spirit." Union Theological Seminary, New York, 1998, unpublished.

————— . *The Female Ancestors of Christ.* Boston: Shambhala, 1993.

————— . *The Feminine in Jungian Psychology and in Christian Theology.* Evanston, IL: Northwestern University Press, 1971.

————— . *The Functioning Transcendent.* Wilmette, IL: Chiron Publications, 1996.

————— . Mending the Mind and Minding the Soul: Explorations Towards the Cure of the Whole Person. *Journal of Religion in Disability and Rehabilitation* 1(1994): 85-101.

————— . *Religion and the Spiritual in Carl G. Jung.* Mahwah, NJ: Paulist Press, 1999.

————— . *The Wisdom of the Psyche.* Cambridge, MA: Cowley Publications, Inc., 1988.

Ulanov, Ann and Ulanov, Barry. *Religion and the Unconscious.* Philadelphia: Westminster Press, 1975.

Underland-Rosow, Vicki. *Shame: Spiritual Suicide.* Shorewood: MN: Waterford Publications, 1995.

Van Aarde, Andries. Social Identity, Status Envy and Jesus' Abba. *Pastoral Psychology* 45(1997): 451-472.

van Deusen Hunsinger, Deborah. *Theology and Pastoral Counseling: A New Interdisciplinary Approach.* Grand Rapids, MI: William B. Eerdmans Publishing Company, 1995.

Vikar, Gyorgy. The Budapest School of Psychoanalysis. In Peter L. Rudnytsky, Antal Bokay, and Patrizia Giampieri-Deutsch (Eds.), *Ferenczi's Turn in Psychoanalysis.* New York: New York University Press, 1996, pp. 60-76.

Weil, Simone. *Waiting for God.* New York: G.P. Putnam's Sons, 1951.

Whitehead, James and Whitehead, Evelyn. *Shadows of the Heart.* New York: Crossroad, 1994.

Williams, Bernard. *Shame and Necessity.* Berkeley: University of California Press, 1993.

Williams, Daniel Day. *The Minister and the Care of Souls*. New York: Harper & Brothers, 1961.

Wimberly, Edward. *Moving from Shame to Self-Worth*. Nashville: Abington Press, 1999.

Winnicott, Donald. Aggression and Its Roots. In C. Winnicott, R. Shepherd, and M. Davis (Eds.), *Deprivation and Delinquency*. New York: Routledge Press, 1984, pp. 84-99.

——— . The Concept of Trauma. In Clare Winnicott, Ray Shepherd, and Madelaine Davis (Eds.), *Psychoanalytic Explorations*. Cambridge, MA: Harvard University Press, 1989, pp. 130-148.

——— . The Development of the Capacity for Concern. In C.Winnicott, R. Shepherd, and M. Davis (Eds.), *Deprivation and Delinquency*. New York: Routledge Press, 1984, pp. 100-105.

——— . Ego Distortion in Terms of True and False Self. In Donald Winnicott (Ed.), *Maturational Processes*. Madison: International Universities Press, Inc., 1965, pp. 140-152.

——— . Fear of Breakdown. In Clare Winnicott, Ray Shepherd, and Madelaine Davis (Eds.), *Psychoanalytic Explorations*. Cambridge, MA: Harvard University Press, 1989, pp. 87-95.

——— . *From Pediatrics to Psychoanalysis*. New York: Basic Books, 1975.

——— . *Holding and Interpretation: Fragment of an Analysis*. New York: Grove Press, 1986.

——— . *Home Is Where We Start From*. New York: W. W. Norton & Company, 1986.

——— . *Human Nature*. Levittown, PA: Brunner/Mazel, 1981.

Wurmser, Leon. *The Mask of Shame*. Northvale, NJ: Jason Aronson, Inc., 1995.

Yarbrough, C. Denise. Fragments of Our Lives. In Roger Alling and David Schlafer (Eds.), *Preaching Through the Year of Mark: Sermons That Work VII*. New York: Morehouse Publishing, 1999, pp. 28-31.

Index

THE HAWORTH PASTORAL PRESS®
Pastoral Care, Ministry, and Spirituality
Richard Dayringer, ThD
Senior Editor

BECOMING A FORGIVING PERSON: A PASTORAL PERSPECTIVE by Henry T. Close. "A rich source of wisdom. I've used many of Henry Close's suggestions on how to help people struggling with issues of unforgiveness. Readers will long remember his stories and practical insights on this subject." *Burrel D. Dinkins, ThD, Johnson Professor of Pastoral Counseling, Asbury Theological Seminary*

TRANSFORMING SHAME: A PASTORAL RESPONSE by Jill L. McNish. "An essential book for pastors and counselors or anyone who has felt the pain of feeling inadequate. Rooted in her experience as a priest, pastor, chaplain, and preacher, Jill McNish argues compellingly that the core ministry of the church does not involve sin and guilt, but the creative transformation of shame." *Rev. D. Andrew Kille, PhD, Co-Chair, Psychology and Biblical Studies Section, Society of Biblical Literature; Author,* Psychological Biblical Criticism

A PASTORAL COUNSELORS MODEL FOR WELLNESS IN THE WORKPLACE: PSYCHOGONOMICS by Robert L. Menz. "This text is a 'must' read for chaplains and pastoral counselors wishing to understand and apply holistic health care to troubled employees, whether they be nurses, physicians, other health care workers, or workers in other industries. This book is filled with practical ideas and tools to help clergy care for the physical, mental, and spiritual needs of employees at the workplace." *Harold G. Koenig, MD, Associate Professor of Psychiatry, Duke University Medical Center; Author,* Chronic Pain: Biomedical and Spiritual Approaches

A THEOLOGY OF PASTORAL PSYCHOTHERAPY: GOD'S PLAY IN SACRED SPACES by Brian W. Grant. "Brian Grant's book is a compassionate and sophisticated synthesis of theology and psychanalysis. His wise, warm grasp binds a community of healers with the personal qualities, responsibilities, and burdens of the pastoral psychotherapies." *David E. Scharff, MD, Co-Director, International Institute of Object Relations Therapy*

LOSSES IN LATER LIFE: A NEW WAY OF WALKING WITH GOD, SECOND EDITION by R. Scott Sullender. "Continues to be a timely and helpful book. There is an empathetic tone throughout, even though the book is a bold challenge to grieve for the sake of growth and maturity and faithfulness. . . . An important book." *Herbert Anderson, PhD, Professor of Pastoral Theology, Catholic Theological Union, Chicago, Illinois*

CARING FOR PEOPLE FROM BIRTH TO DEATH edited by James E. Hightower Jr. "An expertly detailed account of the hopes and hazards folks experience at each stage of their lives. Your empathy will be deepened and your care of people will be highly informed." *Wayne E. Oates, PhD, Professor of Psychiatry Emeritus, School of Medicine, University of Louisville, Kentucky*

HIDDEN ADDICTIONS: A PASTORAL RESPONSE TO THE ABUSE OF LEGAL DRUGS by Bridget Clare McKeever. "This text is a must–read for physicians, pastors, nurses, and counselors. It should be required reading in every seminary and Clinical Pastoral Education program." *Martin C. Helldorfer, DMin, Vice President, Mission, Leadership Development and Corporate Culture, Catholic Health Initiatives— Eastern Region, Pennsylvania*

THE EIGHT MASKS OF MEN: A PRACTICAL GUIDE IN SPIRITUAL GROWTH FOR MEN OF THE CHRISTIAN FAITH by Frederick G. Grosse. "Thoroughly grounded in traditional Christian spirituality and thoughtfully aware of the needs of men in our culture. . . . Close attention could make men's groups once again a vital spiritual force in the church." *Eric O. Springsted, PhD, Chaplain and Professor of Philosophy and Religion, Illinois College, Jacksonville, Illinois*

THE HEART OF PASTORAL COUNSELING: HEALING THROUGH RELATIONSHIP, REVISED EDITION by Richard Dayringer. "Richard Dayringer's revised edition of *The Heart of Pastoral Counseling* is a book for every person's pastor and a pastor's every person." *Glen W. Davidson, Professor, New Mexico Highlands University, Las Vegas, New Mexico*

WHEN LIFE MEETS DEATH: STORIES OF DEATH AND DYING, TRUTH AND COURAGE by Thomas W. Shane. "A kaleidoscope of compassionate, artfully tendered pastoral encounters that evoke in the reader a full range of emotions." *The Rev. Dr. James M. Harper, III, Corporate Director of Clinical Pastoral Education, Health Midwest; Director of Pastoral Care, Baptist Medical Center and Research Medical Center, Kansas City Missouri*

A MEMOIR OF A PASTORAL COUNSELING PRACTICE by Robert L. Menz. "Challenges the reader's belief system. A humorous and abstract book that begs to be read again, and even again." *Richard Dayringer, ThD, Professor and Director, Program in Psychosocial Care, Department of Medical Humanities; Professor and Chief, Division of Behavioral Science, Department of Family and Community Medicine, Southern Illinois University School of Medicine*